Race and Religion in the
Postcolonial British Detective Story

# Race and Religion in the Postcolonial British Detective Story

## Ten Essays

### Edited by JULIE H. KIM

McFarland & Company, Inc., Publishers

*Jefferson, North Carolina, and London*

LIBRARY OF CONGRESS CATALOGUING-IN-PUBLICATION DATA

Race and religion in the postcolonial British detective story : ten
    essays / edited by Julie H. Kim.
        p.      cm.
    Includes bibliographical references and index.

    ISBN 0-7864-2175-4 (softcover : 50# alkaline paper)

    1. Detective and mystery stories, English — History and
criticism.    2. Ethnic relations in literature.    3. Postcolonialism
in literature.    4. Ethnic groups in literature.    5. Ethnicity in
literature.    6. Religion in literature.    7. Race in literature.
I. Kim, Julie H.
PR888.D4R33    2005
823'.0872093552 — dc22                                              2005009220

British Library cataloguing data are available

Cover photograph ©2005 ClipArt.com

Manufactured in the United States of America

*McFarland & Company, Inc., Publishers*
    *Box 611, Jefferson, North Carolina 28640*
        *www.mcfarlandpub.com*

For my family

# Table of Contents

# Introduction:
# Murder and the Other

In 1929, Ronald Knox, a prominent member of the English Detection Club, included in his tongue-in-cheek Ten Commandments for Detective Novelists the rule that "No Chinaman must figure in the story." In 1983, Ruth Rendell published *Speaker of Mandarin*. The intervening years, one might guess, had brought about significant changes not only to detective fiction but more generally to the British cultural landscape. The second half of twentieth century saw sharp immigrant population growth, and the last quarter of the twentieth century is marked by proliferation of ethnic minority characters in British popular culture. Works of detective fiction since the 1970s feature many figures the Golden Age would have considered the Other — figures that I claim as the subject of these essays.

Detective fiction is, of necessity, about the Other. A typical mystery comprises no fewer than *three* others: victim, detective, and culprit. After all, what is more "othering" than to be murdered, no longer a part of the living community — or perhaps not really having been, even in life, part of that community? Detectives, especially the hard-boiled ones, are often outsiders, or even outcasts, of this same community. In fact, despite theories about the conservative strain of detective fiction which posits the criminal as the aberrant element to be disposed of for the health of the morally upright community, many criminals surprise us by being less "other" than one might suppose, or at least less so than the victim or the detective. But, traditionally, mysteries usually ferret out this culprit, thus also eventually othering that individual. In any case, detective fiction cannot escape being about Others.

The following ten essays purport to investigate racial and, to a lesser

extent, religious otherness in British detective fiction. But there is more to
their investigation than these two primary types of otherness. Paul Gilroy,
in his examination of British cultural politics, insists that in Britain (and,
I would add, in the United States as well) "'race' cannot be adequately understood if it is falsely divorced or abstracted from other social relations"[1]; and
it is inevitable that one would encounter otherness related to class, gender,
sexual orientation, culture, and ethnicity in a study of racial and religious otherness. But the essays in this collection will also discuss ways in which those
more prominent forms of otherness intersect with or give rise to marginalization related to anything from political affiliation, domestic status, immigration patterns, exoticized foreignness, and vocational choices to physical
size, hair color, and even sports team loyalties. While it is possible that a too-
broad definition of otherness is being applied, every one of these essays makes
its case for the cultural significance of the specific otherness examined.

## Race

This volume of essays fills a critical gap in the study of Anglo-Amer-
ican detective fiction. When scholars reference notions of otherness, they
tend to focus fairly exclusively on race relations in U.S. detective fiction.
After all, the U.S. has historically been more recognizably multiracial,
and popular minority writers like Walter Mosley or Sherman Alexie or
Barbara Neely explicitly address race relations. In his 1953 essay "Stranger
in the Village," which recounted his isolation during months living in a
remote Swiss village, James Baldwin compared U.S. and European race relations. Baldwin noted that racial conflict was a "comfortingly abstract"
concept for Europeans whose colonies effectively contained those racial
others, providing a physical barrier between empires and those they colonized. "But in America, even as a slave, he [the African-American] was
an inescapable part of the general social fabric and no American could escape having an attitude toward him."[2] Stuart Hall, considered a "founder"
of British cultural studies, appears to endorse Baldwin's conclusions in an
interview. Speaking about the post–World War II wave of immigration
from the Caribbean, Hall suggests that the British "host society" had to
ask: "'Who are these people? How long are they here for? What do we
think about them? Why do they speak English?' 'Because we colonized
them five hundred years ago, that's why.' 'But why are they different?'
'Because they come from Africa.'" He distinguishes himself from the
American popular culture scholar Michael Eric Dyson, "who comes out
of a long, stable, African American community, an African American tradition of resistance and struggle."[3] The provocative title of a Paul Gilroy

work, *"There Ain't No Black in the Union Jack": The Cultural Politics of Race and Nation* (1987), likewise suggests that what James Baldwin postulated about European race relations in 1953 was not entirely obsolete in later twentieth century England.

On the other hand, a shift in British literature and culture has brought about a greater visibility of the racial other in recent fiction — including detective fiction — in an increasingly multiracial Britain. In works of the middle twentieth century, a period when the number of alien residents doubled, we sense an anxiety about national identity — and identity in general — even in the novels of a fairly conservative or traditional writer like Agatha Christie, the most recognizable and still the most popular of British mystery's Golden Age writers. Unease over the fact that World War II has dislocated many individuals and that both English and non–English others are invading the tranquility of the idealized small village is evident in a work such as *A Murder Is Announced* (1950). In John Scaggs' essay, we learn that "in the period from 1966 to 1976, a total of 2,275,000 immigrants, not including a significant number of immigrants from the Republic of Ireland, came to Britain," necessitating a new Race Relations Act in 1976 (see Chapter 6).[4] It is then perhaps no coincidence that earliest primary texts for this collection date from the late 1970s and early 1980s (John Mortimer and Ruth Rendell, for example).

With the increase in minority population and the emergence of disparate ethnic voices, a critical rethinking of racial identity seems to be taking place in both United States and in Britain. As cultural scholars advance and constantly redefine terminology to describe their fields of study, the public is subject to wide-ranging discussions of what *ethnic* means, what *multicultural* describes, why something can be called *postcolonial*. Eliding a few of these catch terms, Adrienne Johnson Gosselin writes, in the introduction to her *Multicultural Detective Fiction,* that each essay in the collection "focuses on detective fiction shaped by multicultural, multiracial, and/or multiethnic worldviews."[5] Within this larger umbrella category, Gina Macdonald and Andrew Macdonald might highlight the contributions of cross-cultural detectives, those "non-mainstream detectives" who "explore cultural differences ... and act as links between cultures, interpreting each to each, mainstream to minority and minority to mainstream."[6] Ed Christian might loosely describe post-colonial detectives as marginalized, "central and sympathetic characters" whose "approaches to criminal investigation are influenced by their cultural attitudes."[7] Perhaps even broader is Stuart Hall's definition of ethnicity. He argues that "because everybody comes from a cultural tradition, a cultural production ... everybody has an ethnicity — including the British: Englishness."[8]

While Stuart Hall concedes that "multiculturalism very much invokes ethnicity," he is careful, especially in the British context, of nuancing his use of the word *multicultural*:

> What I mean by multicultural, then, is that society has been mongrelized. You look out and you don't know whether kids are black or white or North African; it's just the pluralization of kinds of people (not cultures) which now make up a city like London. You have no idea how London has been transformed in fifteen or twenty years; you have no conception. It did not look like this at one time....
>
> ... It's a funny piece of history that the U.S. has a much longer tradition and history of ethnic pluralism — it's made out of it — whereas Britain has always conceived of itself as culturally homogeneous. But the impact of globalization and migration on the two societies has been a little different. In the U.S., recent migration has been absorbed into and has complexified the pluralist hierarchy, whereas in Britain what it has done is simply blur its homogeneous origin.[9]

Essays in this collection support the use of multicultural in the two divergent ways that Hall references above. Earlier essays in the volume appear to suggest that racial or ethnic others are merely blurring the perceived homogeneity of British culture without having greater impact. Later essays — like those on texts written at the turn of the twenty-first century — depict more fully individualized ethnic identities, in the U.S. vein, where the migration has "complexified the pluralist hierarchy."

Two additional thorny issues raised by popular culture critics deserve attention for this volume of essays. In their discussion of U.S. cross-cultural detectives, Gina Macdonald and Andrew Macdonald wonder if the creation of multicultural detectives is a positive development, and their own response is mixed:

> In summary, the explosion of ethnic detective fiction in the last decade or so has had both positive and negative impacts. The heightened interest has produced a good deal of fringe ethnicity in novels that are like old west theatrical entertainments: very mainstream in style and substance but tarted up with backdrops and costumes that are meant to suggest an exotic locale. The other extreme can be seen ... where the ethnic context moves so far afield that the defining elements of the genre are lost.[10]

My own classroom experience supports this ambivalent review. While many students delight in new approaches to (and faces of) detective fiction generated by writers like Barbara Neely and Lucha Corpi, a few bemoan the fact that they are no longer reading so-called traditional murder mystery, defined not by gender or ethnicity of the detective but by the Poe style of ratiocination. While these disappointed readers are not necessarily echoing the sentiments of W. H. Auden, who half-seriously declared that he finds it "very difficult" to read a detective story "that is not set in rural England," they probably do agree with him in wanting the story to "conform to certain formulas."[11] Those readers who prefer conventional mystery or detective fiction to genres such as suspense or thriller are particularly apt to express frustration with the disappearance of (super)detectives in the tradition of Dupin, Holmes, Poirot, or even Wexford or Dalgliesh. The aim of this volume, however, is not to evaluate the popular success of multicultural detective fiction but to study the significant interaction between races—and religions—and examine what the depiction of the other in detective fiction can tell us about contemporary British culture and about the fluid nature of the detective fiction genre.

Perhaps more apropos an issue for this collection might be one raised by Maureen T. Reddy in her *Traces, Codes, and Clues: Reading Race in Crime Fiction*. Like most of the critical works referenced in this introduction about race in detective fiction, Reddy's work focuses on U.S. traditions. In a chapter entitled "Writing the Other," Reddy points to the problem of authors who, though white, are writing about racial others: "One crucial problem in whites' depiction of characters of color relates to the problem of identity itself, which is always relational, never a fixed position. In a white supremacist society, the identity of people of color is always mediated by whiteness."[12] She argues, for instance, that the mystery novels featuring Navajo detectives by Tony Hillerman are not "written for American Indians although they are about them; given the extensive anthropological descriptions in each novel, it is clear that Hillerman assumes a white audience." Because Hillerman remains, according to Reddy, "a kind of cultural tour guide," readers are never asked "to take that other America for granted or to see it as a norm; we are never really inside it."[13] Further, Reddy critiques the critics when she discusses the positive reception of novels by white female Kris Nelscott who writes about a black male detective. Specifically responding to a review which hailed Nelscott's character Smokey Dalton as a more compelling character than African American writer Walter Mosley's Easy Rawlins, Reddy ventures, "Smokey is certainly more accessible to whites than Easy may be and holds views acceptable, even comforting, to the mass of white people."[14] This is not to say that Reddy simply rejects as inauthentic all white-authored works featuring racial others. She singles out for praise writer Barbara Hambly, who is "acutely conscious of her positioning within white discourse" and who deliberately writes "against the demands of the dominant ideology."[15]

Unlike the U.S. detective fiction milieu which Maureen Reddy writes about and which has recently experienced an explosion of ethnic minority writers, British detective fiction still remains a field populated mostly by white writers—with the top of the hierarchy still dominated by the likes of P.D. James or Ruth Rendell. Therefore, essays in this collection deal primarily with white authors "writing the other," with less concentrated references to ethnic minority writers. On the other hand, essayists in this collection articulate the many difficulties in writing about the racial, gendered, or national other, and they explicitly examine the politics of such narratives. For instance, Chapters 3, 4, 9, and 10 discuss problems inherent in depicting the language and thought processes of racially other individuals and communities; and Chapters 4 and 10 delve into the psyche of ethnic minority detectives, one written by a (U.S.) Chicana and the other written by a white male British author. In each of these cases, discussions are enhanced by directly confronting the ways in which these authors' achievements are, according to Peter Clandfield in Chapter 10, both circumscribed but also possibly heightened by the process of writing the other. As more ethnic minority writers take center stage in Britain, we will be able to revisit with greater complexity the politics not only of *writing* the other but also more fully and authentically (and complicatedly) *representing* the other.

## *Religion*

Britain's rich and troubled history with various religions provides another perspective and a correction on the faulty image of a homogeneous Britain. Expulsion of Jews, break with the Catholic Church, Protestant Reformation, and English Revolution encompass only a small portion of Britain's religious heritage — and a relatively compact period in British history at that. New waves of immigration in the second half of the twentieth century also brought new (or renewed) tensions between Christian and Muslim cultures (as Chapter 3 suggests, for example) along with traditional struggles between Protestants, Catholics, and Jews. Therefore, while the issue of racial or ethnic other had previously been more hotly debated, the religious other is also an unavoidable social and political reality in contemporary Britain — and in British detective fiction.

Arguably, detective fiction has always intersected with religious faith. At least as early as 1910 when G. K. Chesterton introduced his priest-detective Father Brown, detective fiction has highlighted traditional morality and Christian orthodoxy. The fact that Chesterton himself converted in 1922 from Anglicanism to Roman Catholicism serves to underscore the significant role of religion in the lives of mystery writers. Robert S. Paul, in *Whatever Happened to Sherlock Holmes: Detective Fiction, Popular The-*

*ology, and Society,* argues that "many of detections' presuppositions are fundamentally theological, such as":

> 1) a belief that our universe is structured on the basis of rational laws; 2) the conviction that 'truth' is real and can be discovered rationally by weighing the evidence; 3) the assumption that if all the facts are known, we can discover meaning in them; 4) the perception that there is real distinction between right and wrong conduct; 5) the assumption that human life is of very great, even of supreme value; 6) the recognition that although people are always capable of goodness, there is also within them an innate capacity for evil; 7) the conviction that we must strive to achieve justice for the sake of society.[16]

In any case, how can a genre of literature which is predicated on sin and probable punishment — and which often emphasizes confessing and repenting — not be religious?

By late twentieth century, the British religious landscape had become crowded. This collection analyzes Catholicism as the "abject other" (Chapter 5) and Calvinist heritage as spiritually troubling (Chapter 8), and depicts how the Jew is culturally alienated (Chapter 6) and the Muslim marginalized as the interloper (Chapter 3). But in addition to treatments of specific religions, essays in this collection discuss ways in which religion itself can be seen as the other. Moral certainty that pervaded early decades of detective fiction — during the fairly conservative Golden Age, for example — is replaced in late twentieth and early twenty-first centuries by skepticism and hostility. Clearly established and institutionalized religions give way to gnosticism, mysticism, and metaphysics. Patricia Merivale and Susan Elizabeth Sweeney define metaphysical detective story as a "text that parodies or subverts traditional detective-story conventions— such as narrative closure and the detective's role as surrogate reader — with the intention, or at least the effect, of asking questions about mysteries of being and knowing which transcend the mere machinations of the mystery plot."[17] Thus, by the time we arrive at Peter Ackroyd's *Hawksmoor* (in Chapter 7), not only traditional notions of faith and spirituality but also expected formulas for the detective fiction genre are upturned. If, as Stuart Hall suggests, a result of multiculturalism in Britain is that "Englishness is increasingly contested,"[18] a result of metaphysical musings in most recent works of detective fiction is that religion and religious faith are also challenged.

## The Chapters

The essays in this collection are extraordinarily varied in perspective and approach as well as in subject matter. It is possible to see a thematic linearity in the ordering of the chapters, starting from discussions of perceived homogeneity and ending with apparent hybridity, but each chapter will also challenge that assumption.

Neil McCaw's essay opens the collection, making us imagine a Christie-esque English village only to pervert that pastoral idyll and the orthodox conception of a rural Englishness. In Caroline Graham's *The Killings at Badger's Drift*, an almost absurdly "cosy" village is presented, where otherness seems initially defined in fairly innocent or parochial terms—such as who has red hair or grew up poor. But McCaw's essay argues that this homogeneity is increasingly in tension with the socio-cultural contexts from which the novel emerges and that this tension effectively pulls the work in different ideological directions. While Graham's book does not actually depict characters who are racially or religiously an other, the novel de-centers English village identity in such a way that everything from sexual perversions to Chinese takeaways is imbued with significance about the mistakenly naïve ways we interpret the English self in relation to the (often absent) other.

In Chapter 2, Brad Buchanan argues that John Mortimer's popular Rumpole of the Bailey series appeals to a widespread nostalgia for a stable British social and cultural identity and that many of the works in the series which directly touch on racial and religious issues reflect a broader conservative tendency in British detective fiction. Buchanan analyzes the way in which *Rumpole's Return*, in particular, hinges on the notion that British identity is (or perhaps should be?) essentially fixed, and he examines the skepticism with which the novel addresses the virtues of multiculturalism, both in England and within the United States where the novel is also partly set. While the novel *Rumpole's Return* is the major focus, this chapter also addresses other works in the series, notably the short stories "Rumpole and the Fascist Beast" and "Rumpole and the Golden Thread," texts which suggest that Britain's turbulent history as an empire results in ambiguous relationships with those colonized others now living in England.

In Chapter 3, Suzanne Penuel compares two Ruth Rendell texts— *Speaker of Mandarin* (1983) and *Simisola* (1995)—in their treatments of the racial other which seem, perhaps unintentionally, to validate the European fear of the mythologized Orient. It is interesting to note the comparison between the more intolerant earlier Wexford and the more benign and willing-to-please later Wexford, both laden with a form of liberal guilt. However, other comparisons are also noteworthy here: Wexford's frustrated and confused attitude toward China versus his longing for the westernized comforts and modernity of Hong Kong; *Simisola*'s portrayals of

English attitudes towards Christian Afro-British versus towards Muslim Arabs; the novel's ambivalent depiction of Wexford's racial sensitivity versus the film version's less flawed hero.

Tim Libretti, in Chapter 4, in an essay comparing Lucha Corpi and Elizabeth George, also offers up a comparison of multiple cultures and the ways in which the dominant culture responds to the minority culture. Examining U.S. white power from the perspective of a Chicana, Lucha Corpi's "other speaks to the center" (outside to inside) but also from within the "belly of the beast" (inside to outside). Elizabeth George, in her *Deception on His Mind,* depicts the Pakistani community in England supposedly from within (in narrative sections going into the minds of Pakistani characters) and from without (in a novel told primarily from the perspective of a white English police officer Barbara Havers). Therefore, we could say that the George novel shows us both the center looking to the periphery and outside-in. Yet, Libretti's "Inside-Out and Outside-In" formulation makes us reconsider the politics of center and periphery when writing *about* or *as* the racial other, especially given that Elizabeth George is an American whose novels are set in Britain. This chapter then examines such nuances of politics of racial and national identity in a world seemingly gone global with the spread of capitalist ideals.

In another essay that examines Elizabeth George's popular series of novels featuring Inspector Thomas Lynley and Detective Barbara Havers, Chapter 5 shifts focus to looking at Catholicism, and religion itself, as the "other." Kate Koppelman suggests that George offers a pointed critique of the place of religion in a contemporary England that is still coming to terms with its own religious past and that, according to George, religious oppression and repression are capable of producing and sanctioning violence in the present. Koppelman draws from both British history and literary theory to develop her ideas that *A Great Deliverance* not only presents us with religion as an other that is merely different from ourselves but also as "the source from which demands and expectations come."

Exploring a trilogy of detective fiction novels set during the 1930s and 1940s Germany, John Scaggs' essay in Chapter 6 combines both the religious and cultural foci of this collection. This chapter examines the fragmentation of the human subject in Philip Kerr's *Berlin Noir* trilogy (1993) as it manifests itself in the themes of missing persons, narrative haunting, and altered identities. Although the novels are set in Berlin during the National Socialist regime, this essay also discusses how Kerr's identification of Jews as "missing persons" makes the cultural alienation of '30s and '40s Germany relevant to a post–1980s British multicultural society where immigration explosions have deconstructed the notion of a stable British identity.

Scaggs' study also involves an intricate discussion of the detective figure as a surrogate, a double, for the missing persons he investigates. Hence this essay serves as a good link to Chapter 7, in which Andrew Ng studies an important doubling between the murderer and the detective in his essay on Peter Ackroyd's *Hawksmoor*. Ng argues that the central character, Nicholas Dyer, presents a paradox of the Christian faith and that Dyer is an occultist whose belief is dependent upon, and duly subverts, established Christian beliefs. The essay concludes that the novel merges its postmodern concerns and its ontological and metaphysical musings to highlight the contentious question of the role and place of religion in a time when boundaries, systems and powers are subverted and deconstructed. Like Kate Koppelman in Chapter 5, Andrew Ng treats not only Dyer's specific religious belief (in occultism) but also religion as a whole as the other.

In a smooth transition, Brian Diemert in Chapter 8 picks up the issue of metaphysical detective fiction. This chapter analyzes Ian Rankin's Inspector Rebus, a figure haunted by his Scottish, Calvinistic heritage and spiritual longing. Diemert argues that the Rebus novels— of which he covers a substantial number — inscribe a vision that is more Gnostic than traditionally Judeo-Christian. In an essay which conveys well the turbulence and the contradictions in Scottish history and culture, Diemert demonstrates how these works which explore Edinburgh's underworld also examine the spiritual, even quasi-occultist, aspects of Rankin's Inspector Rebus and the Gnostic and mythic elements of Rebus's quest for truth and spiritual atonement.

The final two chapters of this collection move us very far away from the quaint English villages of Christie or even of more contemporary Caroline Graham of Chapter 1. Marta Vizcaya Echano's Chapter 9 presents readers with three female writers whose white English protagonists occupy liminal positions in society due to their gender, class, or sexuality. Vizcaya Echano argues that these narratives by Ann Granger, Alma Fritchley, and Cath Staincliffe illustrate how the mystery genre has evolved from the British Golden Age and American hard-boiled fiction and also how the shifting lesbian politics of late twentieth and early twentieth-first century Britain are reflected in detective fiction involving lesbian sleuths. In her examination of racial others, she suggests that the novels' different portrayals of British ethnic communities reflect an increasing social awareness of how these groups' presences are making mainstream society re-imagine itself in both helpful and harmful ways.

In the final chapter of the collection, Peter Clandfield introduces us to "Tartan Noir" and explains what "black" Scots are. Chapter 10 deals with Christopher Brookmyer and Denise Mina, writers of fiction whose exploration of Scottish urban life looks beyond traditional Scottish-English and Catholic-Protestant tensions—although there are plenty of those as well. By examining the ways in which "black" characters play prominent and nuanced roles in these novels, Clandfield demonstrates how Brookmyre and Mina move past binary thinking about ethnicity and religion. He argues that these authors depict contemporary Scotland as not only attaining growing autonomy from England but also undergoing irreversible racial and cultural hybridization. These novels—published 1998, 2000, and 2001—represent the transition to twenty-first century thinking about racial and religious otherness and seem a fitting conclusion to this collection.

## Notes

1. Paul Gilroy, *There Ain't No Black in the Union Jack* (London: Hutchinson Ltd, 1987), p. 14.

2. James Baldwin, "Stranger in the Village" (1953), in *The Winchester Reader*, Donald McQuade and Robert Atwan, eds. (Boston: St. Martin's Press, 1991), pp. 158–168.

3. Julie Drew, "Cultural Composition: Stuart Hall on Ethnicity and the Discursive Turn," in *Race, Rhetoric, and the Postcolonial*, Gary A. Olson and Lynn Worsham, eds. (Albany: State University of New York Press, 1999), p. 217.

4. Peter Clandfield, in Chapter 10, also discusses in detail minority population of Glasgow in particular and Scotland in general.

5. Adrienne Johnson Gosselin, "Multicultural Detective Fiction: Murder with a Message," in *Multicultural Detective Fiction: Murder from the "Other" Side*, Adrienne Johnson Gosselin, ed. (New York: Garland Publishing, Inc., 1999), p. 6.

6. Gina Macdonald and Andrew Macdonald, "Ethnic Detectives in Popular Fiction: New Directions for an American Genre," in *Multicultural Detective Fiction*, p. 60.

7. Ed Christian, "Introducing the Post-Colonial Detective; Putting Marginality to Work," in *The Post-Colonial Detective*, Ed Christian, ed. (Basingstoke: Palgrave, 2001), p. 2.

8. Drew, "Cultural Composition: Stuart Hall on Ethnicity and the Discursive Turn," p. 228.

9. Drew, "Cultural Composition," p. 226.

10. Macdonald and Macdonald, "Ethnic Detectives in Popular Fiction," p. 95.

11. W.H. Auden, *The Dyer's Hand and Other Essays* (New York: Random House, 1948), p. 146.

12. Maureen T. Reddy, *Traces, Codes, and Clues: Reading Race in Crime Fiction* (New Brunswick: Rutgers University Press, 2003), p. 156.

13. Reddy, *Traces*, pp. 169–170.

14. *Ibid.*, p. 179.

15. *Ibid.*, p. 183.

16. Robert S. Paul, *Whatever Happened to Sherlock Holmes: Detective Fiction, Popular Theology, and Society* (Carbondale: Southern Illinois University Press, 1991), p. 14.

17. Patricia Merivale and Susan Elizabeth Sweeney, "The Game's Afoot: On the Trail of the Metaphysical Detective Story," in *Detecting Texts: The Metaphysical Detective Story from Poe to Postmodernism*, Patricia Merivale and Susan Elizabeth Sweeney eds. (Philadelphia: University of Pennsylvania Press, 1999), p. 2.

18. Drew, "Cultural Composition," p. 228.

# 1

## Those Other Villagers: Policing Englishness in Caroline Graham's *The Killings at Badger's Drift*

### NEIL MCCAW

This essay examines the role of the pastoral myth of English village life in defining otherness in the novel and television adaptation of Caroline Graham's *The Killings at Badger's Drift* (1987). The essay highlights the ways in which both novel and adaptation utilize the locality of the fictional Badger's Drift and its incumbent personalities to define the microcosm of an idealized national community, relying upon a myth of communal identity with an intrinsic "sense of harmony and rest about it."[1] This is self-consciously reminiscent of the Golden Age of English crime fiction and of the Miss Marple novels in particular. Furthermore, as in Christie, the apparent permanence of this longstanding social order serves as the backdrop to crimes that puncture the outward complacency of the ideal image. As such, *Badger's Drift* encompasses a "subversion of ... [social] order,"[2] most notably through the depiction of the murder of one of the most traditional characters.

The ensuing narrative sets about trying to suppress the subversion of order by removing anyone whose *difference* poses a threat to the homogeneity of village life. Alternative identities are purged in an attempt to arrive at the "containment of ostensibly subversive pressures."[3] At the heart of this process is a coherent sense of English ethnic identity, an "idea of societal groups, marked especially by shared nationality, tribal affiliation, religious faith, shared language, or cultural and traditional origins."[4] This identity is embodied in the first victim, Emily Simpson, who is an English teacher and an aficionado of Shakespeare, the most potent icon of Englishness. Her life, in terms of the values she represents, marks her out as symbolic of a community as a whole. Even the working-class barmaid Mrs. Sweeney, who notes how Miss Simpson had "not an enemy in the world,"[5] and the errant youth Jake, who publicly stands up for the woman who used to teach him (despite the fact that "he can't read nor write to this day" [p. 49]), vindicate this symbolism.

The Killings at Badger's Drift attempts to uphold the idealized English life Miss Simpson represents by working through a three-stage strategy of "consolidation, subversion and containment" (italics added).[6] Firstly, there is the consolidation of the dominant national identity. Secondly, subversive threats to this ideal are displayed. Thirdly, these perceived threats are shown as overcome or contained, and the harmonious, static social model is then restored. However, in the case of the novel, the strategy of containment is less effective than that evident in the TV adaptation. The novel fails to fully suppress the threats to the imagined ethnic harmony of the English villagers, and instead of purging itself of tension and disquiet, it leaves the reader with an implied vision of a different Englishness in Badger's Drift, one that is potentially more heterogeneous and more diverse than the Golden Age ideal Caroline Graham begins with. Thus we have characters such as Troy and Mrs. Lessiter.

The attempt, yet ultimate failure, to suppress competing identities in The Killings at Badger's Drift will be seen to illustrate how the narrative can be used to work both inside and outside the conservative genre conventions of detective fiction. This duality, John Cawelti has argued, is typical of such popular cultural texts, which

> contain a mixture of two kinds of elements: conventions and inventions. Conventions are elements which are known to both the creator and his audience beforehand — they consist of things like favourite plots, stereotyped characters, accepted ideas, commonly known metaphors and other linguistic devices, etc. Inventions, on the other hand, are elements which are uniquely imagined by the creator such as new kinds of characters, ideas, or linguistic forms.[7]

The TV adaptation of Graham's novel will be seen to be more conventional than inventional; the novel, on the other hand, through challenges to the status quo that are not fully resolved, will be seen to push these conventional limits to the utmost.

There is certainly no doubt that the conservative, conventional instinct of *The Killings at Badger's Drift*, in both novel and adaptation, is strong. The narrative upholds longstanding assumptions about rurality and village life and how central these are to English ethnic identity. It is an ethnic identity built upon a seemingly uncontested value system, rooted in conventional religious practices (the focal point of the church is a notable feature of the Midsomer villages), a dominant conservative morality, a predominant white middle-upper class social orientation, and a valuing of (national) tradition. This conforms to the traditional way in which, as Anita Biressi has pointed out, crime programs "invite an imagined community of viewers to review the measures which they themselves might take in order to shore up their own defences."[8] Ultimately, *Badger's Drift* isolates and projects "cultural guilt upon some scapegoat rather than offer any social analysis or critique."[9] In criminological terms, both novel and adaptation stress "the psychology of the offender" as the root of social deviancy, rather than offering insight as to the "sociological factors leading to crime."[10] In so doing they resist the notion of a criminal class preying upon victims indiscriminately and are specific about the individualized relationships of cause and effect.

Part of the underlying reason for this ideological conservatism is that Caroline Graham writes self-consciously within the formal conventions of detective fiction: "A writer writes (and a reader reads) with an understanding of what is acceptable within the limits of the literary form, of what inventions and experiments are permissible, and what traditions must be observed."[11] For John Nettles, the lead actor in the TV adaptation of the "Midsomer Murders," a self-conscious, almost meta-fictional conformism to genre conventions is fundamental to how Graham's narratives work: "'It's a comedic take on the whodunit, in the glorious English tradition of the detective story, stretching back to Conan Doyle and before. It is almost, but not quite, a send up.'"[12] Nettles sees Graham as relying upon, yet playfully sending up, the Golden Age stereotypes in a kind of pantomimic impersonation of the classical formula; for him the novels (re)present archetypes and images of old with a noticeable tongue-in-cheek and a very large pinch of salt. This conventionalism ensures that *Badger's Drift* offers "fictional reassurance for a middle-class readership,"[13] with Graham identifying village life as "a cultural book of knowledge from which a thousand parables about human nature and motivation can be drawn."[14] Center stage is the "highly focused version of an English archetype,"[15] anchoring the narrative and providing comfort and reassurance to the reader or viewer.

From the opening panning of the camera across the cottage scene, the TV adaptation of *Badger's Drift* establishes an Edenic setting. To emphasize the sense of the paradise-to-be-lost, the viewer is presented with a vision of harmony and quietude. The mock animosity that exists between the characters of Miss Simpson and Miss Bellringer in the novel is expunged from the TV adaptation, and instead of being contesting rivals they are merely elderly friends, gently and amiably living their way through their twilight years. Sergeant Troy's reaction to Miss Bellringer's suspicions about the death of her friend bears out his own sense of the incompatibility between criminality and such an Eden: "[I]t's a waste of time." However, Miss Simpson is murdered and the harmony is shattered, leaving (with self-referential irony) Chief Inspector Barnaby to lament: "[Y]ou wouldn't think that one small village would have so much trouble bubbling under the surface."

Throughout the TV adaptation the producers attempt to maintain the integrity of the English country backdrop. The moral seediness that permeates the novel is downplayed, and deviancy is seen to be the exception rather than the rule. It is a contrived and managed landscape, "a genteel world of immaculate lace curtains, graceful thatched roofs and roses arcing around the door."[16] This patch of England, "chocolate-box pretty and effortlessly green,"[17] is the façade behind which the grim reality of crime is played out, with "homely pots of jam in the larder but rattling skeletons in the cupboard."[18] Despite the hidden horrors of murder, incest, betrayal, and family secrets, the adaptation wholeheartedly upholds the sanctity of its "fabricated piece of England," drawing on as many comforting stereotypes as possible. These stereotypes frame the crimes and provide an effortless contrast between good and evil. As Jeff Evans has noted, "a light touch, a sprinkle of gentle humour, a metaphorical wink at the camera … all ensure viewers know they are in an exaggerated world of make-believe."[19]

The self-regulated comfort of the adaptation situates it as a particular form of media discourse about crime, a discourse that "constitute[s] all viewers as … subject to the fragmented and random danger of criminality, and in so doing provide[s] the preconditions for endless narratives of criminality that rehearse this ever-present danger."[20] The important thing to remember, however, is that the Midsomer Murders do this with an air of safety and reassurance. There may be ever-present danger, but this danger is experienced differently. The fictional world might at first install "paranoia in its images of post-modern society,"[21] exploiting the "very large gap between people's fear of being a victim and their chances of being that victim,"[22] but in the final analysis the Midsomer narratives comfortingly individualize guilt rather than seeing it as an indicator of broader social and national tensions, and the guilty ones are isolated transgressors rather than members of a dissenting collective.

In the early stages of the novel of *The Killings at Badger's Drift,* identities are almost as clear cut. As the backdrop to the first murder, Caroline Graham delineates a stereotypical, idyllic vision of English village life. It is the context for the coherent, apparently unproblematic English ethnicity that is so typified by characters such as Miss Bellringer and Miss Simpson. As part of this idyll, the text supports the notion of a timeless, classical world retaining its grip on universal human and artistic values. When Miss Simpson comes across the two lovers in the woods, her comprehension of the scene is informed by recourse to classical art:

> But Miss Simpson believed deeply that only a truly cultivated mind could offer the stimulus and consolation necessary to a long and happy life and she had, in her time, gazed unflinchingly at great works of art in Italy, France and Vienna. So she knew immediately what was happening in front of her [p. 4].

This easy allusion to ancient archetypes offers Miss Simpson a figurative understanding of the ways in which village life operates, demanding certain codes of behavior and fashioning a shared horizon of expectations: "[S]he had lived in a small village long enough to know that what she had discovered could safely be discussed with no one — not even dear Lucy, who was not a gossip but who had absolutely no idea of concealment" (p. 7). At this point Miss Simpson desires to share her secret with someone outside the village, a non–English other, but the nature of the secret makes this unfeasible: "She could tell her nephew living safely in Australia, but that would mean writing it all down and the very thought made her feel slightly sick" (p. 7). Her nausea is provoked by an underlying sense of impropriety, by the clash between the incestuous behaviour of the Laceys and the value system she sees her world to be founded upon.

The myth of this bucolic, historical Englishness holds sway over much of the novel:

> The Traces went back to Norman times. Effigies of Sir Robert Trayce and his wyffe Ismelda and her cat rested eternally in the cool of the thirteenth-century church. Traces had shed a modest amount of their landowning blood in the two world wars and returned to their squirearchical duties garlanded with honour. The words *security of tenure* were meaningless to them. They had never known anything else [p. 91].

These historical principles are seen to be passed down through generations, distilled into a frozen vision of the past-present: "It had been years since Barnaby had heard such an accent [as Miss Bellringer's]. Not since his early days of going to the pictures. In the postwar years films had been full of clean-cut young Englishmen with straight up and down trousers, all sounding their As like Es" (p. 13).

Such a notion of Englishness underpins the geography and architecture of the village:

> Barnaby turned into the main leg of the T. Church Lane was not as long as the Street and ran very quickly into open country — miles and miles of wheat and barley bisected at one point by a rectangular blaze of rape. The church was thirteenth-century stone and flint, the church hall twentieth-century brick and corrugated iron [p. 26].

Even Miss Simpson's cat bears witness to its feline, historical inheritance: "Barnaby spotted Wellington, a solid cat the colour of iron filings, with four white socks, on top of a grand piano. The name seemed apt" (p. 27). Life is fixed in amber, ahistorical in its resistance to change. Crucially, as shall emerge, outsiders are obliged to recognize the obligations that this timelessness brings with it.

The attempts made within both novel and adaptation to consolidate the village-green Englishness do face challenges. The novel, in particular, embodies a variety of subversive threats to local and national values. At first it is the ebullient, brash Sergeant Troy who reacts against these values most fiercely: "[W]hat on earth was the point of being in the force with all the dreary forms and typing and gormless people endlessly asking you gormless questions" (p. 36). His is a reaction against both the staid conventionalism of the scene, stupefied as if it were a picture postcard, as well as against the inherent insularity of the community he is investigating. Note the contrast between the description of Beehive Cottage as "perfection. The sort of house that turns up on *This England* calendars and tourist posters. The exile's dream of home" (p. 38) and the description of Troy's own childhood, and the class and ethnic identity he represents:

> He remembered his mum cleaning for old Lady Prendicott who always looked as if she dressed in Oxfam rejects. And he remembered wearing her grandson's castoffs: ludicrously expensive clothes from the White House and Harrod's when all he longed for was jeans and a Batman T-shirt [p. 38].

Ethnically, in terms of the "cultural characteristics that connect a particular group or groups of people together,"[23] he does not belong here, and he feels this. Even his physical appearance marks him out as other: "He glanced in the mirror and briefly smoothed his carrot-coloured hair. Surely it was only in romantic novels that girls preferred dark men" (p. 121).

Thus, Troy's estrangement is the result of a clash between differing

English ethnicities: one, rooted in an historical-biological identity handed down through the ages, reliant on mythic ideas of the past (typified by the village of Badger's Drift), and based around certain cultural behaviors; another, more modern, emergent, fundamentally urban identity, which is socially mobile, culturally more ambivalent, and genetically more dilute. Both identities offer fundamentally different life habits and routines. These are most apparent through the lives of the characters that straddle both identities, such as Barnaby, Troy, and Mrs. Lessiter. At times, for instance, it is almost as if Troy has walked onto entirely the wrong set. Barnaby says at one point: "'There's no need to drive as if you're auditioning for *The Sweeney*, Sergeant'" (p. 36). The allusion is to the popular English crime series of the 1970s, a celebration of a more openly working-class, macho form of police hero figure. In the novel Troy is constantly challenged by such ideas of otherness, by the incompatibility between himself and the world around him. It is perhaps what feeds his hostility and drives his aggressive defensiveness; this has to be overcome if he is to fit into the local landscape.

The closest parallel to Troy's incongruous social position is Mrs. Lessiter, who also straddles the ethnic divide of the village, in both class and moral terms: "She'd been born Barbara Wheeler in Uxbridge 'some time in the late fifties,' she told people with coy deceit. Her father was a ganger on the railway, her mother a household drudge" (p. 56). Class insecurity is the motivating force in her life:

> she got a job as a filing clerk in a solicitor's office and, it seemed to her, a precarious toehold on the slippery slope that would lead her out of a slummish and ugly environment into the glossy perfection of middle-class life. A world where you didn't have to go to a park filled with screaming kids and snapping dogs to enjoy grass and trees but had them actually belonging to you, in your own garden [p. 56].

Thus Barbara Lessiter is a social improviser, a woman who adapts to her surroundings, chameleon-like, in order to get on. She partially succeeds, maintaining many of the moral traits that marked her earlier life and yet appropriating many of the espoused ethnic behaviors that so characterize the orthodoxy of the village. This identifies her as a kind of worm in the bud, tainting the supposedly hallowed society from within. In the novel, where her sexuality is more explicit and her disdain for those around her more obvious, this taint is especially apparent.

Caroline Graham also depicts a different form of subversion of the dominant English ethnic identity, one that approximates to a form of *Englishness in foreign clothes*, centring on an alternative sexuality and foreignness in combination. The characters of Dennis and Mrs. Rainbird are the vehicle for this subversion: "The bungalow was called Tranquillada. Barnaby thought this suggested a slightly relaxed version of the Spanish Inquisition" (p. 95). This foreignness, complete with mocking allusion to the historical iniquities of the Catholic church, intrudes upon the landscape of the village. Pointedly, Dennis Rainbird drives a pretentious foreign car: "The silver Porsche was parked in the drive" (p. 96). This sense of strangeness, of dissimilarity between the Rainbirds and the other families they live among, is born out through the depiction of their home, which suspends normal conventions of time and space, and is decorated against accepted standards of taste: "The bungalow seemed much larger than the outside suggested and Dennis led them past several open doors before reaching the lounge. A kitchen that gleamed, a bedroom (all white and gold) that glittered and a second bedroom adorned with lots of red suede and shining brass" (p. 96).

This unfamiliarity emphasizes the sense of Dennis and his mother as freak sideshow attractions:

> She was very, very fat. She spread outwards and towered upwards. At least a quarter of her height seemed to be accounted for by her hair, which was a rigid pagoda-like structure: a landscape of peaks and waves, whorls and curls ending in a sharp point like an inverted ice-cream cone. It was the colour of butterscotch instant whip. She wore a great deal of makeup in excitable colours and a lilac caftan, rather short, revealing bolstery legs and tiny feet [p. 96].

The gross caricature of Mrs. Rainbird, cartoon-like in her unreality, sees her described in terms of pagodas, caftans, a coloured face, and an odd body-shape. Thus the reader is encouraged to see her as foreign to the other characters that live in Badger's drift.

Her son Dennis lives even further beyond conventions of *proper* behavior: "'And what about you, dear?' Dennis danced around Sergeant Troy. 'Don't you want to take the weight off those legs?' Bristling with machismo, Troy selected the hardest chair, sat in it bolt upright and produced his pro-forma pad. A piercing whistle filled the air" (p. 97). Troy's action provokes Dennis to tease him with abandon: "He smiled at Sergeant Troy, a smile as sweet and sickly as the vanilla slice he was consuming. 'I don't think the sergeant likes his marron *Lyonnaise*, Mother'" (p. 99). This precipitates Troy's most vitriolic reaction: "As the two policemen walked down the drive Sergeant Troy said, 'Men like that ought to be castrated'" (p. 105). Crucially, Graham utilizes Troy as part of the process of defining Dennis as other, using his homophobia and repulsion as a standard of *normality* by which to define Dennis's *abnormality*. By implication the narrative of the novel condones Troy's behavior. For Dennis must appear to be odd, is depicted as the stage-queer, and as a consequence the novel cannot fully object to Troy's bigotry without compromising Dennis's perversity. The effect of this is to leave the reader unsure as how to read Troy's blunt assertion of a stereotypical heterosexual masculinity: "Troy thought that if he'd pulled off a double coup like that it'd be drinks all round for the lads and Policewoman Brierley's knickers in his glove compartment before the night was out" (p. 215). This conventionalism, his own sense of fear of penetration by Dennis, strikes the reader most clearly.

Dennis's quasi-pantomimic queerness (which, incidentally, is hardly toned down in the TV adaptation) allows Graham to make the Rainbirds foreign, a threatening other, within the rural idyll. Dennis is the epitome of the perverse, carving his sandwiches into the shapes of the suits of a pack of cards. The strangeness of the relationship between him and his mother and the lifestyle they lead are drawn with explicit and continual reference to their sexuality, and because of this Dennis's outrageous homosexuality is ultimately conflated with incest: "Dennis with his slimy ways" (p. 197). Foreignness is gazed at through the lens of alternative, deviant sexual practice, something that even the more tolerant Barnaby finds problematic:

> Her son poured the tea, his bloodless white fingers flickering over the crockery. He popped an apostle spoon with a large purple stone embedded in the handle in a saucer and handed it, with the cup, to Barnaby. Feeling slightly repelled, the Chief Inspector took it and leaned back rather uncomfortably on his crunchy support [p. 97].

Dennis's foreign sexuality is at the heart of the locals' perception of him. After Mrs. Rainbird is found murdered, "As Barnaby walked away he heard one of the villagers (the one who had made the remark about the library) seize his moment of fame. 'Oh it was horrible! Horrible!' he cried into the microphone. 'The son did it ... he came out covered in blood. They've took him away in an ambulance. They reckon he had a brainstorm. He's queer, you see ... it takes them like that'" (p. 181). The correlation between the Rainbirds' foreignness and a perversion of decent (English) family values is so sustained, marking both mother and son out as convenient soon-to-be-victims, that when Mrs. Rainbird is brutally slain the reader barely raises an eyebrow in surprise.

Despite the challenges to the dominant mode of Englishness they embody, the alternative models of social behavior that are exhibited in *Badger's Drift* are contained by the restoration of the social equilibrium towards which the narrative progresses. This brings a reassertion of an underlying communal identity, the shared activities and social behaviors that allow the barriers to external intrusion to be maintained, offering the reader or viewer closure:

> the detective steps in and, viewing the world ethnographically, shows that, though we may have doubted it, such a culture existed all along. Indeed, the seemingly anarchic terrain of civil society turns out to be not a soulless market but a reassuring culture, exacting unstated obligations, punishing outrageous actions, and rewarding reliable behaviour.[24]

Thus Katherine Lacey, whose afternoons are spent "'in the village hall getting ready for the gymkhana on the Saturday. You know ... putting the trestles up ... sorting things ... I was helping on the WI stall'" (p. 69), is shown as an abuser of the historically sanctioned codes of ethnicity. Katherine's appropriation of these codes of social behavior is revealed to be a perversion, and she pays the ultimate price for her sacrilegious acts. She fails to comprehend that her adopted culture relies upon an inherent sense of ethnic permanence; her sexually incestuous relationship with her brother threatens to undermine the longstanding social and familial structures, polluting the line of genetic inheritance, and so must be expunged. The suicide pact between her and her brother ensures that the Trace family history is not stained by the behavior of this interloper.

The logic of the narrative is that those who do not live according to accepted codes of behavior, who threaten the ethnic harmony, inevitably come to a sticky end. Katherine Lacey is performing a role to which she is not suited, born out in Mrs. Quine's nickname for her: "'Miss Great Britain'" (p. 109). She may live the life of the landed gentry, with an imminent marriage into the hallowed class of the English aristocracy, but at her core she is an outsider, and will never be able to make up the constitutional difference between her and those who are true born. Her aping of expected codes of behavior merely serves to estrange her from all classes. As Mrs. Quine later says of Katherine's voluntary work: "'Women's Institute? Load of cowing snobs. They can stuff their flower arrangements. And their bloody walnut pickle'" (p. 109). Katherine represents an heretical misappropriation of traditional English roles.

As has been mentioned, Troy and Mrs. Lessiter will also never be insiders. Their presence in Badger's Drift represents a subversion of normality that needs to be accommodated. They need to be removed or else suppressed in other ways, in order for the illusion of homogeneity to be maintained. In the case of Mrs. Lessiter, this suppression comes via her partial accommodation into a life of domestic bliss with her husband. In Troy's case, however, he is ultimately contained by being specifically (and ironically) engaged, through his work, in the task of ironing smooth the disturbed landscape of the village, of containing the chaos and upheaval that has shattered the peace. He effectively polices the ideology that threatens to exclude him. He works, alongside Barnaby, to provide a comforting answer to the question as to

> what can hold a society of individuals together *as* individuals and how can it overcome the competing forces that always threaten such an order — such forces, that is, as the ties of blood, family, ethnicity, community, or religion that constitute an alternate image of social responsibility; or the uncontrolled passions, unchecked desires, and unconstrained power that threaten to dissolve any stable order altogether?[25]

The TV adaptation of the novel suppresses Troy's difficult personality more completely. His crass, overbearing bigotry is confronted and eventually regulated by the sobering influence of Chief Inspector Barnaby. So when he first meets Dennis Rainbird, his hostility is allowed to surface. Rainbird himself notices, and begins to play up to it: "'I think you've got a right *cun*stable there,'" he says to Barnaby. Then, when Troy speculates about who it was Miss Simpson saw in the woods he says, "'It could have been arse bandits.'" It is then that Barnaby marks out the parameters of the acceptable for his young Sergeant: "'You are as politically correct as a Nuremburg rally.'" Thus the adaptation tries to create the image of an ignorant, rather than a wholeheartedly unpleasant bigot, someone who will be saved by the guiding influence of his betters. Ultimately Troy becomes more benign, more accepted (and accepting), and takes his place alongside Barnaby as an upholder of the traditional order quite willingly.

The toning down of Troy, making him more amenable to the local landscape, and less offensive to the viewers, is deliberate. As John Nettles recognizes: "'Troy is nowhere near as unpleasant as he is in the novels but there's still a harshness in him.'"[26] The man who brought him to life, actor Daniel Casey, is accepting of the necessary differences in translation: "'Troy's basically a Nazi in the books.... [H]e is racist and sexist and homophobic, and every kind of 'ist' or 'ic' you can think of.'"[27] Yet the television audience is supposed to be interested rather than repulsed: "'I wanted him to be green and inexperienced, as opposed to silly; young and immature, as opposed to deeply prejudiced and offensive.'"[28] Thus for TV, at least, Troy loses much of the harshness and vitriol that so contrasts with Barnaby's own demeanour (which is fully respectful of local sensitivities): "'You know ... gay.' There could not have been more venom in the last word if the couple had been seen devouring children" (p. 128).

The effect of this is to leave Troy in something of a limbo. At times he is clearly delineated as other, and yet sometimes he bears witness to an intolerant, fixed form of Englishness that is much closer (in its fixity) to that of the villagers than might first have been thought. To make matters more complicated, his functional role within the narrative is to police (i. e. maintain, uphold) the traditional English ethnicity that does its best to exclude him. The paradoxes are thus rich. And it is these conflicting images that make Troy such an interesting character in the text. His position illustrates the complexity of the processes of national identity formation, and the difficulty of maintaining the integrity of these in an increasingly multicultural, multiethnic, modern world. The fact that he is implicated, one way or another, in multiple national identities, is testament to that.

Across both novel and adaptation it is made clear that certain behaviors and lifestyles cannot be tolerated. The Laceys commit suicide to escape arrest and trial, Henry Trace's symbolic miscegenation is thwarted, and Miss Simpson is avenged. The Rainbirds are expunged, and family secrets are uncovered and suppressed. Thus the fossilized society of what appears to be an archetypal English detective narrative, rooted in ideas of a stable ethnicity, seems to triumph. The village is a contained world again; a world where everyone knows each other, and where long-lasting unpleasantness is averted. The timeless vision of Englishness remains, the others have been quieted, and the threatened calamity of social upheaval has been averted until the next time. This general triumph of the predominant value system is what, as John Nettles rightly points out, makes the stories work: "'[T]o ensure the ultimate triumph of good over evil and the restoration of peace and tranquility to the small communities. It is a tried and tested formula and, to judge by the viewing figures, one that still works extraordinarily well.'"[29] It perpetuates what Stephen Knight has called "an individualist intellectual quietism."[30] This comfortable coziness has meant that "in the USA, the programme has been screened by the A&E network to millions of loyal viewers who indulge themselves on a sumptuous diet of English stereotypes—thatched cottages, village fêtes, red telephone boxes and wacky country folk."[31] As Betty Willingale (co-producer on the early series) acknowledges: "'This is not cutting edge: it is escapism. Watching *Midsomer Murders* is like reading a good detective story. There is no social comment.'"[32]

And yet, the novel of *The Killings at Badger's Drift* indicates that the strategy of *containment* that is the basis of the adaptation is not all-encompassing. For though it is effective in containing explicit and direct threats to the social status quo, such as the Rainbirds and the Laceys, there is an awkwardness at the heart of the novel's treatment of ethnic difference that is not fully resolved. For when Caroline Graham introduces particular ideas of the foreign, more specifically the Orient, towards the end of the novel, her characters seem rather unsure of themselves. These allusions, which are intended to reinforce the boundaries between the English and the Other, serve to show the conditional nature of such distinctions. The appropriated Oriental culture that emerges through Graham's ironic humor, her "way of coming to terms with the Orient,"as Said would have put it,[33] may not be accessible immediately to the likes of Barnaby, Mrs. Lessiter, or Sergeant Troy, but its presence remains, and its influence, albeit latent, may yet be felt.

The references to China come as the narrative is moving towards the restoration of a coherent, unified vision of imagined English community. The upset of murder, incest, and moral chaos is soon to be calmed. The references to the Orient begin by implying the inevitability of contrast between a more stable, pure ethnic Englishness, and a foreign other. They display an incongruous relationship between life in Badger's drift and alternative cultural traditions; as Edward Said writes, "[N]o identity can ever exist by itself and without an array of opposites, negatives, oppositions."[34] However, they also unwittingly imply a move "beyond nativism ... thinking of local identity as not exhaustive ... with its ceremonies of belonging, its built-in chauvinism, and its limiting sense of security."[35] So, when Barnaby anticipates his wife's notoriously inept culinary skills, he dreams of an Oriental alternative: "It was now almost nine o'clock. He wrote down an order for the Chinese takeaway — Black Bean and Ginger Soup. Sweet and Sour Prawns. Rice and Spring Rolls. Toffee Apples — and had just sent it off when the phone rang" (p. 206). What is important, however, is that this meal is repeatedly deferred through a series of comedic interruptions: "More action forms had come to roost on his desk next to his cold gluey Chinese takeaway" (p. 213). Ultimately, when Barnaby's attention returns to the uneaten meal, "he threw the takeaway into the grey metal waste bin and heaved himself out of his seat. 'I've had it,' he said to the room at large" (p. 214). Symbolically, he decides to settle for the domestic delights of tinned soup, served to him when he gets home.

Yet the narrative continues to imagine lives and worlds beyond the containing frame of Badger's Drift. Of Mrs. Lessiter it is noted that "she could always lie back and think of Capri. Or Ibiza. Or the Côte d'Azur. She gazed out of the window. At the green sweet grass sparkling under the hypnotic sprinklers. At the flowering trees and the terrace with its tables and umbrellas and urns brimming with flowers" (p. 230). She is imagining an escape, mentally conjuring up images of an "other" place to dilute the restrictions and perceived pointlessness of her English domestic incarceration. And it is at this point, when social suffocation seems the only

path her life is likely to follow, that she arrives at her most poignant, entic-
ing image of Otherness: "[T]hen her eyes roamed around the room. Thick
Chinese rugs and puffy sofas and onyx tables, nesting slabs of green and
gold. All she had to do was pretend. She should be able to manage that.
After all she'd been doing it all her life" (p. 230). At the key moment in
her imagining of an alternative world beyond the staid conventionalism
of a continued life with her husband in their English imitation of
respectability, the life of gardens and shopping that has sustained her
(materially, if not spiritually) for years, Barbara Lessiter settles on an image
of the Orient as the absolute point of contrast, of salvation. The foreignness of these Chinese rugs, the "nesting slabs of green and gold" that bring
to her mind alternatives to the pictures of sexual submission and compromise that her husband has painted for her, offer Mrs. Lessiter the
definitive point of difference. It is a symbolized life fundamentally at odds
with the life she presently leads, unmasking the coziness of the domestic
arrangements of English village life and showing them to be a hypocritical sham.

The last allusion to the Orient, again delivered with a comic touch,
comes as Troy is thwarted in his attempts to understand the unfolding of
the case. He is said to be stuck in a restricted mindset, limited by the conventionalism with which he has been associated throughout the novel: "Troy
slammed his fist at the dashboard and winced with pain. Where had he
gone astray? Was he looking at things from completely the wrong angle?"
(p. 240). He then hits upon a potential solution, one of the "faddy Eastern
pursuits" he has been told about by "a colleague at Police Training College
who was heavily into T'ai Ch'I" (p. 11): "That might be it. A spot of lateral
thinking; try a new slant. He would do a bit of Chinese breathing, go calmly
back to the beginning and start again" (p. 240). His thoughts of foreignness suggest that the plain urbanity of Troy's English mind might not be
enough to cope with the intricacies of modern police detection. Looking
at the world in a conventional way has only brought him to the unwelcom-
ing brick wall of a dead end. Lateral thinking, within the logic of the text,
means being willing to look beyond the parameters of this parochial English
mindset, and to embrace cultural diversity. This has the potential to offer
a more enlightened, even sophisticated foreign otherness. However, the
reader is not allowed to contemplate the implications of this for too long;
the narration makes clear that "Troy, whose Chinese breathing and cir-
cumvolutions had got him absolutely nowhere, did not pursue the matter"
(p. 243). Neither does he solve the case. And the fact that Barnaby does,
*without* any Oriental breathing techniques, reinforces the sense that Englishness can, up to a point, police itself, if and when it really has to.

These Oriental *moments* in an otherwise relatively flat and unremark-able cultural landscape are significant because of the light they throw on the processes of identity formation and control within *The Killings at Bad-ger's Drift*. For although these moments do not offer the reader explicit resistance to the dominant Englishness of the natives of the village, they pose questions that are not satisfactorily resolved. Whereas particular and specific deviant behaviors exhibited by characters elsewhere in the text are suppressed or contained, leading to a conclusion where order is re-stored, the recourse to Oriental images through the lives of Barnaby, Les-siter and Troy reveal images of a foreign other that are only deferred — a deferment that guarantees the threatened subversions may occur at a later date. In the case of the comic takeaway meal, the implications of this may be benign; however, in the case of Barbara Lessiter and Gavin Troy, for whom the notion of the Orient represents an opportunity for real social change and advantage, the implications are perhaps more significant. For them, challenge and even escape from the dominant ethnic code are viable (if theoretical) options, and they have the chance to imagine beyond the localized notion of national identity that so characterizes Badger's Drift. As such, if they only knew it, they reveal their latent broader, more com-plex ethnic identities, identities with which the text cannot fully come to terms.

## Notes

1. Agatha Christie, *The Murder at the Vicarage* [1930], in *Miss Marple Omnibus: Volume Three* (London: HarperCollins, 1997), p. 520.
2. Jonathan Dollimore and Alan Sinfield, eds., *Political Shakespeare: Essays in Cul-tural Materialism* (London: Manchester University Press, 1994), p. 10.
3. Dollimore and Sinfield, p. 10.
4. *Webster's Dictionary*, 1911.
5. Caroline Graham, *The Killings at Badger's Drift* [1987] (London: Headline, 1997), p. 49. Subsequent page numbers given in parentheses within the body of the essay.
6. Dollimore and Sinfield, p. 10.
7. John G. Cawelti, "The Concept of Formula in the Study of Popular Literature," [originally from *Journal of Popular Culture*, volume 3, 1969], in Bob Ashley, ed., *Read-ing Popular Narrative: A Source Book* (London: Leicester University Press, 1997), p. 71.
8. Anita Biressi, *Crime, Fear and the Law in True Crime Stories* (Basingstoke: Pal-grave, 2001), p. 76.
9. Ronald R. Thomas, *Detective Fiction and the Rise of Forensic Science* (Cambridge: Cambridge University Press, 1999), p. 42.
10. Thomas, p. 260. See Samuel Walker, *Popular Justice* (New York: Oxford Uni-versity Press, 1997), p. 177 and Michael Gottfredson and Travis Hirschi, *A General Theory of Crime* (Stanford, Calif: Stanford University Press, 1990), (pp. 64–84) on the emerging criminological literature from both sides of the Atlantic in the 1920s.

11. George N. Dove, *The Reader and the Detective Story* (Bowling Green, OH: Bowling Green State University Popular Press, 1997), p. 4.

12. Jeff Evans, *Midsomer Murders: The Making of an English Crime Classic* (London: BT Batsford, 2002), p. 56.

13. Ken Worpole, *Dockers and Detectives — Popular Reading: Popular Writing* (London: Verso, 1983), p. 33.

14. Cora Kaplan, "An Unsuitable Genre for a Feminist?" [originally from *Women's Review*, No. 8, 1986], in Ashley, ed., p. 212.

15. Richard Sparks, "*Inspector Morse*: 'The Last Enemy,'" in George W. Brandt, ed., *British Television Drama in the 1980s* (Cambridge: Cambridge University Press, 1993), p. 97.

16. Evans, p. 5.

17. *Ibid.*, p. 5.

18. *Ibid.*, p. 5.

19. *Ibid.*, p. 6.

20. Richard Osborne, "Crime and the Media: From Media Studies to Post-modernism," in David Kidd-Hewitt and Richard Osborne, eds., *Crime and the Media: The Post-Modern Spectacle* (London: Pluto, 1995), p. 27.

21. Osborne, p. 35.

22. David Kidd-Hewitt, "Crime and the Media: A Criminological Perspective," in Kidd-Hewitt and Osborne, eds., p. 19.

23. *Webster's Dictionary*, 1911.

24. Sean McCann, *Gumshoe America: Hard-Boiled Crime Fiction and the Rise and Fall of New Deal Liberalism* (Durham, N.C., and London: Duke University Press, 2000), p. 10.

25. McCann, p. 7.

26. In Evans, p. 57.

27. *Ibid.*, p. 67.

28. *Ibid.*, p. 70.

29. *Ibid.*, p. 8.

30. Stephen Knight, *Form and Ideology in Crime Fiction* (London: Macmillan, 1980), p. 44.

31. Evans, p. 11.

32. In Evans, p. 15.

33. Edward Said, *Orientalism* (New York: Pantheon Books, 1978), p. 1.

34. Edward Said, *Culture and Imperialism* (London: Vintage, 1994), p. 60.

35. Said, p. 277.

# 2

# A Nice Point of Blood: Race and Religion in *Rumpole's Return*

## Brad Buchanan

In his "Introduction" to *The Best of Rumpole,* John Mortimer describes the genesis of Horace Rumpole (a.k.a. "Rumpole of the Bailey"), his most popular fictional creation: "I thought I needed a character, like Maigret or Sherlock Holmes, to keep me alive in my old age. I wanted a sort of detective."[1] The remarkable international popularity of Mortimer's Rumpole books (and the television series based on them) is undoubtedly due in part to the fact that although Rumpole is a lawyer, he does indeed frequently behave like "a sort of detective," seeking clues to exculpate his own clients. Rumpole idolizes Sherlock Holmes (he has even trained his son Nick in the detection skills Conan Doyle's hero exercises), and his cases frequently seem like mysteries that must be solved either by technical knowledge (Rumpole is an expert on blood and typewriters) or by a combination of faith in the basic tenets of the British legal system and a healthy skepticism about human nature.

Still, the appeal of the Rumpole series lies not merely in its unorthodox yet satisfying detection-plots; Rumpole also appeals to a widespread nostalgia for a stable, homogeneous English racial and cultural identity, though his is a rather downtrodden and self-mocking variety of Englishness. Unlike the cool, obsessively detached and mysterious Holmes, Rumpole is not on the surface a prepossessing figure; his name, for instance, bespeaks a certain excremental quality and is reminiscent of the name "Whorearse Rumphole," which is mentioned in James Joyce's *Ulysses.* Rumpole is a short, overweight, untidy and aging junior barrister with a bullying wife named Hilda (whom he calls, in an invocation of the imperialist fantasist H. Rider Haggard,[2] "She Who Must Be Obeyed"); his lack of any specific career ambitions and distaste for self-promotion have left him to his role as what he calls "an Old Bailey hack." If Sherlock Holmes represented the English empire at its most self-confident and domineering, Rumpole stands for a much-reduced sense of national pride and intellectual identity. Mortimer has claimed that Rumpole is "as resolutely English as boiled beef and carrots,"[3] and one might add that he is every bit as unglamorous as these foodstuffs. Still, Mortimer delights in noting that his squat, cigar-smoking creation's "greatest success" has been in "America and Australia,"[4] suggesting that while English writers may be disillusioned with their own country, the rest of the world is still largely besotted with Englishness.

Although this explanation may satisfy the English themselves and a few Anglophile readers of the Rumpole series, there is another factor to be considered in accounting for Rumpole's success. One of the reasons for his attractiveness both as an icon of English incorruptibility and as a moralistic detective lies in the fact that he is represented as a quasi-religious figure who has set up the basic principles of British law as a sacred or divine text to be followed unquestioningly. Neither Mortimer nor his creation has any apparent faith in Christianity or any other organized religion, but their shared respect for British justice forms a set of guiding principles and tenets that comes to stand in for spiritual beliefs. For Rumpole, the Law, as represented by what he calls "British Justice," is essentially a religion, and he must continually defend it from his dishonest or weak-willed legal colleagues as well as from attacks on its commonsense principles by other false gods and prophets.

Rumpole's relationship to religion is especially interesting when it is juxtaposed with the many other literary detectives who are themselves clergymen (Father Brown, Brother Cadfael) and viewed through the lens of theorists who identify the genre of detective fiction as inherently biased towards a religious perspective. In his article "Religious Cults and the Mystery," Marvin Lachman notes that "detectives who are priests, rabbis, nuns and ministers have long been mainstays of the mystery genre."[5] Lachman makes no attempt to explain or comment on the complex relationship between faith and detective fiction (though he offers an extensive and useful account of mystery stories about exploitative cults), but we may use his insight as the jumping-off point for an analysis of the many (and often conflicting) motives of those who invoke religion in the context of detective stories. On the one hand, we may sympathize with those who would like to combine a religious sensibility with the intellectual clarity of a Sherlock Holmes (whose reliance on pure reason and minute observation is so monomaniacal as to seem almost inhuman); on the other hand, faith seems to be a poor substitute for the rational insight that solves most detective stories.

Still, detective fiction critic Robert Paul has persuasively claimed that "for the greater part of the time since detective fiction began to be popular, it has owned moral assumptions that were grounded in the theologies of Western Christendom."[6] As Paul argues, most detective fiction evinces "perfect confidence that there is a rational explanation" for the mysteries it explores.[7] This confidence is grounded, Paul claims, in a faith that "meaning" can be reliably found in the world, and that the mystery, "like life itself ... must be a game ... in which the rules are already determined."[8] Paul also posits that a faith in the abstract concepts of "justice" and "truth" as "eternally self-justifying" is part of what he calls a "traditionally English point of view."[9] Paul calls this perspective the product of "that sublime but often irritating self-assurance of the Anglo-Saxon race" and claims that for most English readers before the 1960s "it would have been unthinkable that British ... law could have been unjust."[10]

To understand more about what is at stake in the notions of Britishness, Englishness, law and religion in *Rumpole's Return*, it is useful both to put Mortimer's fiction and its controlling ideas into perspective within the genre of detective fiction (as it has been analyzed and criticized by a few important theorists) and to look at some of the other Rumpole stories that deal with these topics. The most obvious place to begin is with Sir Arthur Conan Doyle's Sherlock Holmes narratives. As Jon Thompson argues, the Holmes stories have a "radically conservative vision," in that Conan Doyle's protagonist depends on a "narrow empirical ideology" that demands the marginalization of anyone who threatens his worldview, especially women and non–Europeans.[11]

Robert Paul notes that what he calls "the golden age of detective fiction" is to be found in a time when the English public "felt comfortable with the status quo and supported its ethical foundations."[12] He also quotes Erik Routley, who argues that the ideal reader of detective fiction "is not a lover of violence but a lover of order."[13] Both Paul and Routley acknowledge, however, that detective fiction can also thrive in the period when the accepted order of society is beginning to be challenged or questioned but has not yet been wholly overthrown or discredited. We can speculate that the Rumpole series, begun in the late 1970s and continued through the 1990s, was perhaps in some ways a response to the counter-cultural rebellion against authority in the 1960s. Rumpole's run-in with hippies who are determined to contest drug laws in "Rumpole and the Alternative Society," for instance, clearly indicates that such protests against the legal system as a whole are fruitless. In the story, a charming young woman is browbeaten by her dogmatic boyfriend into pleading guilty to selling marijuana (as a protest against her brother's imprisonment on drug charges), even though Rumpole could have won her acquittal quite fairly within the existing rules of evidence.

It might at first appear that *Rumpole's Return* is another neo-conservative indictment of counter-culture as well as religious hypocrisy and delusions. Its plot revolves around the activities of a religious cult that dupes its members and kills those who threaten to expose its secrets. Yet there is more to the cult than mere faith; the cult is a transatlantic, racially diverse global organization that represents the pieties of postmodern multicultural society. Its most dedicated adherent is an African-American woman named Tiffany who was once a sociologist (like Rumpole's son, who has himself been deracinated and Americanized). Thus what appears to be a fringe religious group ends up representing the sociological wave of the future, as Mortimer sees it: it is an ideology that threatens the integrity of individual identity, not to mention justice, by positing a fraudulently utopian racial homogeneity. Our last glimpse of Tiffany is a sad one; she complains that she has to "work so hard" to be the fully integrated, assimilated person the cult wants her to be.[14] Better to "return," as Rumpole and his client both end up doing, to one's cultural and racial origins, than to try unsuccessfully to be something or someone that one is not.

Yet, there is more to *Rumpole's Return*, the longest and most ambitious of Mortimer's lawyer-as-detective narratives, than mere nostalgia for a vanishing ideal of English purity, as a summary of its plot will suggest. We first see Rumpole attempting to relax in Florida, having given up his thankless pursuit of justice in Britain and retired to live with his son Nick, who has taken an academic job in the United States, and Nick's wife Erica. Predictably enough, however, he is lured back to London to defend a timid and fatalistic client, Percival Simpson, who is accused of murdering an aristocratic young man named Rory Canter. Simpson unwittingly leads Rumpole to uncover a peculiar cult named "The Children of the Sun," which forces its adherents to write a pledge in their own blood. The case turns on one such document that appears to be written in the murder victim's blood, though the truth is that Simpson wrote it in his own blood much earlier. When this pledge is found in Simpson's possession, it is taken by nearly everyone as evidence of his guilt; the suggestible Simpson himself becomes convinced that the cultists have somehow mysteriously altered the blood type to punish him.

Rumpole's lifelong fascination with blood enables him to solve the problem, since he points out that blood becomes increasingly difficult to identify over time. With sleuth-like acumen, he proves that a document written long ago in his client's own blood might later appear to contain the victim's blood instead. As he asks during his cross-examination of the prosecution's expert witness:

> ...supposing it had been written months before.... Suppose my client joined a somewhat dotty religious sect ... which required him to write an oath or motto in drops of his own blood ... wouldn't the antigens have perhaps faded in their strength...? The various constituents of blood fade in time, don't they...? And blood become more difficult to classify?[15]

The witness is forced to agree with Rumpole's assessment of the situation, and finally admits that the blood on the paper could well have been the defendant's, and not the victim's. Rumpole has used his specialized knowledge to clear away the misunderstandings that produced a belief in the miraculous; his legal and scientific mind has triumphed, in classic Holmesian fashion, over ignorance and superstition. He has also destroyed another rival to his own code of beliefs, showing that the law and its rational principle of evidence is a more powerful instrument of truth than is Simpson's (or anyone's) willingness to believe the miraculous. There is no room for divine intervention or supernatural occurrences in Rumpole's world, and he advises Simpson to face this fact when he takes the stand in his own defense, if only "for the sake of a lot of lonely people ... who go out looking for miracles."[16] Thanks to Rumpole's brilliant performance, Simpson is at last disabused of his faith in the cult's power to "change the blood on a paper"[17] and tells us what really happened: he had joined the cult as an accountant, had concluded that it was a swindle and deserted his post, and he had then been attacked by the alleged victim, who had been persuaded to exact revenge on the cult's behalf.

In hitting upon this explanation for what seemed like a miracle, Rumpole unwittingly offers an interesting symbolic picture of the nature of national identity (and what threatens it). The blood that cannot be "changed" on the paper plainly symbolizes Englishness (an identity Rumpole himself seems to have come close to shedding at the start of the novella by retiring to Florida to become "an orange," as he puts it [52]) and its essentially fixed, if ambiguous, character as well as its necessarily textual nature. English identity is about blood, but more importantly, it is about blood on paper; it is, essentially, a written object that requires expert interpretation. It is more or less like the system of law that the English have evolved over the centuries; it is certainly not a magical or mutable substance that can, as Simpson initially believes, be changed or change itself to become something else.

Not surprisingly, given his insight into nice questions of blood, Rumpole often functions as a kind of microcosm of England itself, nowhere more so than in *Rumpole's Return*. Rumpole himself is symbolically threatened with extinction as a result of his encounters with the foreign. Although he claims that his existence in Florida is "neither life nor death,"[18] it plainly represents a posthumous existence for an "Old Bailey hack," in which he feels himself reduced to the senseless condition of a passive fruit "gently ripening to a roseate hue" in the sun.[19] Rumpole's near-deathly condition seems to stem from the threat America poses to his identity; he notes that his daughter-in-law is "expecting the first ever Rumpole to become a citizen of the United States,"[20] and he himself is compared to George Washington by a well-meaning Tiffany Jones, who refers light-heartedly to the wigs worn by English barristers in court. Not surprisingly, Rumpole's death-like absence from England seems to have ushered in a state of moral chaos and social upheaval at home, at least in his own mind, as he asks, "What's an honorable doing down the tube, like a common barrister?"[21]

To make a stand against this world turned upside-down, Rumpole must solve the riddle of Canter's death, and of course he must return to England to do so.

To suggest the emotional and even spiritual importance of this journey back across the Atlantic, Mortimer uses the last three stanzas of Ben Jonson's "A Farewell to the World" as the epigraph for *Rumpole's Return*:

> Else I my state should much mistake
> To harbour a divided thought
> From all my kind — that, for my sake,
> There should a miracle be wrought.
>
> No, I do know that I was born
> To age, misfortune, sickness, grief:
> But I will bear these with that scorn
> As shall not need thy false relief.
>
> Nor for my peace will I go far,
> As wanderers do, that still do roam;
> But make my strengths, such as they are,
> Here in my bosom, and at home.

In these stanzas Jonson refuses to entertain the belief that "a miracle" might be "wrought" for his sake (a stoical stance Rumpole forces Simpson to accept, as we have seen). Jonson also expresses a determination to "make" his "strengths ... at home," a feeling that Mortimer no doubt wishes us to see echoed in Rumpole's escape from America back to England. English-ness and the non-miraculous go hand in hand in *Rumpole's Return*, whereas miracles and America seem strongly allied. One might even construct the following chain of reasoning using Mortimer's works: Englishness is defined by a respect for justice; justice depends on the application of laws; laws depend on our ability to recognize reality; and reality is based on a refusal of miracles.

As such a formula might suggest, Rumpole must do more to rescue himself and Englishness from the clutches of religious madness and for-eigness than merely return "home."[22] He must first shake his client's gullible faith in the supernatural. When Simpson marvels, "About the blood ... that must be a miracle," Rumpole politely responds, "If you have one fault, Mr. Simpson ... it is that you are a touch too ready to assume the miraculous."[23] Rumpole's mild tone belies the seriousness of his accu-sation; for a lawyer who deals in facts and reasonable doubts, a readiness to assume the miraculous is anathema. Rumpole forces Simpson to face the fact that "[t]here is a perfectly clear, scientific explanation" for the mis-understanding about his own blood,[24] and he induces Simpson to clear his name by exposing the cult as a fraud. In his final speech to the jury, Rumpole emphasizes the psychological attractions of irrational religious faith, and describes the brainwashed victim as a would-be murderer in his own right, a man "more dangerous than any thief or sexual molester ... a man who believed he had God on his side."[25] Such a message is by no means unique to *Rumpole's Return*; we also see Mortimer warning us of the dangers of moral witch-hunts or religious crusades in a story entitled "Rumpole and the Children of the Devil."[26]

To clear Simpson's name and restore order to the chaos that first inspired Simpson to seek help from supernatural sources, Rumpole must also face his nemesis, Judge Roger Bullingham. Bullingham is a combat-ive, rubicund oaf whose name may contain a reference to John Bull, the symbol of a powerful, self-confident England (and who is thus an ironic contrast to the emasculated Simpson, a pale and weak-minded milque-toast whose nickname is "Duchess").[27] Rumpole's task, symbolically speak-ing, is to bring these opposing images of Englishness closer together; he must restore Simpson's faith in his own identity and bring Bullingham's animal vigor to heel. Rumpole succeeds in bringing Simpson and Bulling-ham into an unlikely harmony; he inspires the taciturn Simpson to tell his story in court and sees the usually irascible Bullingham receive his client's account of his own innocence with respectful attention. As Bullingham says, "I think we must let Mr. Simpson tell his story."[28] Such a response, Rumpole realizes, cannot be due to the Mad Bull's own virtues; it must be that respect for the Law has managed to win out over prejudice and stupidity at last.

Such happy outcomes as we find in *Rumpole's Return* are not always to be found in Mortimer's detective stories, especially when the issues of race, nationality and religion are concerned, and it is possible to argue that *Rumpole's Return* offers an unusually positive resolution of the tensions these problems create. Indeed, the irony of Rumpole's profession is that he frequently manages to punish his morally guilty clients more effectively by getting them acquitted by a court of law. This is certainly true in "Rumpole and the Fascist Beast," in the case of one Colonel Rex Parkin, a member of the racist "Britain First Party," whom Rumpole defends on a charge of inciting violence. Rumpole succeeds in getting his client acquitted, even though Parkin (inspired, ironically, by the example of Gandhi) earnestly desires martyrdom for his dubious cause. Humiliated by the belittling though exculpatory speech Rumpole gives in his defense, and attacked for disloyalty by his fellow party members, Parkin commits suicide. The details of Parkin's case are remarkable for more than their irony, however; they are also directly relevant to the issues of race and nationality raised in *Rumpole's Return*.

Parkin makes what Rumpole calls a "regrettable speech" in which he "had recommended repatriation of all migrants ('We want our tinted friends to be thoroughly at home. In their homes, my friends, not ours')."[29] According to police records (which Rumpole later shows to be slightly but crucially mistaken), Parkin's speech ends with an apparent call for violence: "The answer, my friends, is ... Blood."[30] In arguing for Parkin's innocence, Rumpole suggests that Parkin may have said "The answer is *in* the blood" and may therefore have been making an "innocuous" statement implying that the source of "some supposed difference in racial characteristics" is in the blood.[31] The repeated mention of "blood" as an equivocal word implying both violence and racial difference is reminiscent of Enoch Powell's infamous speech in which the right-wing politician predicted that unrestricted immigration would lead to "rivers of blood" flowing in the streets of London. It also looks ahead to *Rumpole's Return*, and forces us to look at the centrality of the question of blood in that story with special attention to its racial connotations. Indeed, in *Rumpole's Return* Rumpole himself uses more or less the same phrase as Rex Parkin when discussing the murder case in question: "The answer lies in the blood."[32] Whether he believes that such remarks—even if they are clearly not incitements to violence—are truly "innocuous" is difficult to say, since Rumpole seldom expresses an extra-legal opinion on issues of race and nationality. Even his use of the word "regrettable" to describe Parkin's speech echoes other instances in his narratives when he terms any statement by a client imply-ing his or her guilt is "regrettable" or "unfortunate" from an advocate's point of view.

Clear from this story is that Rumpole's attitudes towards race are complex and conflicted. When his wife Hilda herself occasionally expresses racist views, Rumpole professes discomfiture: "'Hardly a white face to be seen. Down by the tube station.' Oh dear. 'She' does come out with these embarrassing remarks occasionally."[33] He also assumes a typically lawyer-like pose as a cross-examiner, treating his wife as a hostile "witness" to be put "on the defensive" by a suggestion of her hypocrisy in racial matters. At one point he asks her, "You didn't get the supper at Chatterjee's Gen-eral Stores by any chance?"[34] She confesses that she did, albeit reluctantly, since "[e]verywhere else was shut."[35] When Hilda invokes her Aunt Fran, who would "turn in her grave if she could see London nowadays," Rumpole reminds her that the sight of Indians and Pakistanis would hardly have been a shock to her by itself, since Aunt Fran lived in the Punjab for many years and "spent her life running up curries and kedgerees."[36] Rumpole is, of course, ignoring the subtext of Hilda's objection, which is not to the sight of non-whites *per se*, but to their visible and seemingly permanent pres-ence in the English capital.

Hilda's views, we see, are exactly those of Rex Parkin, and we are invited to see her also as the "Fascist Beast" of the story's title. Rumpole even manages to enlist his new pupil, a Pakistani named Lutaf Ali Khan, to assist him in his covert but deliberate attempt to twit both Hilda's and Parkin's prejudices. Rumpole invites Khan to sit in on his interview with an outraged Parkin, and brings Khan home for a roast beef dinner with a less hostile but still uncomfortable Hilda. This show of political correct-ness is clearly undertaken mainly out of a spirit of mischief; Rumpole confesses that when Parkin sees Khan, Rumpole's prospective pupil, "there was such a sharp disapproving intake of breath from Captain Parkin that I couldn't resist taking the young Pakistani there and then."[37] Khan repays this equivocal favor handsomely; he flatters Rumpole by his fervent devotion to the law ("I am mustard keen, I must say...."[38]) and his syco-phantic assertion that Rumpole is overdue for a judgeship. More problem-atically, Khan also proves to be a faithful mirror for wounded British imperial pride, as we see in his expression of nostalgia for the British Raj: "We had some sensible fellows in the government then. Not these silly asses we have now."[39] In other words, Khan makes up for his transgres-sive presence on English soil by endorsing an implied narrative of English superiority; indeed, perhaps the most authoritarian sentiment in the story is expressed by Khan, whose annoyance with the "dreadful Pakistani students" whom he suspects have stolen his radio is expressed in a wish to see them summarily imprisoned: "I'd send them inside, double-quick pronto."[40]

The subtext of Khan's brief but disturbing presence in "Rumpole and the Fascist Beast" is essentially that Pakistani immigrants like him are hard-working, deferential caricatures of Englishness, but the rhetorical implications of the story suggest that they are a wave of invaders every bit as alarming to the native English as a fascist invasion would have been during World War II. When Rumpole reads newspaper accounts of fascist marches and race riots in London, he immediately associates them with World War II–era imagery of "jackboots marching into Czechoslovakia."[41] His fantasies of reliving the privations of the Blitz ("they'll give us dried eggs. Whale steak"[42]) evince his nostalgia for a past that guarantees the "moral and spiritual" purity that Robert Paul associates with Winston Churchill and the struggle against Hitler. As Paul notes, Winston Churchill symbolized a period when "the British people were more ready to believe that the struggle in which they were engaged was essentially moral and spiritual" than at any other time.[43] Incidentally, Mortimer repeatedly associates Rumpole with Churchill; descriptions of Rumpole "puffing a small cigar" and walking with his "old mac flapping in the wind" are allusions to the familiar Churchillian stride.[44] Mortimer also describes Rumpole's characteristic outfit as a tribute to his own father's, which was "rather like that which Mr. Churchill used to wear in the war."[45]

In this sense, Rumpole's own attitude towards the past is not entirely different from that of the "fascist beast" he is to defend; indeed, the label "fascist beast" hardly seems appropriate as a description of the ramrod-straight, sincere and disciplined Rex Parkin. Parkin is a racist, but Mortimer suggests that his wish to defend Britain against what he sees as a new wave of invaders is not particularly bestial or even fascistic. Indeed, Rumpole's initial impulse to take up his wartime post and re-enlist in the RAF ground-staff is a satirical but clear parallel to Parkin's reversion to a militaristic ethos in the face of the threat he sees from "our tinted brothers."[46] Although Rumpole seems at times to have a racially motivated distaste for Khan's less well-behaved countrypeople (in "Rumpole and the Alternative Society" he complains about having to "defend some over-excited Pakistani accused of raping his social worker"[47]), he is arguably just as hostile towards other, less visible, minorities who are encroaching on English soil and legal affairs. For instance, in "Rumpole and the Fascist Beast," despite Rumpole's own attempts to ridicule Parkin's xenophobia, he can't resist expressing disapproval of "Welsh solicitors" and, when he is rebuked, making an irreverent and inappropriate mention of "the Race Relations act."[48]

This animus against foreigners becomes an important theme in *Rumpole's Return*, where two unwelcome strangers invade Rumpole's chambers (no doubt as revenge for Rumpole's desertion of England). The first of these, Ken Cracknell, is a hypocritical "radical barrister" whose careerism wears a mask of "democratic principle."[49] Although in many ways a stereotypically resentful product of the English lower classes, Cracknell is marked by non–English signifiers; he rides an "overpowered Japanese Honda" motorcycle[50] and wears an outfit that makes him look "as though he's dropped in from Mars," according to the elderly barristers of his chambers.[51] He is also nicknamed "The Dirt Track Rider" and "The Speedway King," titles suggesting American motorcycle racing culture rather than anything recognizably English.[52]

The other usurper of Rumpole's place is Owen Glendour-Owen, whose name is reminiscent of Owen Glendower, a Welsh nationalist rebel, and implies strong anti–English sentiment. Rumpole comes briefly into conflict with Owen over shared space in chambers, and is forced to endure Owen's gloating enjoyment of a rare defeat for Rumpole: "It seems Rumpole spouted Wordsworth at the jury. It went down like a lead balloon."[53] The trial Owen is referring to happened in a provincial town called Grimble, where Rumpole is faced with the fact that some of what he takes to be core English values are under threat; he concedes, "I made the mistake of appealing to the old English sense of freedom. Freedom's gone out of fashion in Grimble."[54] Grimble is the geographical counterpart of Percival Simpson; it represents an England out of touch with its identity and traditional virtues. In any case, Owen, like Khan before him, is removed from Rumpole's sphere by a combination of ambition and the favorable attitude of the Lord Chancellor's office; both foreigners are safely assimilated and exalted by the legal hierarchy without forcing Rumpole to deal with a permanent foreign presence in his professional life.

However, Rumpole's battles with un–English foes are by no means confined to his interchanges with Owen; yet another familiar foreigner, the Scottish doctor Angus MacClintock, impinges on Rumpole's consciousness at intervals, having been (mistakenly) informed by Hilda that Rumpole is an avid reader of pornography. This stereotypically "dour and anxious Scot"[55] offers various embarrassing bits of enigmatic advice to a mildly puzzled Rumpole before the misunderstanding is cleared up. The case Rumpole is trying to solve in *Rumpole's Return* also presents a suitably exotic enemy — the leader of the Children of the Sun cult is described as "a cleric with crinkly white hair, kindly eyes beaming behind rimless glasses, and a deep and healthy suntan."[56] While Mortimer is not explicit about the leader's race, his non–European ancestry is strongly implied in the "crinkly" hair and dark skin. If this man is European, Mortimer implies, he has done his best to shed this identity. As part of his membership in this cult Simpson possesses a "curved Moroccan dagger,"[57] an object that is both another sign of the cult's foreignness[58] and an implicit indication of the violence that such foreign religious traditions entail. Rumpole's most decisive legal battle with foreignness comes in his confrontation with Professor Andrew Ackerman, the expert whose testimony on bloodstains has been especially damning to Simpson's defense and morale. Ackerman's "Edinburgh upbringing" is only faintly discernible in his mild Scottish accent,[59] but it is enough to make him a worthy antagonist. Symbolically enough, Ackerman has made a rare mistake where blood is concerned, and Rumpole proves that Ackerman's conclusion (that Simpson wrote the letter in his alleged victim Rory Canter's blood) is not only debatable but deeply flawed.

Even Rumpole's family is not free from the taint of the foreign; his American daughter-in-law Erica, with her dogmatic views and homespun clothing, seems like a leader of a cult of her own.[60] In conceiving a child with Erica, Nick has essentially created a blood-covenant with America rather similar to Simpson's pledge of allegiance to the cult. Rumpole tries to explain his need to return to England to his son, and at first can only say (rather confusingly, from Nick's point of view): "It's about blood."[61] He later reminisces with Nick about their old closeness as father and son: "We used to track Indian spoor and swear to be blood-brothers."[62] Nick doesn't recall such explicitly blood-oriented bonds, and is not terribly eager to revisit his early years. Mortimer makes it plain that Nick has chosen to leave England for America and has therefore allowed his blood to be "changed" in America, metaphorically speaking, in something of the same way that Simpson believes his blood was changed by the cult.

Furthermore, the basic conflict between immigrants and Englishness is visible in a crucial scene from *Rumpole's Return*. The only witnesses to the aftermath of the struggle between Percival Simpson and Roderick Canter (the man Simpson is accused of murdering) are Byron MacDonald, a "Jamaican guard," and two (presumably English-born) teenagers wearing "a job lot of Iron Crosses and other emblems of the Wehrmacht."[63] The fatal confrontation between Simpson and Canter is arguably a displacement of the more socially charged confrontation between a minority whose non–English origin is proclaimed by his skin color (and emphasized by Mortimer) and the apparently racist skinheads who, if their attire is any indication of their ferocity, would presumably wish to murder him.

Mortimer employs a plotline similar to that of *Rumpole's Return* in "Rumpole and the Confession of Guilt," which describes the trial of another young man accused of stabbing an apparent stranger in a public place. Here the hints of racial violence in the stabbing portrayed in displaced form in *Rumpole's Return* and incited in "Rumpole and the Fascist Beast" are made explicit, since the accused himself is of Jamaican ancestry and his alleged victim is a white Englishman. In "Rumpole and the Confession of Guilt," Rumpole quickly becomes impatient with his instructing solicitor's view that the defense should accuse the police of "racialism … based on strong feelings of sexual jealousy"[64] and seems hostile to his own client:

> Try as I might, I couldn't find a satisfactory explanation for Oswald Gladstone. I mean, I believe in Mutual Aid, Universal Tolerance, and the Supreme Individual. At heart, I've long suspected I'm an anarchist. Man is born free and is everywhere in chains. But … jolly Jean-Jacques Rousseau, or even that old sweetheart, Prince Peter Kropotkin, would have drawn the line at shoving a flick-knife into a complete stranger.[65]

Rumpole's pessimism is only deepened by the fact that Gladstone has signed a confession, but this document is proven invalid when Rumpole forces his client to admit that he can't read. In other words, Gladstone is saved from jail only by another kind of humiliating isolation — his racial otherness and the illiteracy that accompanies it.

Gladstone's family has abandoned him to the state, and the only father figure in his life is a priest named Eldred Pickersgill, whose claims to religious authority seem as tenuous as Gladstone's claims to English identity (despite his last name, which is a reminder of a famous liberal prime minister); Pickersgill will only give testimony on the condition that he isn't asked to swear on the Bible.[66] Rumpole is not impressed with Pickersgill or his supportive attitude towards Gladstone, but the father-son bond between the two is clearly an important one, and it is a central theme of the story, as it is in *Rumpole's Return*. Not surprisingly, Rumpole's own son Nick figures prominently in both stories, playing the role of a foil to his father's clients: In "Rumpole and the Confession of Guilt," he expresses distaste for his father's profession and abruptly leaves to "start a new sort of life in another country"[67] whereas his counterpart, Gladstone, is freed to pursue his life in England. In *Rumpole's Return*, of course, Nick is already established in America, and while still there he joins his father's legal adventures, as if both to compensate for his defection and to offset the plotline revolving around Simpson's abortive American odyssey and near-fatal return to England.

As Nick's sleuthing suggests, Mortimer is strongly attracted to the idea that British justice and skill in detection can be exported beyond Britain's borders. Moreover, Mortimer drew upon his own experiences as a lawyer working abroad for Amnesty International in writing "Rumpole and the Golden Thread," a story inspired by Mortimer's own real-life defense of (now Nobel Laureate) Wole Soyinka on a charge of murder in Nigeria.[68] Rumpole is asked to defend a politician named David Mazenze on a trumped-up charge of murder. Mazenze, a revolutionary leader in the fictional country of Neranga, asks Rumpole to represent him partly because Mazenze fondly recalls his own days in England, and partly because Rumpole is deemed "typical of British justice" precisely because he is so "perfectly lowly" and "ordinary."[69]

Despite the undoubted benevolence of Mortimer's involvement with Soyinka's cause, the fictional story contains some problematic assumptions about the relationship between law and empire. Firstly, its title, "Rumpole and the Golden Thread" (an allusion to the presumption of innocence that is, according to Rumpole, "the Golden Thread which runs through the whole history of our Criminal Law"[70]), is associated with the "Golden Journey to Samarkand," a phrase from James Elroy Flecker's poem "Samarkand" that Rumpole quotes early in the story.[71] Thus the central principle of British justice becomes a kind of accompaniment to Flecker's fantasy of travel, conquest and trade in exotic lands, making law itself a tool of imperial profiteering, at least in a symbolic sense. Even more tellingly, when recalling his relationship with David Mazenze (a former student, who has become a would-be revolutionary in the fictional country of Neranga) Rumpole says, "There was something to be said for the old days of the Empire. Almost all African politicians were students in the Temple."[72] As befits a non–European pupil of Rumpole's, Mazenze himself is nostalgic about his time in Britain ("I think of England so often…. I long for your Cotswolds") and makes a rather mawkish allusion to Rupert Brooke's "The Soldier" to imply his sense of vicarious Englishness: "If I'm hanged, think of this, Horace. There is some corner of a Nerangan jail house that is forever Moreton-on-Marsh."[73]

Despite his flattery, Mazenze points out some contradictions in the British justice system he admires: "We have no jury…. You British abolished juries in murder cases when Neranga was still 'New Somerset.'"[74] Naturally, Rumpole is doubly "appalled" when he hears this; in the first place, it will make his own task more difficult, and in the second place, this exercise of colonial power threatens his own faith in the British commitment to justice: "*We* did that?"[75] In these passages we can see the complexity of Mortimer's attitudes towards law and Britishness once again. On the one hand, he clearly identifies the system of British justice as a positive good that has come from (and partly justifies) the British Empire, and, on the other hand, he shows how its principles have been compromised here and there by political considerations (some no doubt based on racism or paternalism).

As we can see, Mortimer's own political attitudes are seldom obvious, but he occasionally plays the role of the disillusioned liberal who has gravitated towards conservative points of view on some social and cultural matters along with the rest of English society (especially during the Thatcher era, the time in which his stories became popular). He uses the Rumpole stories to suggest that multiculturalism and leftist social activism have gone much too far, though they may have begun with the best of intentions. His pet peeves, as he has listed them in his introduction to *The Best of Rumpole*, include "the power of social workers," "euthanasia" and "political correctness."[76] For instance, in a story called "Rumpole and the Miscarriage of Justice" Rumpole falls afoul of a civil rights lawyer named Miles Crudgington, whom he accuses of caring about "human rights" only when they are afforded to "a carefully selected minority" that does not include Rumpole's Caucasian client.[77] Rumpole's racial attitudes are far from politically correct. The case of Oswald Gladstone, for instance, prompts Rumpole to some cynical, even potentially racist musings: when a priest claims that "[t]here's good in that lad ... real good in him, deep down somewhere," Rumpole responds with uncharacteristic misanthropy: "Pity he doesn't bring it up and give it an airing occasionally."[78] What is ironic here is that Rumpole has switched places with the prosecutors, who usually greet his own protestations about his clients' goodness with skepticism.

Usually, however, the central tenet of Rumpole's (and, indeed, of Mortimer's) creed is a respect for individual liberty. In "Rumpole and the Honorable Member," Rumpole opines: "I can think of no social theory which could possibly account for such sports as Rumpole and She Who Must Be Obeyed, and I honestly don't believe we're exceptions, being surrounded by a sea of most most peculiar, and unclassifiable individuals."[79] This sentiment may sound attractively innocuous, but in the context of detective fiction (as analyzed by theorists such as Moretti and Paul, cited above), it has a conservative subtext. Rumpole appears to be denying the possibility of applying any sort of collective theory to the English people, thereby effectively forestalling the idea that they could be guilty of anything as a group. Even if we disagree with Moretti's and Paul's political critiques of the genre of detective fiction, their views underline the fact that Rumpole's staunch belief in individual autonomy makes him the ideal detective; he is determined to deal with people purely as individuals, regardless of what kinds of social pressures have made them what they are, and regardless of what injustices await them after they are convicted and imprisoned. They are English, and are therefore individuals in the legal and moral sense; indeed, Rumpole often seems to echo the cliché that England is a nation of eccentrics which cannot be transformed into any truly collective identity. In one story Rumpole meditates ruefully on "the number of different countries, all speaking private languages and with no diplomatic relations, into which England is divided."[80] Given this paradoxical, divided image of the nation to which he belongs, it is perhaps not surprising that in the end (as we shall see) Rumpole is driven to embrace a modified sort of religious discourse to recuperate and justify his wholly irrational sense of national identity and his conviction that it is embodied in a fixed set of laws and principles.

At first glance, it would seem unlikely that Rumpole would have recourse to any religious sentiments whatsoever; he despises anything that smacks of the holier-than-thou, and his most hated foe is described by Mortimer as "the intolerably pompous Sam Ballard, Q.C., leading light of the Lawyers as Christians Society."[81] Rumpole's attitude towards religion is partly a result of his upbringing; he informs us that his father, the Reverend Wilfred Rumpole, "came reluctantly to the conclusion that he no longer believed any one of the Thirty-nine Articles" but nevertheless "soldiered on" as a Church of England clergyman.[82] Having seen firsthand the dismal existence produced by an attempt to live by an evidently false set of beliefs, Rumpole muses that it is better to be a lawyer who appeals to doubt, than to be "a cleric" and deal in "improbable beliefs."[83]

Nevertheless, Mortimer clearly wishes to draw upon a religious vocabulary to enshrine and dignify Rumpole's humanistic faith in British law. Rumpole muses on his delight at walking to work one morning by paraphrasing Robert Browning's lines "God's in his heaven / All's right with the world." Rumpole's own sense that he is in the right place (i.e., on his way to his chambers) is reinforced by his intuition that "God was in his heaven,"[84] and Rumpole's own placid benevolence is compared to God's.[85] Mortimer implies that Rumpole's quasi-sacred status is partly a necessary compensation for the degradation of actual religious figures who are supposed to provide spiritual and moral guidance. The story shows Rumpole wrestling with the paradoxes of the powers he has assumed as a barrister; he notes that "lawyers get to know more than is good for them about their fellow human beings."[86] This intimate knowledge, as Mortimer too has noted, was once the special province of the clergy,[87] but Rumpole's client is so apparently naïve and innocent that Rumpole condescends to him quite mercilessly, telling his client, the Reverend Mordred Skinner, that "[j]uries are like the Almighty God.... Totally unpredictable."[88] Rumpole's implication here is that he understands both rather better than the average priest seems to.

Rumpole's limitations as priestly or quasi-divine figure, however, are made quite plain by the events of the story. Rumpole's expert but still imperfect understanding of the mysteries of the legal system is emphasized when his arch-enemy, Judge Roger Bullingham, ends up agreeing with him and advising the jury to find Rev. Skinner not guilty. Faced with this inexplicable demonstration of fairness by the Mad Bull, as Rumpole calls his nemesis, Rumpole can only call the end of the case a "miracle" comparable only to the parting of the Red Sea.[89] Skinner is duly acquitted, but seems a bit disappointed, reflecting on the possibility of being "unfrocked": "It might have been extremely restful. Not to have to pretend to any sort of sanctity."[90] Rumpole is left wondering about his career choice too: "Perhaps I should have taken up as a vicar…. Faith not facts, is what we need."[91]

The complexity of Mortimer's attitudes towards detective fiction, the law and religion may be seen in an episode from *The Trials of Rumpole* in which Rumpole is asked about the prospect of becoming a judge and sentencing criminals to prison. With typical anti-establishment reflexes, Rumpole bristles: "Don't ask silly questions…. I'd start every Sentence [sic] with, 'There but for the grace of God goes Horace Rumpole.'"[92] Here Rumpole echoes Holmes's words in "The Boscombe Valley Mystery": "I never hear of such a case as this that I do not think of Baxter's words, and say, 'There, but for the grace of God, goes Sherlock Holmes.'"[93] While some might argue that such sentiments amount to no more than the typical bad-faith bourgeois *frisson* at another's misfortune, they do contain the unmistakable suggestion that society produces criminals arbitrarily, without any special regard for the inherent moral character of the individual. At any rate, it seems to take "the grace of God" (something Rumpole himself doesn't believe in, as he frequently states) to guarantee the freedom of the citizen. As we can see, religious language, if not actual piety, supplements Rumpole's usually unshakeable faith in the justice system. This faith extends to Rumpole's clients; he has established a cult-like following among the minor criminals of London, as we are told: "my regular clients … smile with everlasting hope when their solicitors breathe the magic words, 'We're taking in Horace Rumpole.'"[94] When we cast our minds back to the systematic debunking of the magical in *Rumpole's Return*, the irony of the little personality cult that Rumpole has produced is keen.

Another instance of religious language creeping into Rumpole's life occurs after the successful conclusion of the case in *Rumpole's Return*. Happily reinstalled in his London home, Rumpole celebrates Christmas with Hilda, rescuing religious vocabulary from the cult's fanaticism by attending her performance of "O Come All Ye Faithful" and calling himself one of "the faithful."[95] By these gestures Rumpole shows himself to be willing to forgive and recuperate the various defections and deviations from his secular ethic of legal Englishness, as long as he is permitted to retain the illusion that his law-driven, rational worldview will ultimately triumph. This belief is what makes Rumpole one of the "faithful" even though his faith is certainly of a peculiar sort. Despite the fact that it is religion that lures the English away from their pragmatic, empirical point of view and towards either a self-destructive altruism (as in the case of Mordred Skinner) or murderous fanaticism (as in the case of Rory Canter), Rumpole cannot afford to abandon its postures of devotion entirely. After all, he too must come to terms with what he calls a "Higher Tribunal," a transcendent law-giving identity that he can neither understand nor repudiate.[96] This higher tribunal is concerned with more than just the fact of innocence and guilt that obsesses the detective; as one of Mortimer's characters, a man named (perhaps symbolically, given Mortimer's obsession with "Britishness") Bill Britwell, who was once a writer of murder mysteries and is now a clergyman, claims, "[S]ince I've been concerned with the greatest mystery of all, I've lost interest in detective stories."[97] Yet where the answer to this "greatest mystery" lies is never made quite clear, and this is, no doubt, as Mortimer would wish it. In using Rumpole to meditate upon issues of race, religion and nationality, he clearly prefers to take old-fashioned British empiricism as far as it can go, and then abandon himself to his faith that justice, like God's will in the eyes of a believer, is at least merciful where it is incomprehensible.

## Notes

1. John Mortimer, *The Best of Rumpole* (New York: Viking, 1993), 1.
2. H. Rider Haggard was greatly admired by Mortimer's father, and Mortimer himself calls Haggard the pre-eminent author of "the myths of the Englishman's Africa." John Mortimer, *Clinging to the Wreckage* (London: Penguin, 1986), 24.
3. Mortimer, *Best*, 4.
4. Mortimer, *Best*, 4.
5. Marvin Lachmann, "Religious Cults and the Mystery," in *Synod of Sleuths: Essays on Judeo-Christian Detective Fiction*, ed. Jon L. Breen and Martin H. Greenberg (Metuchen, NJ: The Scarecrow Press, 1990), 79. Lachmann goes on to posit a counter-trend that is more relevant for readers of *Rumpole's Return*: "there is a reverse side to religion in the mystery, and a surprisingly large number of books and stories depend on cults which are by their nature irreligious, with leaders who prey on their flocks for power and/or financial gain."
6. Robert S. Paul. *Whatever Happened to Sherlock Holmes?: Detective Fiction, Popular Theology, and Society* (Carbondale, IL: Southern Illinois University Press, 1991), 9.
7. Paul, 17.
8. Paul, 17.

9. Paul, 20.

10. Paul, 21. In a similar vein, Franco Moretti has argued persuasively that "Detective Fiction ... exists expressly to dispel the doubt that guilt might be impersonal, and therefore collective and social"; Franco Moretti, *Signs Taken for Wonders: Essays in the Sociology of Literary Form* (London: NLB, 1983), 135. This observation might usefully be applied to the detective element in the Rumpole series. Because Rumpole is so firmly committed to reaffirming Englishness and its connection to the ideal of a universal justice, it is unthinkable that English identity as a whole could itself be based on injustice, whether it be economic, class-based or race-based. Jon Thompson also contends that "[t]he myth of Sherlock Holmes is ... a myth of England as well" in that Holmes's world is "a world in which crime is intriguing, individual, and eminently soluble, not an ugly social problem; a world in which urban squalor makes a quaint constrast to the elegance of London hansom cabs and gas street lamps; a world undisturbed by conflict, whether sexual or social"; Jon Thompson, *Fiction, Crime, and Empire: Clues to Modernity and Postmodernism* (Urbana and Chicago: University of Illinois Press, 1993), 77. It is very tempting to make the same argument about Mortimer's Rumpole fictions, which, as we will see, displace social, religious and racial conflict into isolated and discrete "cases" that do not necessarily have much bearing on the social world around them. In other words, both the Holmes and Rumpole stories refuse to critique the central institutions of English society, preferring to concentrate on the criminal acts that occur within them, treating these transgressions not as the logical outcomes of an unjust society (which critics such as Thompson clearly assume it is) but as aberrations to be dealt with within the framework of existing social institutions (the law courts, in Rumpole's case).

11. Thompson, 75. Thompson also notes that "whatever cameo roles Indians have in the Sherlock Holmes stories, they are invariably represented stereotypically, as unfathomable exotics of the East. Behind these stereotypes is the assumption that foreigners, especially dark ones, are only important enough to warrant a quick 'snapshot' characterization"; Thompson, 69. Unfortunately, the same is essentially true of the Rumpole stories, which feature minorities either as clients or temporary colleagues (like Khan in "Rumpole and the Fascist Beast"); they, like the Holmes tales, are concerned with English people and their ideas and institutions, not with outsiders who may or may not fit into them.

12. Paul, 64.

13. Erik Routley, *The Puritan Pleasures of the Detective Story* (London: Gollancz, 1972), 223.

14. John Mortimer, *Rumpole's Return* (New York: Penguin 1980), 115.

15. Mortimer, *Return*, 148

16. Mortimer, *Return*, 150.

17. Mortimer, *Return*, 73.

18. Mortimer, *Return*, 12.

19. Mortimer, *Return*, 12.

20. Mortimer, *Return*, 25.

21. Mortimer, *Return*, 15.

22. "Home" is a very contested and ambiguous word in *Rumpole's Return*; set against the English "home" Rumpole flees Florida to reoccupy is the "home" provided for Tiffany and (very briefly) for Nick by the Children of the Sun; Mortimer, *Return*, 113.

23. Mortimer, *Return*, 96.

24. Mortimer, *Return*, 150.

25. Mortimer, *Return*, 154.

26. This tale concerns an overzealous social worker named Mirabelle Jones, who

accuses a man of devil worship after seeing his daughter in a demonic mask at school. As he exposes Ms. Jones's paranoia as unfounded, Rumpole manages to antagonize the pious Sam Ballard and exacerbate his colleague's Christian disapproval of a rival lawyer, all the while learning to dance. Indeed, as she watches him caper, Hilda comes to associate her own husband with the Satanic principle he has been simultaneously ridiculing and manipulating throughout the story: "You are an old devil, Rumpole!" Mortimer, *Best*, 235.

27. Simpson's nickname, "The Duchess," is an allusion to Wallis Simpson, the American divorcée who induced King Edward VII to abdicate the throne. Simpson is cast in a similar role *vis-à-vis* Rumpole by Ken Cracknell, who schemes to use the hopeless-looking murder case to discourage Rumpole from continuing to practice law.

28. Mortimer, *Return*, 152.

29. John Mortimer, *The Trials of Rumpole* (London: Penguin, 1979), 83.

30. Mortimer, *Trials*, 83.

31. Mortimer, *Trials*, 91.

32. Mortimer, *Return*, 94.

33. Mortimer, *Trials*, 81.

34. Mortimer, *Trials*, 81.

35. Mortimer, *Trials*, 81.

36. Mortimer, *Trials*, 81.

37. Mortimer, *Trials*, 83.

38. Mortimer, *Trials*, 84.

39. Mortimer, *Trials*, 88.

40. Mortimer, *Trials*, 89.

41. Mortimer, *Trials*, 79.

42. Mortimer, *Trials*, 79.

43. Paul, 26.

44. Mortimer, *Best*, 16.

45. Mortimer, *Best*, 1–2.

46. Mortimer, *Best*, 83.

47. John Mortimer, *Rumpole of the Bailey* (London: Penguin, 1978), 69.

48. Mortimer, *Trials*, 97.

49. Mortimer, *Return*, 18.

50. Mortimer, *Return*, 17.

51. Mortimer, *Return*, 21.

52. Mortimer, *Return*, 17.

53. Mortimer, *Return*, 93. The central claim of the Wordsworth passage in question reads: "It is not to be thought of that the flood of British freedom … should perish"; Mortimer, *Return*, 81.

54. Mortimer, *Return*, 84.

55. Mortimer, *Return*, 66.

56. Mortimer, *Return*, 30.

57. Mortimer, *Return*, 30.

58. The cult has also made inroads into England, where it is seen as a "foreign" company, "ruining local businesses by employing no strangers and keeping completely to themselves" (Mortimer, *Return*, 121–22).

59. Mortimer, *Return*, 146.

60. Such a reading is implicitly endorsed by Mortimer's description of the Sun cult, which has spuriously adopted the vocabulary of the family; the "Parents in Love" greet each "child" as he or she is received into the group; Mortimer, *Return*, 114.

61. Mortimer, *Return*, 41.

62. Mortimer, *Return*, 41. Rumpole's obsession with lineage and identity is manifested indirectly in his legal reminiscences about cases that "turned on a nice point of blood"; Mortimer, *Return*, 29.

63. Mortimer, *Return*, 10–11.

64. John Mortimer, *The Second Rumpole Omnibus* (London: Penguin, 1988), 16.

65. Mortimer, *Second*, 14.

66. Mortimer, *Second*, 26.

67. Mortimer, *Second*, 38.

68. Mortimer writes: "In the countries which have received our law it often proves a most durable commodity, keeping a flicker of freedom alive when all else has broken down. Driving away from Ibadan I had the unoriginal thought that British law might, together with Shakespeare, Wordsworth, Lord Byron and the herbaceous border, be one of our great contributions to the world"; Mortimer, *Clinging*, 199.

69. Mortimer, *Second*, 250.

70. Mortimer, *Second*, 274.

71. Mortimer, *Second*, 240.

72. Mortimer, *Second*, 247.

73. Mortimer, *Second*, 253.

74. Mortimer, *Second*, 255.

75. Mortimer, *Second*, 255.

76. Mortimer, *Best*, 5.

77. John Mortimer, *Rumpole on Trial* (New York: Viking, 1992), 103.

78. Mortimer, *Second*, 25.

79. Mortimer, *Bailey*, 87.

80. Mortimer, *Bailey*, 48.

81. Mortimer, *Best*, 4.

82. Mortimer, *Best*, 9.

83. Mortimer, *Second*, 32.

84. Mortimer, *Trials*, 11.

85. As if to reinforce the idea that Rumpole is a semi-divine figure, this passage ends with Claude Erskine-Brown (one of Rumpole's less admired colleagues) telling Rumpole "I saw a priest going into your room"; Mortimer, *Trials*, 11. Clearly, Mortimer is implying that Rumpole himself is a priestly figure of sorts, whose room in chambers is a spiritual sanctuary where God can be found. The irony of such implications is immediately underlined by another exchange between Rumpole, Erskine-Brown and their clerk, Henry: "'That's your con, Mr. Rumpole,' said Henry, explaining the curious manifestation of a Holy Man. 'Your con*version*? Have you seen the light, Rumpole? Is Number 3 Equity Court your road to Damascus?'" Mortimer, *Trials*, 11.

86. Mortimer, *Trials*, 9.

87. Mortimer himself has pointed out the degree to which the clergy's functions have been taken over by trained professionals such as lawyers: "At one period of history we might have put our affairs in the hands of priests or vicars. Nowadays the dissolution of marriage seems to be attended by grave and sympathetic chartered accountants"; Mortimer, *Clinging*, 201. His own upbringing bought this truth home to him rather forcefully: "I saw my father, the doyen of the divorce bar, in a rare role, that of the confessor, imposing a few Hail Marys and a period of abstinence"; Mortimer, *Clinging*, 133. Mortimer has plainly spent some time musing on the relationship between the tasks of the lawyer and the religious believer, and makes the following comparison: "The advocate has this much in common with the religious mystic, he can only operate successfully when he is able to suspend his disbelief"; Mortimer, *Clinging*, 128. Not too surprisingly, however, Mortimer goes on to imply that a sus-

pended disbelief is a healthier condition for a defense lawyer than active belief: "Indeed belief, for the advocate, is something which is best kept in a permanent state of suspension. There is no lawyer so ineffectual as one who is passionately convinced of his client's innocence"; Mortimer, *Clinging*, 128.

88. Mortimer, *Trials*, 15.
89. Mortimer, *Trials*, 34.
90. Mortimer, *Trials*, 35.
91. Mortimer, *Trials*, 41.
92. Mortimer, *Trials*, 41.
93. Quoted in Paul, 48.
94. Mortimer, *Trials*, 9. No doubt because of such expectations in his clients' minds, Rumpole is frequently made "to feel the awful burden on the defending lawyer, the need to work miracles"; Mortimer, *Second*, 257. He compares his courtroom performance with spiritualist seances in terms of their power of evoking unlikely results: "We go through all that mumbo jumbo ... 'My Lord, I Humbly submit.'... Abracadabra"; Mortimer, *Bailey*, 206.
95. Mortimer, *Return*, 157.
96. Mortimer, *Second*, 426.
97. John Mortimer, *Rumpole à la Carte* (London: Penguin, 1990), 129.

# 3

# Relocating the Heart of Darkness in Ruth Rendell

## SUZANNE PENUEL

### Orientalism *and Its Uses*

Before I discuss Ruth Rendell's novels *Speaker of Mandarin* (1983) and *Simisola* (1994), I will engage in a bit of rhetorical space-clearing. This gesture, though ritual, has like other rituals a functional component: although writers of genre fiction do not usually cause bitter arguments among academics, overtly political authors do become hotly contested territories. Rendell fits in both categories, particularly since being appointed to the House of Lords as a life peer. Increasingly a subject of critical attention, Rendell runs a slight risk of being claimed by one of several occasionally skirmishing academic camps, and I wish to establish claims for all of those parties before examining specific texts.[1]

Students of postcolonialism may find much to discuss in Rendell's novels of British encounters with Asia and Africa, and the long shadow of Edward Said hangs over any treatment of postcolonial themes. (This is even truer after Said's recent death, which has prompted conference panels, symposia, and special journal issues devoted to reexamining his work, particularly of *Orientalism*.) But Said, as various respondents have pointed out, downplays class conflict, preferring to concentrate on the interplay of different nations and ethnicities. Ahmad Aijaz, in fact, argues that Said and his followers neglect class conflict unjustly. In Aijaz's response to Edward Said and other theorists of the intersections of East and West, those theorists' accusations of Orientalism appear as a career move:

> Those [Asian immigrants to Europe and the United States after the late
> 1960s] who came as graduate students and then joined the faculties, especially
> in the Humanities and Social Sciences, tended to come from upper classes in
> their home countries. In the process of relocating themselves in the metropol-
> itan countries, they needed documents of their assertion, proof that they
> had always been oppressed. Books that connected oppression with class were
> not very useful, because *they* neither came from the working class nor were
> intending to join that class in their new country.... What the upwardly mobile
> professionals in this new immigration needed were narratives of oppression
> that would get them preferential treatment, reserved jobs, higher salaries
> in the social position they already occupied: namely, *as* middle-class pro-
> fessionals, mostly male. For such purposes *Orientalism* was the perfect nar-
> rative.[2]

I am not qualified to discuss the histories and motives of the academics
Aijaz discusses so passionately. His account of *Orientalism*'s influence, at
any rate, unfairly singles out those who moved to the West — Western-born
academics, too, responded positively to the text. However, Aijaz's general
concerns are hardly irrelevant: In producing Said-influenced readings, academics of *any* ethnic or geographical identification may be giving cruelly
short shrift to the effects of social rank and class that structure life among
both colonized and colonizing, including the lives of Western academics.
And the British detective novel in particular is one of the most class-
obsessed of genres; its concerns have generally been seen as intranational,
not international. For that matter, Rendell, a socialist baroness in the
House of Lords, speaks frankly in interviews about the importance of class
to her work. Susan Rowland, in her study of six twentieth-century British
crime and detective novelists, sees Rendell as addressing class as the *primary* locus of social tension.[3]

   *Orientalism* and other first-wave postcolonial criticism, stringently
anti–Marxist blind spots or not, still seems a relevant lens through which
to view Rendell's novels. Said's preferred analytical categories of nation
and race often blend with the category of class, though not explicitly in
his work. In a global marketplace, class allegiances and divisions can straddle borders and oceans; in economies in which the bulk of money is
acquired through inheritance, class can be as biologically framed as race.
In other words, class and race are not the same thing, but similar dynamics can structure both arenas. Not all of Said's poststructuralist tendencies, such as his pessimism about the capacity of language to represent
reality, need be accepted wholesale in order for the text to provide a spring-
board for readers of class as well as of race, religion, and nation.[4] For as
Said points out, Orientalist discourse is not usually about the Orient in
any real sense. Instead, it is about a vaguely examined other.

In 1991, Tony Giffone argued for Ruth Rendell's *Speaker of Mandarin* as a traditionally Orientalizing text. It and similar narratives of British encounters with China, Giffone writes, "merely reinforce all the [ethno-centric] suppositions in their readers, most of whom have probably never been to China." Giffone claims that for Rendell's characters, the "encounter with the Other has produced no new insights into their lives, no transfor-mation.[5] But writing about Rendell ten years later, Susan Rowland finds something quite different: "The energy of the detecting narrative is directed towards a *utopian social order*, one not achieved or even coherently imag-ined, but characterized by social progressiveness and liberal tolerance." Rowland describes Rendell's corpus as the only one among the six British crime fiction writers she examines that posits a "quest object for liberal politics"; that is, a world in which outdated hierarchies are defeated and in which conservatism no longer oppresses the populace and leads to crim-inal impulse.[6]

How to reconcile Giffone's indictment with Rowland's approbation? We may claim that Rendell changes; that 1983's *Speaker of Mandarin* is indeed racist, and that 1994's *Simisola*— Rowland discusses this text, but not *Speaker of Mandarin*— is part of a Great Leap Forward in Rendell's rep-resentation of the non-white, non–British subject. Alternatively, the change may be in Rendell's narrator, Chief Inspector Wexford. Giffone implicitly identifies Wexford with Rendell, but Rendell herself has said that she has to fight the temptation to kill him off.[7] The misanthropy of detective fiction is an open secret. After all, the genre requires violence, suspicion, and deception. Either the victims earn their bloody deaths to some degree, or the villains represent the worst impulses of humanity; more often, both are true. Wexford, who succeeds in his profession largely through his pow-ers of mistrust and social skepticism, is no exception to the misanthropic rule, but we need not assume that he voices Rendell's thoughts.

In *Speaker of Mandarin* and *Simisola*, Rendell directs Wexford's habit-ual distemper toward what are to him foreign lands: In the first novel, the People's Republic of China, in the second, an England of increasing racial and religious heterogeneity. The first novel refuses to validate the tradi-tional European fear of the mythologized Orient. The second text, part of a revitalized anti–Arab Western discourse that encompasses both the British detective novel and the second Gulf War, does validate that fear. It deploys yet a third racial-geographic term, that of Africanness, in order to do so. Rendell's rewriting of an English Orientalist myth paradoxically mobilizes late-twentieth-century ideals of racial parity in service of that Orientalism. Both narratives, though, also draw a parallel between West-ern imperialism and British domestic violence: the murders of women in their homes mirror the destructive involvement of the English in other countries. In *Simisola*, much more than in *Speaker of Mandarin*, the problems of imperialism emerge as a present-day British responsibility; in the first novel, the history of British imperialism is a potent memory.

## The Return of the Native

Part One of *Speaker of Mandarin* involves a twentieth-century parody of imperialism, the tour group. Wexford goes to China as part of an English delegation giving advice on crime prevention and detection to Chinese law enforcement. In his spare time, he travels with a motley assortment of tourists, British and Australian, who eat, drink, and shop their way through the People's Republic. When a Chinese man on the group's riverboat drowns after going overboard, Wexford dithers about going to the local police, finally deciding not to because "[s]uch an action would smack of 'putting himself forward', of showing off his greater sophistication and that of the nation he came from."[8] Ironically, Wexford's postcolonial angst and liberal self-consciousness cuts him off from his Chinese colleagues. Too, his perception of British expertise in matters of police work suggests that England is a lawless, violent place. Before going to China, Wexford assumes that the Chinese will wish to engage in the "favourite communist pastime of showing off national institutions—in this case, probably, police stations, courts, prisons" (9). But as it turns out, Wexford's guide shows him a museum, a cinema, and some impressive countryside. It is only in England that Wexford must spend time in institutions that exist because people commit crimes. However, when Wexford leaves China for the then–British territory of Hong Kong, it is with relief: "The cool airy train raced pleasantly back towards the Crown Colony, back to luxury, ordinariness, a 'too high' standard of living, soft beds, capitalism" (68).

*Speaker of Mandarin* oscillates between subverting racist Western stereotypes and offering a fairly uncritical treatment of Wexford's racial hostility. Early on, the detective derides his Chinese tour guide as "pink-cheeked baby-faced slant-eyed Mr Sung" (4). Sung is "inscrutable" and "enigmatic," he is "fanatical" about Mao Zedong, and his sense of duty to his government job overwhelms his hapless British client (4, 7, 5). True to Western stereotypes of Asian imitativeness, Sung even borrows Wexford's travel guide and quotes long passages back to Wexford the following day as if they were improvised. *Speaker of Mandarin* does suggest at times that Wexford's perceptions of Sung are unduly harsh — when Sung uses the phrase "let's go" once too many, the narrative identifies Wexford's response of "I wish you wouldn't keep saying that" as "irritable" (4). And when Wexford, grumpy about being bitten by mosquitoes, makes a knowingly incomprehensible joke to Sung about it ("I am particularly attractive to *anopheles* but the passion isn't mutual"), our sympathy is mostly with the tour guide, whose English is basic and who reacts with "amiability" to Wexford's intentionally alienating use of language (6–7). But Rendell also undercuts that sympathy, encouraging us to share Wexford's perception of Sung as someone to be mocked. While the novel does not render into dialogue Wexford's few fumbling attempts at Chinese, Sung's Rs turn into Ls in a way that is almost inevitably amusing to readers whose first language is English: "Velly well. I hope you not leglet." "I aflaid you be solly." "You take malaria pill evly Fliday?" (5–6). Here the novel falls into an Orientalizing trap: Sung is no longer one of Rendell's celebrated psychologically realistic characters, but rather turns into a figure of amusement for the West.[9]

For Said, Western illusions of knowing the Orient form a major part of Orientalist discourse.[10] In *Speaker of Mandarin*, on the other hand, Western racism aggressively denies knowledge. The "inscrutable" and "enigmatic" qualities that *Speaker of Mandarin* ascribes in part to Wexford, but mostly to the Chinese, are of course stereotypical. Wexford muses, "The truth is never really known about China, and that's not new, it's always been so" (62). His use of passive voice in the first clause absolves him, and other non–Chinese, of responsibility for knowledge. The undesirability of inscrutability becomes clear when Wexford's fellow tourist Lois refers to her tour guide as "that inscrutable little Yu"— Lois does not bemoan her own inability to read Yu, but rather cites inscrutability as a fundamental and irritating part of his character (25). (Permanent inscrutability is a particularly serious offense in detective fiction, whose teleology is one of secrets made public.) In any case, this British disowning of knowledge is also a disavowal of responsibility, an anti–Orientalism that nevertheless presents the East as alien, just as Said's Orientalism does. In Rendell's postcolonial setting, the British must deny knowledge, because the knowledge they have of China is self-incriminating imperialist memory. By contrast, in the accounts of Said's colonizing Orientalists of the nineteenth and eighteenth centuries, the will to power is still relatively free of guilt; knowledge, however dubious, is valuable currency.

Near the end of *Speaker of Mandarin*, Wexford looks at Hsia Yu-seng, a Chinese immigrant to London, and complicates the accusation of inscrutability: "Wexford looked at him, the bland parchment-coloured face, the still features that have led to 'inscrutable' being the adjective invariably associated with the Chinese" (163–4). The passive voice once again conceals the identity of the people who associate inscrutability with the Chinese; it absolves any particular person or group of responsibility for that association. In fact, the passage only assigns responsibility to the facial features themselves. Here, a physical quality, the "features," creates a social dynamic. Race is apparently no mere social construct, no biological fiction. Instead, the sentence implies, the biological reality of race has led to Ruth Rendell's fiction. However, the indirectness of the passage's *active* voice indicates a hesitancy about its own claims—"still features that have led" is a roundabout, evasive phrase (164). Also, its implicit acknowledgment that the perception of inscrutability must be explained suggests a defensiveness, an awareness that the perceptive capacity of those who call the Chinese "inscrutable" may be limited. Even as the passage justifies the presumably Western description of the Chinese, it hints that a different description is possible, if unlikely in the British context. Wexford and the Watson to his Holmes, Inspector Burden, in fact, have been fooled by what they see as Hsia's gentle appearance. Hsia Yu-seng is a criminal, and hardly an inscrutable one, since he confesses ("sings") to the crime and gives the two policemen his life history.

Wexford initially experiences Hsia as another stereotype of the non-Westerner, "impassive" (161), and this idea, too, proves inaccurate. Wexford has already described another Chinese man as "impassive" (51), but the reader realizes the unreliability of that label when the second "impassive" Chinese man turns out to be a rapist. The term, though, does not only mean "not passionate or demonstrative." As its root suggests, it also means "not *suffering*." Just as supposed Chinese inscrutability allows the British to disavow unpleasant knowledge, supposed Chinese impassivity allows the British to believe that the Chinese do not suffer from Western acts. The Chinese man who drowns is pushed overboard by an English tourist, but the circumstances of his death remain suppressed for most of the novel. The tourists cannot find his body, nor can they identify him. "Who is it?" Wexford asks (48); however, the man no longer exists in the present tense. Once again, Wexford's verb selection is questionable. The inspector's ignorance of the man's death and identity paves the way for the drowning victim's narrative replacement by a figure who bears no obvious connection to the novel's plot other than to console both tourists and readers with his very presence. The drowned man dies a painful death while still young; the replacement figure, who appears on the shore just after the tourists cease their search of the river, has lived the full span of life denied to the drowned man, and he seems to feel no pain at all. "The old man," the narrative reassures us, "looked at the people from the West with a kind of impassive polite curiosity" (51). The tourists rapidly forget the other man's death and suffering. Back in England, then, the "impassive" Hsia's "parchment" face also serves an imperialist textual fantasy, a *tabula rasa* ripe for any narrative the British may wish to write upon it.

With one or two exceptions, *Speaker of Mandarin* avoids explicit allusion to the larger history of the British in China. Nonetheless, the novel's twentieth-century British tourists end up reenacting nineteenth-century imperialism. The British Hong Kong to which Wexford gratefully returns is a prize of the Opium Wars, whose tensions over addiction, narcosis, smuggling, and international trade reappear in Wexford's compulsive consumption of hallucinatory tea and in his fellow traveler Vinald's carefully rationalized antiques smuggling.[11] Once back in England, Vinald declares, "When I hear sentimentalists groaning over our so-called thefts from China in, say, the Boxer Rebellion, I thank God for those — appropriations. Thank God we do have the Dowager Empress's throne in the British Museum. What do you suppose the Red Guards would have done with that?" (133–4). The antiques dealer's casual references to God reframe the conflict as one of Christian values versus godless destruction, and his question about the Red Guards is unanswerable. However, Vinald, who has profited substantially from his smuggling activities, eventually overstates the case: "The end here is to save priceless art treasures for the world. And these are not China's but indisputably the property *of all mankind*. They are our heritage, for in art all men are brothers" (134). His previous excuse to Wexford ("China is an extremely long way away and pretty alien to us anyway") makes the insincerity of his idealism patent (133). The tour group leaves China with more wealth than it brings in, plunder destined for the non–Chinese consumer. Though the Opium Wars are traditionally represented in the West as instances of the inevitable economic superiority of capitalist Europe to backward China, *Speaker of Mandarin* rewrites English economic gain from China as repellently exploitative, simple theft.

Wexford's green-tea-induced hallucinations indicate a similarly repressed guilt about the British presence in China. Continually imagining that he sees an old Chinese woman with bound feet, Wexford never realizes why he hallucinates that particular image, though his musings demand that we identify her: "Out of what recesses of experience, unconscious processes, even trauma, was his mind conjuring an old Chinese woman?" (54). Her metaphorical identity as China becomes clear when Vinald, in a trope that both objectifies the feminine and feminizes the East, refers to China itself as "she" (62). Wexford, who initially fantasizes the "trauma" as his own victimization, revises his understanding of the hallucination so far as to recall a Somerset Maugham story about an

Englishman in the Far East who is tormented by the spirit of a Sumatran man he has harmed.[12] Although in the Maugham story the emotional focus of the trauma narrative is still the Westerner, the original cause of that trauma is the Westerner too. But the Chief Inspector is indignant at the implication: "He, Wexford, had never done any sort of injury to an old Chinese woman" (63). In a projection-laden colonization nightmare that is inspired both by Britain's guilty imperial history in China and by Wexford's own status as the penetrating foreigner, he fears that the hallucination will invade his domestic space: "He lay on the bed, thinking about schizophrenia, wondering what he was going to do if she moved in with him, if she came into his room in the night and lay down in the other bed. Presumably, the truth was that she had never existed at all" (54).

In fact, on a few occasions Wexford's hallucination is real: one old woman with bound feet *does* seek him out, though Wexford assumes that she is a pre-twentieth-century phantasm. The text's pattern of references to time slippage suggests, despite the customary detective-novel concern with establishing what happened when, that it is difficult to distinguish past and present, colonial and postcolonial.[13] In one version of this temporal confusion, what seems relatively new and present in the novel is actually rooted in history. Only an expert can date the Chinese antiques accurately; others think thousand-year-old *objets* are from the 1900s. Hsia Yu-seng inadvertently uses present tense to indicate past events. Wexford mistakes the adult prostitute who appears in his office one day for a child. In the second version of chronological slippage, the past-present divide simply cannot be maintained. Hsia's listener remembers that "Mandarin has no tenses" (165). Two weeks after Wexford's arrival, he is thrilled to be in China, but he calls it by the obsolete names of "Tartary" and "Cathay" (8). The Chief Inspector experiences intense déjà vu when the barrister Knighton, who has arranged his wife Adela's death, is also found dead; on that second occasion, "if the sun was a little higher because the clocks had gone back an hour, only a purist would have noticed" (168). When Wexford sees a young woman, she reminds him of "some famous beauty of thirty years back" (171). The barrister resumes an affair with that woman's mother after a quarter of a century, but the time lapse "might never have been"; "history [was] repeating itself" (181). The temporal blurring is particularly strong when it comes to China and to women, a phenomenon I discuss below.

The "Chinese" qualities alluded to several times in the text, primary among them inscrutability and interchangeability, end up being English qualities after all. The English, in fact, are the ones who look alike, even to the other English. The silver-haired barrister who wants his wife dead is hard to tell apart from the silver-haired criminal he asks to kill her; the corrupt English antiques dealer is mistaken for the English son-in-law who shoots Adela before Knighton's man can. The Westerners in the novel are considerably harder to separate from the Chinese than they initially appear; even the eponymous and deadly speaker of Mandarin is revealed to be an Englishman, not the exoticized feudal Chinese woman pictured on the cover of the Ballantine paperback edition. Lois, the tourist from Gibraltar, has "red nails as long as a Manchu's," and Wexford has a dream that he is a young Chinese man (26, 11). Hsia's "parchment" face is anticipated by Knighton's "paper-white" face when he finds that his wife has been shot (163, 80). Like explosive powder, whose origins we are reminded of when Wexford sees a Chinese boy holding a firecracker (58), parchment is a Chinese invention whose Western derivative the text links to violence. The innocent Chinese firecracker turns into dangerous Western gunpowder, and the novel ultimately figures Western technological progression as social regression. Not only are the British not so different from the Chinese, *Speaker of Mandarin* at times implies; they're worse.

China's similarity to England in *Mandarin* is in part a fear of postcolonial revenge, a phobic fantasy of the well-taught colonized turning the tables on the colonizer. The trope of imperialism as rape is a constant in colonial and postcolonial texts.[14] The women with bound feet, for example, initially suggest the most extreme form of passivity and sexual objectification to Wexford; on seeing for the first time a woman who "could do no more than hobble," he muses that in China's past "no man would have wanted a wife with normal feet" (13). He is ambivalent, but ultimately, the section tells us, "fascination conquered revulsion, pity, and distaste, and Wexford stared" (13–4). Even as Wexford ponders the woman's immobility, though, "all the pain she had suffered, the curtailment of movement" (14), he decides she likes it that way: "[N]o doubt," he thinks, she looks down on women with fully developed feet and "with a sniff of snobbish contempt shuffled the more proudly" (14). His assumption justifies whatever pain she might suffer.

Wexford himself is aware that his gaze is transgressive. But he does not acknowledge that his theories about the woman's relationship to her body and about Chinese women's dependence on men are sexually presumptuous (the woman at whom he stares is actually holding the arm of another woman, not a man). His imagination, at any rate, ultimately relocates his own Western sexualized aggression away from the West onto the Chinese. Wexford's concern with Chinese sexual life, fascination with the woman's physical appearance, and dangerous confidence about her feelings reappear in Hsia, whose participation in a gang rape manifests Wexford's impulses taken to an extreme. Hsia, confessing his part in the crime, begins like Wexford with a narrative of Chinese sexual subjugation and reads a woman's gait as indicative of her willingness to be part of a socio-sexual exchange: "You don't know how it was, the life there, the depriva-tion, the oppresssion, the repression. This girl, she asked us, you see, she teased us, it was an invitation with the eyes, the walk" (163). Wexford does not recognize the similarities between his misreading of the Chinese woman and Hsia's misreading. Nor can he distinguish the woman with bound feet whom he hallucinates in his bedroom, the one he fears will take the bed next to his, from the mother of the Chinese rapist who moves to England. In the chain of events and perceptions that links the figures, the first woman, a representation of feminized Chinese otherness, is subject to Wexford's male Western sexual gaze. She blurs in Wexford's mind with an imagined invader of his bedroom, who in turn blurs with a woman who gives birth to a sexually predatory Chinese man. Hsia leaves China because rape is a capital crime under Mao's régime, but in England, Wex-ford hears his confession and can do nothing. Hsia is an assiduous neo-colonizer, and his economic self-assertion is a relatively benign echo of his sexual aggression. Once in London, he becomes prosperous working for the Kowloon and Fuchow Bank, which draws money from England and sends its profits to headquarters in Hong Kong.

The popular rhetoric of imperialism is almost always one of enlight-enment and liberation. Anglo-Chinese similarity, in that paradigm, should be a positive effect of colonization: the successful Hsia, for example, is proud to send his two sons to boarding school in the English tradition. The sub-tle counterpart to the rhetoric of improvement, though — what Conrad explores in *Heart of Darkness*— is that one will go native. Instead of the col-onized people's rise to the level of the benign imperialists, the imperialists will sink to the level of the benighted colonized, who are in this case the denizens of the ostensibly cruel, misogynistic East. The image of the inva-sive racial-national other with bound feet, then, represents both the fright-eningly invasive nature of imperialism *and* the perceived backwardness that serves as justification for imperialism, backwardness that may pollute the imperialists themselves. *Speaker of Mandarin* figures the journey to the East as a corrupting voyage for the English. The chivalrously named Knighton (Wexford remarks, "I certainly wouldn't have expected an English gentle-man like Knighton to shoot anyone, let alone his wife, through the back of the head" [77]) decides to have his wife killed after a decades-long mar-riage only once he has been to China. Recalling her ill-fated decision to take Knighton back, his lover explains, "In China ... everything seemed sim-ple" (180). The Chinese love poetry Knighton reads, with its reference to shooting, presages the romantic self-indulgence that leads him to have his wife shot. Knighton also reads English love poetry, and by the erotically rebellious Elizabeth Barrett at that, but it is *Sonnets from the Portuguese*. The volume's name connects passion to a foreign country, not England. Once Wexford is back in England he insists on a Chinese restaurant called the Many-Splendored Dragon; his partner complains, "Oh, God, I can see it in your face, you want to go Chinese again" (86).

In going native, *Mandarin*'s British do not exactly become like the natives of another land. On Knighton's bedside table rests Thomas Hardy's *Return of the Native*, and as the word "return" suggests, the British representation of Chinese who seem like the British does not *only* indicate fear of postcolonial revenge or anxiety about becoming like marginalized foreign others. Instead, Rendell's "native" is the innermost Self and repressed libidinal impulses that have always been present. The novel uses the Chinese other primarily to mirror that Western self, an Orientalist tendency that Said bemoans as an inevitably reductive way to read Eastern cultures.[15] It is, of course, a more effective way to read Western ones, and this is Rendell's project. The aspect of British selfhood that appears most tellingly in *Speaker of Mandarin* is the proclivity for violence against women and its connection to the objectification of the racial other.

Three different British men, two of them representatives of the legal establishment, attempt the death of Adela Knighton. The "English gentleman" Adam Knighton does so because he is hesitant to pay the social price of divorce; his very English class consciousness, and more specifically, his gentility, leads to brutality. Knighton has already defended a client on charges of rape and stabbing in such a way that the female victim is humiliated. The client, however, is ungrateful: "All that carry-on, that telling the jury the girl was asking for it, that wasn't to help me, that was just for show. Using a lot of long words and making her colour up and getting a laugh, that was for show" (138). As it turns out, the ridicule does not help the defendant, who is found guilty. Making the girl "colour up," then, functions primarily as sexual sadism; it also distinguishes her from Knighton. The girl's blush connects her to the "baby-faced pink-cheeked" Sung (4). But Knighton's consistently pale face announces both his Europeanness and his apparent invulnerability to irrational emotions of the sort felt by women and non–Westerners. His acquaintance Irene, who appreciates a "true-born Englishman," muses of Knighton's younger self that "there's nothing to beat a really good-looking *fair* man.... [H]e was like a god in a painting" (116–17).[16] *Speaker of Mandarin* marks Knighton's decision to dispose of his unloved wife as a murder born not merely of passion but also Knighton's conviction of superiority—Adela, with her "thick red hands," lacks Knighton's sophistication (48). Rendell links the condescension that marks Knighton's attitude to women to Wexford's attitude to the Chinese.

Adela Knighton's body is not the first woman's corpse that appears in *Speaker of Mandarin*. Its precursor, the two-thousand-year-old body of a Chinese woman called the Marquise of Tai, opens the novel; it is on display for tourists. The Marquise is dressed in silk and her face is "waxen" (4). The dead silk-clad Adela, too, has a face with a "look of half-melted wax" (73–4). Knighton has commanded her death merely by saying the code word "mandarin" to a deputy; that her son-in-law kills her first is mere chance. Knighton chooses "mandarin" because of an old question: "[I]f by raising your hand you could acquire a million pounds and kill a Chinaman, would you do it?" (167). Adela, for Knighton and the other men who want her dead, is the same as a Chinaman — insignificant. Her death is violence both domestic and imperial, and *Mandarin* suggests that the Western violence toward the Chinese, past or present, is of a piece with contemporary male violence against women.

*Speaker of Mandarin*'s analogy between male aggression toward women and British aggression toward the East unites feminism with the struggle for postcolonial liberation. However, this link is politically problematic both in the world of the text (Adela herself is particularly nasty about the Chinese) and in the world outside it. Critics such as Sara Suleri, discussing the figure of the third-world woman, warn against an easy alliance between feminism and postcolonialism, arguing that "each term serves to reify the potential pietism of the other."[17] Rendell's work generally minimizes pietism, and *Mandarin* hardly falls prey to the trap of liberal-feminist imperialism.[18] One may, though, protest that the novel's critique of national chauvinism and its confrontation with imperial history are largely abandoned once Wexford has unraveled the mystery of Adela's death. Certainly, China recedes from Wexford's memory and from the pages of the text. As Jenny Sharpe argues, using female-targeted violence as the dominant trope for both misogyny and colonialism "keeps the colonized hidden from history."[19] But when Knighton commits suicide, Wexford observes that his "yellowish-white waxen face looked as long dead as the Marquise of Tai's. It looked as if it were made of porcelain" (169). *Speaker of Mandarin*, then, effaces history only to emphasizes the return of the repressed, whether female or East.

## Postscript: Arabs, Africans, English

Published more than a decade after *Speaker of Mandarin*, *Simisola* is Rendell's first "political Wexford," she claims.[20] The chief inspector is almost entirely oblivious to racial stereotype in the earlier novel. But in *Simisola*, he struggles with issues of race in the increasingly multicultural town of Kingsmarkham. Apart from a brief reference to Blake's "The Little Black Boy" and a mention of a "hook-nosed" and stereotypically wealthy Arab man (17, 120)—a sophisticated late-twentieth-century author would probably hesitate to let Wexford describe a Jew in these terms—*Speaker of Mandarin* is primarily biracial. In the 1983 novel, English means white, and stands in opposition to the equally ethnically undifferentiated Chinese.[21] In *Simisola*, East and West are no longer simple binaries.

*Simisola*'s immediate racial others to Wexford are black (the novel problematizes the term "black" when Wexford realizes that the word bears no stable connection to observable reality; ultimately, though, the novel associates blackness with African origins). The Epsons are an irresponsible interracial couple who neglect their children in a literalization of the old argument against interracial marriage —"But the children will have no place in society!" Euan Sinclair is an even less responsible "Afro-Caribbean," as he is identified.[22] Mhonum Ling, a hard-working and prosperous woman from Nigeria, is dehumanizingly compared to a "lioness on the loose" (292). But more central are Dr. and Mrs. Akande ("wellborn"), emigrated from Nigeria and Sierra Leone. In Raymond Akande's waiting room, the distinction between the physician from Nigeria and the two other doctors is apparent before Wexford even sees Akande: the others, who are not numbered among Kingsmarkham's eighteen black people, are named Moss and Wolf (1). The organic quality of those names, along with their place in the English lexicon, naturalizes the two doctors and emphasizes Akande's foreignness to the reader, though Wexford does not comment on the linguistic difference. Of his relationship to Akande, which has only extended to two office visits, the novel reveals Wexford's unease:

> He liked to believe there had been some sort of rapport between them, that they had taken to each other. And then he castigated himself for thinking this way, for caring, because he knew damned well he wouldn't have involved himself with likings or dislikings if Akande had been other than he was [3].

That is, if Dr. Akande were not black. His African birth seems beside the point. Wexford knows that he and the rest of England are unintentionally or intentionally racist, as he tells Inspector Burden later, and he is so self-conscious about this racism that he has difficulty communicating with Akande at times (13, 5). *Simisola* sets up this difficulty as the central agon of the novel.

To readers of American detective fiction, though not to devotees of P. D. James, Wexford may well appear an odd fictive policeman — unnecessarily literate, and unexpectedly liberal. Mike Burden, on the other hand, is instantly recognizable as the cliché tough cop, not given much to introspection or to sympathy. His name suggests Kipling's infamous "white man's burden," the lament of the European imperialist: "Take up the White Man's Burden —/ And reap his old reward / The blame of those ye better, / The hate of those ye guard."[23] We are unsurprised when Burden, whose racism is overt in the novel, responds to Wexford's gloomy observation that "[w]e're all racist in this country" with indignation: "Oh, come on. I'm not. You're not" (13). Burden is in part a splitting off of the social impulses that Wexford denies. His precursor in *Speaker of Mandarin* is a loud Australian whom Wexford holds in some disdain but who nonetheless gets to make vociferous complaints about Chinese politics that Wexford is too sophisticated to voice aloud. That the earlier novel's crude ethnocentrist is a native of another former British colony is hardly irrelevant; English conversational restraint appears superior to Australian bluntness, just as Western democracy appears superior to Chinese oligarchy. The splitting lets Wexford — and sympathetic readers— have their cake and eat it too. Likewise with Wexford and Burden: Burden unconsciously avoids a man because of his brown skin, the narrator notes disapprovingly (50). Wexford also dislikes this man, but does not comment explicitly on his ethnicity. As Wexford's subordinate, Burden perhaps represents a past Wexford, an inferior Wexford. Through Burden's commentary, the narrative allows words such as "darky" and "nigger" even as it lets us relish Wexford's superiority to Burden, and, by extension, our own superiority to Burden (14).

The disappearance of Raymond and Laurette Akande's twenty-two-year-old daughter Melanie ("dark") ultimately occasions a crisis in Wexford's progressivism and in the Akandes' trust in him. Scrutinizing Melanie's photograph, Wexford is discomfited by her difference: "There was nothing Caucasian about the face in the photograph. Melanie Elizabeth Akande had a low forehead, a broad, rather flat nose, and full, thick, protuberant lips. Nothing of her mother's classical cast of feature showed in that face." He does not find her attractive, but understands that millions of other people might (25). The contrast between Melanie and her mother that Wexford notes underscores *internal* difference among the Afro-British, too; whereas *Speaker of Mandarin* delights in recurring patterns and similarities between characters, *Simisola* is scrupulously careful to demonstrate that not all black people are alike. However, Wexford's awareness of this fact flickers. When the body of a black girl turns up, he immediately assumes that it is Melanie's. The Akandes are asked to identify the body of someone who looks very little like their daughter, and they react with intense hostility when they realize that Wexford's carelessness in the matter is caused by his racism.[24]

Wexford eventually finds the real Melanie alive. She is on all fours when he sees her, acting as maid and nanny, cleaning up after someone more prosperous (301). Wexford's discovery of Melanie allows him some degree of reconciliation with her parents, whose upstanding professionalism, self-discipline, and intense involvement in their children's social futures render them spotless British citizens. In removing Melanie from the company of a predatory white man who desires her and returning her to her parents, Wexford neatly reverses the family-destroying trajectory of the slave trade. The gender dynamic is crucial here: Melanie's specifically female vulnerability makes Wexford seem chivalric; were she a male character, Wexford would perhaps appear a condescending neocolonialist, emasculating the dark-skinned male subject by the very act of rescuing him. Wexford redeems his earlier inability to find Melanie attractive by deciding that she is "at once pretty and charming" (306), but we never wonder if Wexford himself will be sexually predatory, since he immediately drops the topic and returns to his professional self.

In *Allegories of Empire*, Jenny Sharpe writes, "Britain's moral stand against slavery underwrote its self-designated mission to free enslaved peoples across the globe. As the first European nation to abolish slavery, it saw itself as a more humanitarian master."[25] Expanding into India with this rationale, the English let their distaste for the exploitation of Africans lead to more destructive confrontations with the Orient. To some degree, *Simisola* mirrors that pattern. Wexford's reconciliation with the black other highlights his familiar unease with the other from the East. In *Simisola*'s version of the Orient, though, the Near East replaces the Far East, and the Near East comes to England. The anti–Arab, anti–Muslim sentiments only hinted at in *Speaker of Mandarin* gain strength in the later novel, although its celebration of the somewhat tenuous black-white bond initially camouflages the text's Orientalism. A religious bond between Wexford and Dr. Akande (in Akande's office, the two men share a Christian in-joke about the road to Damascus) underscores the foreignness of the Egypt-born Khooris, whose Arab identity renders them more threatening in *Simisola* than the reassuringly Christian African English. The Khooris are among other things supermarket developers—their Islamic-looking chain is called Crescent supermarkets, with minarets visible from the English highways. Like the Akandes, the Khooris are prosperous; unlike the Akandes, they tear down an old English house and replace it with a new one, with a hallway like an Arab "desert" (334). And unlike the Afro-British in the novel, Wexford thinks the Middle Easterners look interchangeable from the start: Wael Khoori and a man Wexford assumes to be his brother "each had the handsome Semite's face, hook-nosed, narrow-lipped, the eyes close-set" (190). But the handsomeness of "the face" (Wexford's phrasing suggests that there is only one kind of Semitic good looks) does not translate to pleasingness. Wexford is repulsed by two other Arab-British, Wael's beautiful wife Anouk and Osman Messaoud, a Muslim man who is stereotypically unable to deal with women. Wexford's need for the Akandes' approval does not extend to the Khooris. Even when it becomes clear that they are not murderers, as he has suspected, the novel represents them as repellently unlikable.

As with *Speaker of Mandarin*, flaws that are perceived as Eastern — misogyny, concentration of wealth, patriarchal despotism — also turn out to be Western. Wexford suspects the Khooris of having held captive and killed the teenage girl whom he originally mistakes for Melanie Akande. However, the real killers are the ultra–European doctor Swithun Riding and his son Christopher, who is "like his father with the same straw-colored hair and Nordic looks" (133).[26] The eponymous Simisola is a modern-day Yoruba-speaking slave, and she is raped, beaten, and ultimately killed in complete secrecy in an English mansion. The East, nonetheless, mediates the English evil of the Ridings: living in Kuwait before the first Gulf War, they get Simisola after "a Kuwaiti man bought her from her father in Calabar, Nigeria, for five pounds" (368). Though the Ridings' daughter Sophie tells Wexford that the Kuwaiti man, before his death, had meant to educate Simisola and treat her "like a daughter" (368), the chronology suggests that *non*–Westerners are the ultimate cause of Simisola's exploitation. And although the novel gives precise detail about the disturbing transaction between the Nigerian man and the Kuwaiti man, we never find out exactly how Simisola comes to the Ridings. The lack of information softens the scenario; the absence of words such as "bought," "traded," and "abducted" allows the reader to imagine Simisola as other than enslaved, and the Ridings as other than enslaving.

The Ridings do, after all, treat Simisola "like a daughter" (368); they ultimately keep Sophie, too, in a position of financial dependence and try to restrict her movement. As in *Speaker of Mandarin*, Rendell represents English participation in the exploitation of the people of other countries as a domestic problem. The violence done to Englishwomen as well as to African and Asian people in both novels brings seemingly remote concerns much closer to home. Christopher Riding's twin sister, whose "corn-coloured" European hair reflects Laurette Akande's "corn-coloured"

African palms (356, 21), eventually experiences physical violence at the hands of her father and brother too; she then turns them in for Simisola's murder and rape. The very scope of the exploitative patriarchal structures proves their undoing, since the Riding men's cruelty toward a female family member exposes their neocolonial savagery as well.

In showing Swithun and Christopher to behave brutally to their daughter and sister only after Simisola's death, the novel raises the possibility that Simisola's existence has somehow protected Sophie, sheltering her from her family's malice. The frightening counterpart to that suggestion, though, is that Simisola's victimization is *necessary* for the intrafamilial harmony previously enjoyed by the Ridings. Simisola's social value and her suffering are inextricably linked, and not just for the Ridings. Her death, more than her life, is part of Wexford's bread and butter as a policeman, and the representation of her death is part of Rendell's as a writer. Even reading the novel for enjoyment, perhaps, is an act of sadism at worst, complicity at best. Rendell's inclusion of the Roman archeological site where Simisola's body is discovered is a particularly pessimistic touch, though an apposite reminder of England's *other* imperial heritage as colonized land. "Numerous remains of female infants unearthed by archaeologists ... suggest that the Romans practiced infanticide among the Regnenses [the indigenous Celtic tribe] with a view to maintaining a male work force," the passage tells us (195). The location of Simisola's body at the site suggests that not enough has changed. The man who finds Simisola's body while looking for Roman gold and keeps digging anyway encounters only a "Victorian halfpenny" as reward (197); the coin is a reminder of the racial distinctions that informed England's nineteenth-century colonialism as well, perhaps, as the enslavement of the Regnenses fourteen centuries before. The narrative does inform us of the "romantic" belief that the Romans in the area buried the gold because they were "forced to flee" (195), thereby discounting the historical accuracy of the resistance scenario even as it puts forward the possibility. What emerges as historical fact, rather, is that "[t]he Romans had never come back and the Dark Ages began" (195). Hardly an optimistic vision of history, the novel here suggests that subjugation of cultural others is what Western cultures, at least, are founded on.

## Conclusion

Recent critics such as Maureen Reddy have objected that late-twentieth-century crime fiction, including Rendell's, has been largely unable to escape the limiting perspective of "all-pervasive" whiteness.[27] *Simisola* itself acknowledges a similar point. Wexford says his own racism is "ineradicable" (14). Also, when Anouk Khoori seeks Laurette Akande's vote in an election, she, like Wexford in *Speaker of Mandarin*, appropriates Blake's "The Little Black Boy" in a way Laurette and Wexford both find unconvincing. "'My skin is white,'" Laurette reports her to say, "'But oh, my soul is black'" (268). Blake's rhetoric of racial parity, and by extension Anouk's, Wexford's, and perhaps that of any white author, lacks in force, undermined by its own dependence on traditional binaries of white and black, self and other. Still, Susan Rowland's view of Rendell as something of a social visionary may be justified. The young women Melanie and Sophie break with the past, Sophie more successfully than Melanie. Their ruptures with family are also ruptures with oppressive racial and class hierarchies (Melanie flees her parents because they expect her to function as a member of the "ebony élite"). In *Simisola*'s severing of generational bonds, Rendell offers not necessarily a tragic outlook on human connections, but rather, a prospect of history that does not control present and future, as it does in both novels. In the wrenching asunder of blood ties, Rendell delineates not only psychic damage but also the potential for a society not rigidly based on biologism. These transformations are disruptive and traumatic realignments, *Simisola* acknowledges. Nonetheless, the novel presents them as both possible and desirable.

## Notes

I would like to thank all the students in my summer 2004 British literature seminar for clarifying my thoughts on *Simisola*.

1. In addition to this collection, see Maureen T. Reddy, *Traces, Codes, and Clues: Reading Race in Crime Fiction* (New Brunswick, NJ: Rutgers University Press, 2003); Peter Hühn, "The Crime Novels of Patricia Highsmith and Ruth Rendell: Reflections on a Genre," *Literatur in Wissenschaft und Unterricht* 32.1 (2000): 17–30; Urzsula Clark and Sonia Zyngier, "Women Beware Women: Detective Fiction and Critical Discourse Stylistics," *Language and Literature* 7.2 (1998): 2141–58; and Lisa Kadonaga, "Strange Countries and Secret Worlds in Ruth Rendell's Crime Novels," *Geographical Review* 88.3 (1998): 413–28, among others.

2. See Ahmad Aijaz, "*Orientalism* and After," in *Colonial Discourse and Post-Colonial Theory: A Reader*, ed. Patrick Williams and Laura Chrisman (New York: Columbia University Press, 1994), 162–71, quotation on 166.

3. Susan Rowland, *From Agatha Christie to Ruth Rendell: British Women Writers in Detective and Crime Fiction* ( New York: Palgrave, 2001). See esp. 39, 41, and 193.

4. As Aijaz points out, Said is not entirely consistent in this pessimism (as indeed, few people can be); see "*Orientalism* and After," esp. 164.

5. "Disoriented in the Orient: the Representation of the Chinese in Two Contemporary Mystery Novels," in *Cultural Power/Cultural Literacy: Selected Papers from the Fourteenth Annual Florida State University Conference on Literature and Film*, ed. Bonnie Braendlin (Gainesville: University of Florida Press, 1991), 143–51, quotation on 146.

6. See Rowland, *From Agatha Christie to Ruth Rendell*, esp. 40, 13.
7. See Giffone, "Disoriented in the Orient," esp. 148. On Rendell's irritation with Wexford, see Sarah Lyall, "Mysteries, of Course, But Ruth Rendell Also Sees Real Evil." *New York Times*, 10 April 1995, late edition, sec. C.
8. Ruth Rendell, *Speaker of Mandarin* (New York: Ballantine, 1983), 65. All subsequent citations of *Speaker of Mandarin* are parenthetical.
9. See Edward W. Said, *Orientalism* (New York: Vintage, 1979), 71: the language of Orientalism puts the Orient on a "theatrical stage whose audience, manager, and actors are *for* Europe, and only for Europe."
10. See Said, *Orientalism*, esp. 49–72.
11. The first Opium War was fought between China and Britain from 1839 to 1842; the second, sparked by an incident in which Cantonese police charged the British of smuggling, between China and Great Britain and France from 1856 to 1860. The extent to which opium addiction was a problem for the Chinese, apart from international conflicts over its financial ramifications, remains unclear. For a reading of the Opium Wars that emphasizes the disruptive effects of British controls over the traditional drug, see Frank Dikötter, Lars Laamann, and Zhou Xun's *Narcotic Culture: A History of Drugs in China* (Chicago: University of Chicago Press, 2004). *Opium Regimes: China, Britain, and Japan, 1839–1952*, ed. Timothy Brook and Bob Tadashi Wakabayashi (Berkeley: University of California Press, 2000), presents a multifaceted picture of the relationship between Western *and* Eastern imperialism in China and the opium trade.
12. The story is "The End of the Flight" (1926), and both Maugham and Rendell refer to the man from Sumatra as "Achinese," a term that makes Wexford's association process more clear. As with Maugham's fable "Appointment in Samarra" from the play *Sheppey* (1933), "The End of the Flight" represents the East as a mystical place of fate and death.
13. The "timelessness" of the Orient in general and China in particular is also a stereotype, of course. See for example Dun J. Li, *The Ageless Chinese, a History* (New York: Scribner, 1965).
14. For a discussion of the trope's workings in colonial India, see Jenny Sharpe, *Allegories of Empire: The Figure of Woman in the Colonial Text* (Minneapolis: University of Minnesota Press, 1993), esp. 118–127 and 137–57.
15. Not coincidentally, the examples Said cites of this tendency use the Orient as a reflection of a Western *weakness*— rarely, it seems, does the East mirror something in a positive light. See *Orientalism*, esp. 209–10.
16. "Fairness" indicates Knighton's blond hair as well as his skin color. In *A Dark-Adapted Eye* (1986) Rendell, writing as Barbara Vine, discusses the English preference for blond hair in women and its effect on social relations.
17. See Sara Suleri, *The Rhetoric of English India* (Chicago: University of Chicago Press, 1992), p. 274. Quoted in Leela Gandhi, *Postcolonial Theory: A Critical Introduction* (New York: Columbia University Press, 1998), 83.
18. For a cogent overview of postcolonial critics' analyses of feminist imperialism, see Gandhi, chap. 5, "Postcolonialism and Feminism."
19. See Sharpe, *Allegories of Empire*, 130.
20. See Rowland, *From Agatha Christie to Ruth Rendell*, 193, 195.
21. The first four lines of the 1789 Blake poem: "My mother bore me in a southern wild, / And I am black, but O! my soul is white; / White as an angel is the English child, / But I am black, as if bereav'd of light." When Wexford cannot stomach the Chinese heat, he appropriates the speaker's rhetoric of marginalization, though he domesticates "wild": "My mother bore me in a northern clime."
22. Ruth Rendell, *Simisola* (London: Arrow for Random House, 1995), 26. All subsequent references to *Simisola* are parenthetical.

23. The 1899 poem, though written after clashes between Americans and Filipinos, clearly alludes to British trouble with the East in the form of India.

24. The television adaptation of *Simisola* puts viewers in the awkward position of sympathizing with Wexford's error — in the brief shots of Melanie's photograph and of the eponymous Simisola, the difference between the two is noticeable, but still slight enough to be attributed to the changes that accompany violent death and several days of decomposition. The adaptation also eliminates the novel's discussion of the discrepancies between the heights and ages of Melanie and Simisola, so that viewers are encouraged into complicity with Wexford and are likely to perceive Laurette Akande's rage as an unjustifiably extreme reaction. These differences may suggest that television executives think that viewers want to approve of the film's protagonist at all times, and that overt racial discrimination on Wexford's part will be unpalatable to those viewers. However, the exculpation of Wexford turns Laurette into the stereotypical angry black woman. See *Simisola*, dir. Jim Goddard, Wellspring Media, 2003, DVD.

25. See Sharpe, *Allegories of Empire*, 27.

26. Here the film again departs from the novel — in Goddard's adaptation, Christopher is dark-haired, and does not look especially northern European or resemble his blond sister. The casting choices link darkness with malevolence, lightness with benignity.

27. See *Traces, Codes, and Clues*, cited in note 1 above, 107.

# 4

# Detecting Empire from Inside-Out and Outside-In: The Politics of Detection in the Fiction of Elizabeth George and Lucha Corpi

## TIM LIBRETTI

The recent tag-teaming of British Prime Minister Tony Blair and U.S. President George W. Bush against Iraq provides a charged and perhaps clarifying context in which to study comparatively Elizabeth George's 1997 best-selling detective thriller *Deception on His Mind*, which takes place in Britain, and Lucha Corpi's detective fiction, such as her novels *Eulogy for a Brown Angel* (1992) and *Cactus Blood* (1995), which take place in the United States. Both George's novel and Corpi's fiction treat many of the volatile issues concerning imperialism, race, and cultural and religious difference and otherness that have received intensified scrutiny in the context of recent historical developments. George, for example, represents an Islamic Pakistani culture and community in Britain and narrates its investigation by the Anglo detective Barbara Havers. In doing so, she interestingly occupies the position of many Westerners who, in working to develop a multicultural awareness and understanding of the racial and cultural other, must cautiously negotiate the risky prospect of evaluating and representing racial, cultural and religious others from the assumed position of Western cultural superiority which has often underwritten projects of colonial domination and empire-building. Corpi, on the other hand, writing from the perspective of the Chicano/a people who view themselves as a colonized nation within the U.S. imperialist nation-state, writes not so much to acquire an understanding of otherness but moreso to highlight the cultural and historical consciousness of the colonized other and the very role that the process of othering plays in maintaining an economic system that features racial exploitation and oppression.

In the works of these two authors, we see two different deployments of multiculturalism in the context of treating the thematics of empire in the supposedly new global age. An American writer, George sets the events of her novel in England, interestingly displacing onto British soil the treatment of such volatile issues of race and empire — issues wholly germane and rather ripe both to the history of U.S. nation-formation and to the contemporary socio-political situation. Reading the novel backwards from the context of the Bush-Blair partnership, however, a context that reveals that empires themselves are perhaps no longer nationally discrete but new kinds of multi-national corporate entities or alliances, we might argue that George's novel does not so much displace these volatile themes as adumbrate a new conceptualization of the global or multinational capitalism that, from a postcolonial theoretical perspective, has putatively displaced older nation-based imperialist projects. Thus, to write about Britain, for George, is not a displacement but rather an expansion of American imperial thematics. Indeed, George's novel engages in a discursive reconfiguration of the traditional cultural logic of the British empire which valorized English culture over all others and saw cultural and racial otherness as threats to English imperial identity and dominance. We see this logic expressed in extreme form in the words of the infamous right-wing member of Parliament Enoch Powell in his 1971 declaration, "It is ... truly when he looks into the eyes of Asia that the Englishman comes face to face with those who would dispute with him the possession of his native land."[1] George takes on this fear of the alien within informing British imperial logic and attempts in her novel to reconceptualize empire and multiculturalism as compatible. Indeed, as we will see, it is her character Agatha Shaw, believing that the Pakistani's need "to start acting English ... dressing English ... worshipping English ... [and] bringing up their children English"[2] who represents an outmoded and counterproductive cultural attitude in the novel. The new sensitive empire has room for all nations, races, and peoples who wish to take part harmoniously in the culture of global capitalism.

Corpi, however, eschews this postcolonial enthusiasm that hails prematurely the pastness of colonial or imperial enterprises that seek economic dominance of racialized others through cultural domination that entails the erasure or disappearance of the other's culture. In solving crimes in Corpi's novels, the detective Gloria Damasco invariably ends up engaging in some way the history of the Chicano movement of the 1960s and 1970s which figured itself as a Third World anti-imperialist movement against U.S. colonization. As she engages this history, she reconnects with the political perspective and cultural consciousness in a way that connects past and present, highlighting not the transformation of empire into a genuinely kinder and gentler global capitalism but rather the continuity and persistence of the colonizing practices of multinational capitalism. Corpi explores ways in which such a multinational capitalism seeks to spread a uniform global capitalist culture that harmonizes *racial* differences by eliminating *cultural* differences that register alternative historical understandings and promote other ways of life, other socio-economic systems and sets of social and production relationships. Thus, Corpi's multiculturalism is not a harmonizing one but one that registers different cultures as entailing differing and not necessarily compatible ways of life and ways of knowing. Her brand of multiculturalism understands cultures as deeply entrenched in power struggles as colonized peoples continue to resist the drive to cultural domination and racial labor exploitation that characterize, in Corpi's representation, the behavior of the putatively new global capitalism just as it characterized the "old" imperialism.

As these authors engage cultural struggle and the politics of cultural difference, we can see them as taking part in what has been identified as a new development in detective fiction, namely the encoding of and participation in multiculturalism, the ideology of diversity. This development is so prevalent in individual works that the genre has for all intents and purposes evolved into nothing less than a site of intense contestation not just over racial political issues but, more pointedly, over the meaning of multiculturalism itself as an ideology. Gina Macdonald and Andrew Macdonald, for example, highlighting how "popular culture's concern with the ethnic is clearly established by the recent explosion of cross-cultural detectives," suggest that contemporary detective fiction has often as its primary aim the treatment and indeed harmonizing of potentially or actively divisive cultural differences, asserting that it "attempts to bridge the developing gap between traditional American culture and the new, much less European and/or nontraditional culture."[3] Kathleen Gregory Klein seconds this identification of the predominance of multiculturalism in the genre, noting, "Detective fiction's current integration of multicultural social concerns occurs as frequently in plot or setting as in characters or criminal investigation"[4]; so much so, in fact, that Klein advocates the pedagogical usefulness of detective fiction to help fulfill "the increasing responsibility of educational institutions to address America's multicultural society."[5] Readings of detective fiction, she forwards, can be useful for "illustrating diversity."[6] Thus, what we begin to see in contemporary detective fiction, according to these critical treatments, is both a focus on the cultural if not racial (depending on interpretations of multiculturalism) diversity of society against the illusion of a supposedly common culture and also a pluralist objective of mediating or bridging differences in the name of cultural understanding.

The crime novel as a literary form has even been identified as particularly suited to representing comprehensively the full range of cultural diversity in U.S. society. Andrew Pepper, for example, mobilizing Bakhtin's concept of heteroglossia to describe the linguistic dynamics of not just of the novel generally but the crime novel specifically, writes,

> Whereas sociology, in Bakhtin's terms, aspires towards a unitary language or an overall perspective that is arguably noncontradictory, the novel welcomes diversity. In fact, the contemporary American detective novel, in particular, has sought to depict society in all its diversity — as the detective attempts to discover who has done what, he or she necessarily comes into contact with individuals drawn from different backgrounds and cultures. And while there might ultimately be only one "language of truth," that of the hard-boiled investigator, his or her voice, according to Bakhtin at least, will necessarily reflect the full diversity of his or her social milieu because language is constructed via a process of what he calls "dialogics" (whereby each voice of utterance only takes its meaning in relation to other voices or utterances and therefore reflects all the voices in a given society).[7]

One element of Bakhtin's theory of novelistic dialogism that Pepper overlooks, however, is Bakhtin's insistence that the novel, while inevitably heteroglossic, also organizes and hierarchizes the range of social voices into an ideological structure, imagining the proper relation of those various voices to one another. Indeed, one objective of novelistic interpretation for Bakhtin is to decode a work's ideological imagination of class relations. Thus, while contemporary detective fiction might portray diverse cultural perspectives, what require interrogation in studying this fiction are the ideological dimensions of individual works in terms of how they represent the socio-economic relationships of diverse voices and social positions, how they construct and understand difference, how they define otherness in their systems of characters and represent the relationship between self and other, center and periphery. In short, we need to study individual works in terms of the multiculturalist ideology which informs them and which they forward.

In comparing George's *Deception on His Mind* with Corpi's fiction, I will look precisely at how their novels ideologically organize and hierar-

chize diverse voices. As I have been suggesting, what we call multiculturalism has many incarnations, from its development in the 1960s Third
World movements as a radical critique of U.S. colonialism and internal
colonialism to its appropriation in the workplace and market where diversity is focused on as a kind of management technique for controlling
difference and recruiting workers. As detective fiction has traditionally
been a conservative form, committed in plot and structure not to social
transformation but to narratives that restore the social order, the comparison of George and Corpi will in part focus on how the form can be used
to represent diversity. Will the form be another way of policing or managing diversity to maintain social order against racial upheaval? Or does
the form have the potential to be used to rethink conventional conceptions
of law and order, which, we must admit, have historically been quite racist?
As I look at the fiction of Corpi, who writes from within "the belly of the
beast" and detects empire from inside out, and that of George, who detects
empire from outside in with her representation of the Islamic Pakistani
community, I will explore how each uses the crime novel form to explore
volatile issues of cultural difference and their impact on the fate of empire
around the globe.

## Detecting Empire from Inside the Belly of Beast

In *Eulogy for a Brown Angel* and *Cactus Blood,* Corpi appropriates the
popular genre of detective fiction in order to subject to critique dominant
cultural and legalistic conceptions of crime and injustice and to forward
new conceptions informed by an historical perspective of the racial experience in the U.S. In solving crimes in Corpi's novels, the Chicana detective Gloria Damasco inevitably finds herself looking beyond the isolated
individual acts of violence or murder into the deeper socio-historical
causes as a way of uncovering the larger structural and historical patterns
of injustice perpetrated against people of color. As Gloria Damasco says
in *Eulogy for a Brown Angel* when four people are killed in a 1970 Chicano
uprising in L.A. and their bodies are raised onto slabs for autopsies, "In
time, perhaps someone would admit to the *real* cause of what happened
that day. But perhaps we already knew the name of that insidious disease
that had claimed three, perhaps four, more lives that late August afternoon."[8] The novelistic autopsy Corpi performs, obviously, is one that
identifies the disease of racism upholding the exploitive and oppressive
racial order of U.S. society and political economy. The system itself and
those who endorse, perpetuate, and underwrite it are the real criminals.
If, as Franco Moretti argues, traditionally detective fiction has restored

social order by finding individuals guilty so that society can declare itself innocent,[9] Corpi's fiction incriminates society itself, but without necessarily uncritically acquitting individuals who commit crimes. Rather, her fiction develops a much more complex relation between the individual and society, recognizing the material and discursive social practices that produce criminals and the discourse of criminality itself.

In carrying through these arguments and explorations, I will focus schematically on key features of Lucha Corpi's *Cactus Blood* and *Eulogy for a Brown Angel* and make a series of arguments with respect to the ways in which Corpi's Chicana political perspective rethinks issues of criminality and injustice. *Eulogy for a Brown Angel* opens with the murder of a small child, taking place seemingly peripherally to the 1970 L.A. Chicano March. In the process of detection, however, the novel really becomes a rethinking and diagnosis of the movement from a contemporary perspective. Gloria Damasco is still working on solving the crime eighteen years later and is beginning to piece together the crime as part of an international corporate plan encompassing areas of the globe from Germany to Brazil, suggesting that the assault on Chicanos/as in the U.S. is bound up with imperialist aggression towards Third World peoples globally. And, indeed, the murder of the child, while again an event seemingly peripheral to the events of the movement, becomes intimately imbricated in the assault on the movement. As Damasco says, "In the summer of 1970 everything anyone of us did had to be considered according to its political impact on the Chicano community"(64). It is this sentiment that fuels Corpi's rethinking of "criminality" and, in particular, of the way in which she defines the difficult task for the writer of color in using the crime fiction genre. Historically, people of color have been criminalized in the U.S., so the writer of color must negotiate carefully between reinforcing this stereotypical criminalization, especially in this case in which the individual murderer of the child — insofar as the cause of murder can be reduced to an individual act — is in fact Chicano, and rethinking criminality altogether. Hence, Damasco supports "the unwritten rule that forbade Chicanos to go public on any issues that could be used to justify discrimination against us.... In some ways, I realized our movement for racial equality and self-determination was no different from others like it in other parts of the world. But we were a people within nation. Our behavior was constantly under scrutiny, our culture relentlessly under siege"(64). Through her detection, Damasco begins to refocus the investigation of the crime, understanding the crime less as the individual action of the Chicano paid off by European corporate culture and more as a crime that is part of the larger crimes against people of color committed through the mechanisms of colonialism and internal colonialism. What Damasco finally uncovers is the history of racial oppression, and what she demystifies are the ideologies of "race"(criminalization, colonization, discrimination, etc.) which under-write those mechanisms.

Indeed, in *Eulogy for a Brown Angel,* that Gloria Damasco's quest to solve the murder of a young child at the 1970 Chicano Moratorium march in East Los Angeles continues for eighteen years, suggests that one cannot have done with history and that it will continue to erupt in and inform the present such that the political models of the past developed to under-stand experience and resist the conditions of existence defining that expe-rience must not be forgotten. Such a narrative of detection does not only *not* repress history, it calls attention to and continually calls up history. The detection process not only propels and keeps alive an historical con-ciousness into the present but it also pushes Damasco further back into the past to the very colonization of California itself. Similarly, in *Cactus Blood,* the death of Damasco's friend and former Chicano Movement activist Sonny which motivates the narrative turns out not to be a mur-der but an accident, if not a suicide, such that the "crime" itself which Damasco seeks to solve throughout the novel turns out to be a red her-ring. What is important in the narrative, then, is not so much the crime or even its solution as the process of detection itself and the exploration and interpretation of clues because of the psycho-historical therapeutic recovery and analysis to which the characters subject themselves.

In *Cactus Blood,* for example, the central task in solving the putative death of Sonny is finding the character Carlota Navarro, who had been seen leaving his apartment. Yet the search for Carlota, who has nothing to do with Sonny's suicide, figuratively signifies the search and eventual encounter with the Chicana/o historical past as well as with the political exigencies persistently defining the present. As an illegal immigrant and undocumented worker who is raped by the husband of the family for which she works as a domestic and is poisoned when, in flight from the family, she runs through a pesticide-ridden field, Carlota becomes the embodi-ment of the Chicana/o history of racial/national oppression and coloniza-tion, labor super-exploitation, and sexual violence within the racial patriarchal class structure. What Damasco rediscovers in locating Carlota and learning her history are all of the issues that informed Chicana/o polit-ical consciousness and identity and motivated the Chicana/o Civil Rights movements in the 1960s and 1970s. She functions as the living voice and repository of historical memory, a point Corpi underlines as Damasco finds Carlota's story on a tape made by her deceased friend Luisa who had been engaged in interviewing Chicanas for a project entitled "The Chi-

cana Experience," which was to document the Chicano Civil Rights Movement from the perspective of Chicanas.

In particular, Carlota registers the tradition of Chicana/o protest and
resistance to the conditions of national oppression or internal colonization while also magnifying and questioning the waning of Chicana/o
activism and political commitment in the wake of the movement's hey-
day and in the face of these persisting conditions. While driving with Carlota through Sonoma at one moment in the story, for example, Damasco
recounts seeing the houses of General Mariano Vallejo and his brother
Salvador Vallejo and engages in an historical reflection which I will quote
at length for its usefulness, first, in demonstrating Corpi's incorporation
of historical documentary and historical consciousness into the plot of
detection and, second, in creating within the plot the setting and context
that highlights Carlota's heightened and Damasco's diminishing political
sensitivity:

> I had never before been in Sonoma, the heart of the wine country and the
> site of historical events that changed the fate of Mexicans in California for-
> ever. Forgetting the urgent reasons that had brought us to the Valley of the
> Moon, I let my excitement at being there grow for a moment. Doing research
> at the Oakland History Room to uncover the lives of the Peraltas, an old Oak-
> land Californio family, I had also discovered the Vallejo family, friends of the
> Peraltas.
>
> I saw the mission of San Francisco Solano, which stood kitty-corner to us
> and the Bear Flag Revolt Monument. The monument had been erected in
> honor of those who fought against the Mexican Army to take control of Cal-
> ifornia. The building across from the mission and the monument had been the
> Mexican barracks. I knew they had been occupied by the Bear Flag rebels after
> the Mexican Army, led by General Vallejo, laid down their arms. A short time
> after Vallejo's surrender, California became a U.S. territory and every gold-
> digger's rainbow's end.[10]

Damasco's interior narration here of her perceptions of Sonoma is
revealing not just because it uncovers the perhaps often overlooked or
repressed history of the colonization of the Californios by Anglo settlers
but also because of the cultural terms in which this moment of historical
documentary is inserted into the narrative. The narrative here swings like
a pendulum between the Anglo or dominant U.S. cultural and historical
perspective and the Chicana/o one. For example, Damasco first describes
Sonoma in terms of its importance from an economic perspective of consumption, in terms of what the land now means within the capitalist economy of commodity production, as "the heart of the wine country," a
description that effectively enacts a type of commodity fetishism. This per-

spective is quickly countered, however, by Damasco's qualification from a Chicana/o perspective that Sonoma is also "the site of historical events that changed the fate of Mexicans in California forever." Similarly, Damasco's vision moves from the Mexican monument of the mission of San Francisco Solano to the monument memorializing the conquest and colonization of California, the Bear Flag Revolt Monument, registering the history of cultural strife and land struggles between indigenous Mexicans and invading Anglo settlers in California.

The passage itself effectively calls up that historical consciousness and even shrewdly and economically reveals the cultural struggle and the process of the commodification — and commodity fetishism — of the land that resulted in the repression of the Chicana/o historical perspective in the face of the instrumentality of capitalist cultural and economic imperatives. Yet, as a narrative representation of Damasco's consciousness it seems significantly to indicate the extent to which she is vacillating between these two cultural perspectives which seem ambivalently and alternately to inform her cultural and historical consciousness. She seems to inhabit a Chicana/o past but an Anglo present; that is, she has a clear and committed understanding of U.S. history from the Chicana/o perspective of internal colonization, but this understanding seems to apply only to the events of the past and not to inform her decoding of the present. Her "forgetting the urgent reasons that had brought us to the Valley of Moon" in order to remember the historical research she did (for solving the crime in *Eulogy for a Brown Angel*) exemplifies this dissociation of past and present in Damasco's mind. Even the language she uses here marks this cultural duality, as she speaks of Sonoma, apart from her recovery of California history from a Chicana/o perspective, as the "Valley of the Moon," calling up an almost Jack Londonesque cultural figuration of Sonoma. Damasco fails to realize that solving crimes in the present requires understanding them both as crimes with a history and as crimes of history. Indeed, Corpi implicitly diagnoses her detective's flawed investigative techniques as ahistorical. Damasco must connect past and present, a lost connection which for Damasco results from a sense her lost political consciousness.

The detection process, in psychotherapuetically recovering the repressed history of Chicana/o struggle against racial oppression and class exploitation, performs a dereification of consciousness that brings both characters and reader back to the scene of labor that produces our world and is the motor of history. The questions Carlota raises and the history of racial and sexual oppression and labor exploitation she embodies as an undocumented worker, an "illegal alien" in her own colonized land, are ones that the formulaic plot of detective fiction as discussed by Moretti and others cannot make disappear. Indeed, Corpi recursively brings the plot back to the scene of labor, as when earlier in the novel Damasco's friend Victor, a physician, diagnoses Carlota's illness as caused by poisonous pesticides: "'I've read reports in medical journals about the effect of pesticides and herbicides on human beings. Ironically, people still feel it's a problem only for the farm worker ... I always tell Irma there is a human price to be paid for the unblemished apple or grape. But that's what we consumers demand.... The proverbial poisoned apple. Amazing, isn't it?'" (114). Through the orchestration of character and plot Corpi invokes a perspective of production and critiques the dominant perspective of consumption informing U.S. capitalist culture which is a function of, in Marxist terms, the reification of consciousness and the fetishism of the commodity that effectively mystifies and eliminates labor from the purview of U.S. social vision. Thus, while Moretti argues that "Money is always the motive of crime in detective fiction, yet the genre is wholly silent about *production*: that unequal exchange between labour-power and wages which is the true source of social wealth" and condemns detective fiction as performing "a cultural fetishism,"[11] Corpi's detective fiction overturns these conventions by making the solution of the crime the discovery of history itself, of the functioning of the racial patriarchal capitalist system as it has historically and in the present shaped racial and class struggle and criminally impacted individual lives such as Carlota's as well as the collective lives of workers and people of color generally. Indeed, while Ernest Mandel identifies the "reification of death ... at the heart of the crime story,"[12] referring to the process by which death becomes an isolated, individualized experience divorced from social circumstances or problems, Corpi indicts the systemic structure of racial capitalism and its productive relations which consign people of color to the worst jobs and to inhumane and deadly work conditions.

Corpi thus reworks the typical detective fiction formula by displacing the importance of the individual crime to what she identifies as the larger source of criminality: the social structure itself. No innocence, as in Moretti's narrative, is ever restored. In fact, as the plot progresses it uncovers only more guilt and more evidence of the fallen condition of the social order. Indeed, as Corpi structures the narrative, the crime is not revealed at the beginning of the narrative but rather discovered at the end, inverting the traditional formula of the detective novel. The solution of the actual crime in the novel offers no significant closure because it serves more to motivate the plot than to constitute a central event in the plot.

The murder in the novel, again, is not that of Sonny, who presumably committed suicide. The murder in the novel is committed by Carlota's friend Josie Baldomar who, by her confession, accidentally murdered her Anglo husband because, she knew, he had been planning to leave her for another woman. She had been intending to murder him and with these intentions had been at work creating the circumstances that would allow her to frame an old Chicano activist, Ramon Caballos, of whom she is jealous because she views him as a rival for Carlota's affection. During a farmworkers' strike in 1973, Ramon had wanted to explode a pesticide tank and had conspired with Art Bello and Sonny to carry out the mission. Art and Sonny, however, had misgivings, deciding it would be politically counterproductive to the ends of the strike, and attempted to persuade Ramon not to execute his plan. When he did anyway, Art and Sonny, in a moment of ambivalence, testified against him, believing it best for the movement, although their sense of ambivalence never diminishes and they continue to harbor guilt for having betrayed a comrade. Aware of these events, Josie leaves poisoned grapes in the refrigerators of Art and Sonny, steals some significant photographs of the strike hanging on Art's wall, and leaves a rattlesnake in Art's yard to make them believe that Ramon is seeking revenge upon them, her logic being that given such circumstances she will be able to frame Ramon for any murder she commits.

While this is but a partial recapitulation of the complexities of the plot, it should make apparent that the actual murder Josie commits is irrelevant in comparison to the chain of events her attempt to frame Ramon triggers. Damasco, in fact, is never even attempting to solve the murder of Josie's husband but rather the death of Sonny, which she mistakenly believes to have been a murder. But Josie's actions motivate the central elements of the plot, the characters' meditations on their political pasts and their examination of the strength and persistence of their political commitment in the present. Art, for example, must come to grips with his having testified against Ramon. And Sonny, it is speculated, committed suicide after seeing the tape depicting events from sixteen years ago because of a sense of political failure. Indeed, the search for the missing photographs from Art's walls which document past Chicano struggles symbolizes this urgency to recover the pieces of the past and reassess one's present position — and the state of the movement as well — in light of that history. This aspect of the plot and its relative dissociation from Josie's murder of her husband become clear in the climactic scene near the end which takes place in a Native American ritual site. At this point, Art still suspects that Ramon Caballos is still behind Sonny's death and the other events and sees this culmination as a referendum of sorts on the outcomes of the movement. He says, "'I feel as if a cycle that started back in 1973 is coming to a close. I just hope this cycle doesn't end with my own demise.... For the cycle to end like it began, those of us who were involved in the action of sixteen years ago would have to be here at the same time. Aren't cycles supposed to work that way?'"(190).

But the cycle does not end, at least not as Moretti has theorized the cycle of detective fiction as a return to the beginning and to the status quo with nothing changed and nothing learned. Through the ritualized process of detection, the characters work through the difficult political questions of the past, the conflict between Ramon and Art is resolved, and Damasco also has her political commitment restored. Josie, who exploited the past and the movement, is brought to book, and the conditions of possibility for a Third World working-class solidarity are renewed. The questions and awareness raised by Carlota remain, not at all dissipated or overshadowed by Josie's being brought to justice, for the novel recasts concepts of justice and criminality in much broader terms. The re-establishment of political solidarity and the re-recognition that, as Damasco asserts early in *Eulogy for a Brown Angel*, "we were a people within a nation," signifies not a closure but a renewed beginning which is not a return to the beginning but a recognition that the conditions of internal colonization persist in the 1990s and that the Third World Movements of the 1960s and early 1970s provide fruitful models of resistance. In the terms in which the novel defines justice, as the end of racial, class, and sexual oppression and exploitation, the quest for justice is just beginning. Apprehending the criminal means overhauling a social and economic system that is itself criminal through and through.

In *Eulogy for a Brown Angel*, Damasco is still trying to the solve the crime of 1971 eighteen years later. Although the individual murderer, a Chicano Vietnam veteran who had turned against the movement, had been apprehended in 1971, Damasco uncovers in 1989 the conspiracy with which he was linked, a multinational corporation, signifying the continuation of imperialism and global capitalism into what Mandel has termed "late capitalism." In short, she discovers not just that "we were a people within a nation" but that Chicanas/os and other racial minorities still are peoples within the U.S. nation and that an anti-colonial nationalist politics must still constitute the enabling conditions of literary practice and political resistance. Yet, as we have seen, Corpi's novels address the U.S. Third World national audiences and support the Third World political status quo which calls for the revolutionary transformation of the racial and economic order.

## Detecting and Protecting Empire: From Outside In

The engagement with multiculturalism we see in Corpi's detective fiction is that in which the other speaks to the center, highlighting more complex historical comprehensions that engender a critique of the U.S. racial order and the role of the legal system and police in underwriting and sustaining that order. In contrast, George's work participates in the multiculturalism project geared toward managing diversity within the marketplaces and workplaces of global capitalism in ways complicit with the maintenance and re-ritualization of empire in the new global order, in the age of globalization. If First and Third Worlds ever were entirely distinct geographic spaces, Michael Hardt and Antonio Negri argue that the onset of globalization has seen the increasing interpenetration of these worlds, requiring a reconceptualization of empire and imperialist practice. "The Third World," they write, "does not really disappear in the process of unification of the world market but enters into the First, establishes itself at the heart as ghetto, shantytown, favela, always again produced and reproduced."[13] George's novel *Deception on his Mind* (1997) registers and responds to this global development, treating the presence of Pakistani immigrant communities in England and centering the novel on the murder of a Pakistani, Haytham Querashi, who has recently come both to assume an executive position in a condiment factory and to marry Sahlah Malik, the daughter of the factory's founder and owner, Akram Malik. Through a cast of characters ranging across a broad spectrum of social and cultural positions, George represents a corresponding range of racial attitudes as well as a range of possible homicidal motivations (from the economic, to the cultural, to the familial, to the romantic and erotic) brought to the surface in the community by the murder and the ensuing investigation led by the racist Emily Barlow and monitored by Barbara Havers, the putatively more culturally sensitive officer who tries to mediate the Pakistani and Anglo cultural communities. As the novel represents these attitudes, it effectively manages and polices them, in a sense disarming them by portraying them as merely idiosyncratic and sometimes historically residual individual attitudes not linked to or informing the larger systemic structures that organize contemporary social relationships or condition economic interests.

Indeed, as we will see, the Pakistani community George represents is not one located in the ghetto or shantytown; rather she represents primarily the extended Malik family as inhabiting an upper-class social milieu of wealth, corporate ownership, and a social status (Akram is a member of the city council) held despite the racist views of other leading citizens, such as Agatha Shaw. This fact is important as we see George reconfigure relationships between First and Third Worlds in a way that elides the content of racial labor exploitation and political disenfranchisement typically informing that relationship, thereby divorcing understandings of racial difference from material economic or neo-colonial relationships of inequality. The racism George represents in the novel, again, tends to be expressed in the attitudes of individuals which are at odds with the systemic structures of English socio-political and economic life, as George represents them, and which are often checked or counter-balanced by other characters in the novel who are represented as more humane and culturally sensitive or more aware of the fact that racism does not serve the economic interests of the community. While Corpi, for example, links racism to a history of U.S. capitalist development through colonialist domination of people of color, which requires a cultural conquest that entails the criminalization of people of color through dominant legalistic and police discourses and practices, George represents racism not as linked to but as hostile to progressive capitalist global economic development. The culture of capitalism George represents, then, is decidedly anti-racist. Thus, while for Corpi anti-racist and anti-exploitation politics requires the infusion of a different cultural perspective and value system from that of capitalism, for George the importance of multiculturalism — represented in the novel as an awareness and sensitivity to the values, practices, and worldviews of other cultures— lies in the way it enables us to understand and hence resolve social conflicts that are merely the result of cultural misunderstandings, not deep material economic divisions. In *Deception on His Mind*, capitalism harmonizes and manages relationships between peoples of different cultural backgrounds, promoting tolerance of the private practice of the other's cultural rituals and the public sharing of and participation in a common set of social values and practices rooted in a common economic interest. The ideology of multiculturalism forwarded implicitly by the novel is one that standardizes a Western epistemological and cultural framework in the processing of information and evidence and in the construction of knowledge about others in a way that maintains the racial or imperial law and order of the status quo, explicitly, as we will see, re-inscribing its superiority.

Thus, George narrates Havers's solution of the murder case as a process of her developing an understanding of and sensitivity to Pakistani culture and of her confronting her own cultural and sexist stereotypes of Pakistani women. It needs to be stressed, however, that her multiculturalist epiphany occurs in the process of effectively policing another culture, such that the functionality of multiculturalism in this instance is very much linked to the procedures and project of social management, of the maintenance of law and order according to the mandates and values of the existing social system, the status quo. To cut to the chase, Havers finally discovers that Yumn, the wife of Akram Malik's son Muhannad, murdered Haytham Querashi because her only source of power as a woman in the Malik household would disappear should Sahlah marry Querashi. As relations stood, as an unmarried woman Sahlah was effectively the servant of Yumn, a relationship that would cease to exist once Sahlah married. In fact, as merely the daughter-in-law of the Maliks, she would hold a rank even lower than Sahlah. When Yumn orders Sahlah to do her duty and confirm her lie in front of Barbara, the stereotypes that blinded Barbara become clear to her:

> And there it was…. The motive. Buried deep within a culture she knew so little about that she had failed to see it. But she saw it now. And she saw how it had worked its desperate energy within the mind of a woman who had nothing else to recommend herself to her in-laws but a sizable dowry and the ability to reproduce. She said, "But Sahlah wouldn't have had to obey any longer if she married Querashi, would she? Only you would be left having to do that, Yumn. Obeying your husband, obeying your mother-in-law, obeying everyone, including your own sons eventually" [705–6].

In the context of her police work, Barbara putatively achieves a higher order of perception and multicultural awareness, developing a deep cultural understanding as she is able genuinely, as George represents it, to enter empathically into the consciousness of the other, of Yumn, and to apprehend her mental and emotional states. The value of this achieved understanding, however, lies finally in its acquisition — or extraction — of a kind of cultural surplus value, of cultural capital, that furthers the exploitation of peoples of color, of racial, religious, and cultural others in the name of law and order, in the prosecution of justice. Thus, while in Corpi's work the purpose of recalling and highlighting an alternative historical and cultural consciousness was in part to challenge the dominant conceptions of law and order and the criminalization of people of color, in George's novel the function of apprehending an alternative cultural consciousness (often devoid of an historical dimension in George's writing) is precisely to uphold the dominant conceptions of law, order, and criminality and the socio-economic system they underwrite and ratify.

This moment of Havers's epiphany provides a key index of the novel's narrative patterns and ideological strategies for processing multicultural content and simultaneously transforming crude and obvious racial and cultural stereotypes into supposedly enlightened and genuine cultural information codified in politic and sensitive modes of expression. The novel frequently at once dismisses crude stereotypes only to validate them in another form at another point in the novel — at times through linguistic metamorphosis and at other times through plot developments that countervale expressed attitudes or narratives of a character's transformation of consciousness. Havers's behaviors offer a powerful example of this gesture, particularly because she seems to serve as the novel's conscience for George, undertaking a self-critical look at the limitations of a Western vision. In reflecting on the murder and her and Barlow's inability to see the facts, she humbly admits, "'We never thought it could have been the means to an end having nothing to do with anything that we — as Westerners, as bloody *Westerners*—could possibly hope to understand'"(698). She thinks to herself that all the clues had been before them: "They'd merely been incapable of seeing them, blinded by their own preconceptions of what sort of woman would submit herself to an arranged marriage" (697). She articulates to Barlow the stereotypes they as Western women harbor which have led them astray in the case:

> "Just look at us. Look at how we think. We never even asked her for an alibi. We never asked any one of them. And why? Because they're Asian women. Because in our eyes they allow their men to dominate them, to decide their fates, and to determine their futures. They cover their bodies cooperatively. They cook and clean. They bow and scrape. They never complain. They have, we think, no lives of their own. So they have, we think, no minds of their own" [699].

While supposedly processing her prejudices and overcoming them here, Havers's self-castigating consciousness-raising moment functions in the novel really as a kind of catharsis that provides the illusion of meaningful self-criticism and concomitant transformation while similar stereotypes are merely re-inscribed on the level of plot.

For the novel, solving Querashi's murder involves seeing beyond stereotypes to other "genuine" cultural attributes the novel figures as backwards. As we will see repeatedly, the novel critically addresses, even skewers, what it figures as a kind of brash, exaggerated, ignorant racism only to uphold later a more sensitive, sophisticated, cosmopolitan racism or culturalism masquerading as scientific knowledge. Indeed, it is not stretching, I think, to characterize the narrative of the novel as emplotting the progressive development from prejudicially convicting and criminalizing people of color to convicting and criminalizing them on more "reasoned" and culturally sensitive grounds. The verdict of the novel is not substantially different from those verdicts the racist and colonialist justice system reaches in criminalizing people of color, but the rationalizing, understanding, culturally sensitive forensic procedures do mark a difference, supposedly, thereby re-inscribing with a newfound validity the same old racist processes. Thus, the plot validates the stereotypical criminal justice narratives that the detectives putatively overcome in identifying criminals.

Moreover, in the case of Yumn, her portrayal does not alter significantly from a pejorative stereotype. While it is true that Havers moves beyond simply seeing her as a victim of her situation who is docile and accepting to granting her the potential of social agency, of taking action within her situation, the enlightened understanding Havers achieves still figures Yumn's agency as incredibly limited by her acceptance of cultural norms. Yumn's agency extends as far as her ability to act to uphold the very system that victimizes her and to secure what little sense of power it can afford her. Thus, her having a mind of her own means, in George's terms, having the ability to participate actively in one's victimization.

In this sense, for all of Havers's epiphanies through which she supposedly learns to think beyond stereotypes and grant critical subjectivity to Third World women, George in actuality does little to transcend what Chandra Talpade Mohanty still labels a First Worldist feminist view that comprehends and represents Third World women only as victims, a perspective she labels the "feminist-as-tourist-model."[14] This model Mohanty describes provides a useful explanatory framework for George's novel. The perspective is one that, in Mohanty's words, "could also be called the 'feminist as international consumer' or, in less charitable terms, the 'white women's burden or colonial discourse' model."[15] This mode of inquiry, as Mohanty identifies it, particularly as it is manifested in curricula and syllabi, tends to make "brief forays" into "non-Euro-American cultures" in the study of sexist cultural practices but tends to sustain a "Eurocentric women's studies gaze." The study of "Third World/South cultures" is added on as supplemental narrative rather than incorporated into, in a way that would necessarily radically alter, a feminist liberation narrative. Spending a week studying Indonesian women workers in Nike factories, matriarchal cultures in precolonial West Africa, or dowry deaths in India without inquiring into the power dynamics between First and Third Worlds that condition relations between First and Third World women, Mohanty argues, leaves "power relations and hierarchies" as well as "the fundamental identity of the Euro-American feminist on her way to liberation untouched" since "ideas about center and periphery are reproduced along Eurocentric lines."[16] Moreover, she argues, this approach tends to depict Third World women in monolithic and static terms, often figuring them only as victims of backwards sexist cultural practices, in contrast to "images of Euro-American women who are vital, changing, complex, and central subjects."[17]

George's representational strategy very much replicates in *Deception on His Mind* this pedagogical strategy Mohanty outlines here. First, George reproduces dominant Eurocentric conceptions of center and periphery, in cultural terms absolutely locating a Western epistemology as the central intelligence, so to speak, the normative central knowing and apprehending consciousness through which the process of detection and policing takes place. Indeed, the crime tale becomes one not of a drama of clashing cultural differences or of a multicultural encounter characterized by a mutual discovery and hence elimination of otherness but of the tensions created by the internal power dynamics and struggles within Pakistani culture that the Anglo detective must acquire the cultural capital to decipher. The murder is not committed out of, say, a conflict between romantic love and familial duty — a conflict raised throughout the novel — but out of Yumn's desire to maintain power *within* the patriarchal kinship network and sexual economy of Pakistani cultural norms. Thus, despite Havers's celebrations of her altered and expanded consciousness, the Western self in the novel does, in fact (consistent with Mohanty's diagnosis of the "feminist-as-international-consumer"), remain untouched. The non–Western other is studied and understood from the perspective of criminal anthropology, not out of a desire for cross-cultural understanding, much less communication or solidarity. Nothing new, then, in terms of a cultural dynamic is produced out of this supposed multi-cultural encounter, as the encounter is the one-sided Western consumption of the Third World other.

Moreover, further consistent with Mohanty's analysis of the white woman's burden, is the representation of Euro-American women as "vital, changing, complex, and central subjects" against their object of study — Third World women — who are static and represented in culturally homogeneous terms; that is, George represents them as wholly representative of their cultural belief systems. While it is true that Sahlah is romantically involved in a love affair with Theo Shaw, she is insistent she will not disobey her father's wishes she marry Querashi and never forgoes her commitment to arranged marriages in favor of a Western ideal of romantic love. With both Sahlah and Yumn, their characters and behaviors are represented and understood always in relation to or against Pakistani patriarchal culture, its internal hierarchies, and its practice of arranging marriages to serve the economic and social interests of the patriarchal family. The representation of these women differs vastly from the representations, say, of Barbara Havers or Emily Barlow. In fact, it is interesting to note here that Barbara Havers takes center-stage in this particular novel while others in the series depict her assisting her male superior, aristocrat Inspector Thomas Lynley. In this novel, George represents the police-women — especially Emily Barlow — as independent, unmarried professionals who certainly have to negotiate sexism and patriarchy in the workplace but who also have private lives in which they make their own economic and sexual choices without the influence of the patriarchal family structure. Barlow, for example, is represented as very sexually aggressive and as having sex with men not in the context of committed, family-oriented romantic relationships but merely to satisfy her healthy sexual appetite, a behavior generally identified as masculine. Indeed, while Havers's ailing mother figures prominently in earlier novels in the series, neither Havers nor Emily Barlow are seen in familial relationships in *Deception on His Mind*. In stark contrast, Sahlah and Yumn have no identities apart from the family structure and make no decision or take any action uninfluenced by family expectations.

The terms of the novel are clear that this story is not about the conflicts or opportunities generated by two cultures coming into contact and learning about and influencing one another. Clearly, the English culture constitutes the normative position against which difference is defined and which requires no sociological or anthropological explanations. Havers and Barlow are not seen in any way as cultural representatives, as actors whose romantic, sexual, and economic behaviors are strongly conditioned by something identified as a particularly British culture that we need to come to understand in the novel. Rather, they are merely individuals making their own choices and living their own lives apart from any strenuously determining context like that in which Sahlah and Yumn live. Here, again, we can see that the novel does not escape deploying and reinforcing criminalizing racial stereotypes notwithstanding Havers's discovery that Asian women might just have minds of their own. Even these minds, the novel suggests, are hopelessly constrained and tragically informed by their culture. Surely, Sahlah and Yumn have lives of their own and are thinking, acting beings, but the choices they make and lives they lead are finally absolutely conditioned by the oppressive family structure and values of their culture. Thus, their "free-thinking" is limited to replicating the beliefs, attitudes, and values of the Pakistani patriarchal culture into which they have been, irretrievably it seems, interpellated. What is criminalized, finally, then, is the "other" Pakistani culture itself for its constraining of passions in the name of unviable conceptions of duty the repressiveness of which fosters an untoward and anti-social release of the libidinal and romantic energies that will always and inevitably out.

Indeed, as much as George might try to give an even-handed, sympathetic representation of Pakistani patriarchal culture and to understand Sahlah's commitment to her culture's values, finally the plot resolutions betray this sympathy and valorize English culture as superior and more desirable because it is somewhat more amenable to individual liberties and more accommodative to the free expression of human desires and inclinations. Taymullah Azhar, for example, a London professor and Havers's neighbor whom she follows when he is called by Muhannad Malik to come to Balford le Nez to mediate between the Pakistani community and the Anglo police, is represented sympathetically by the novel for enduring being outcast from his family for marrying a white woman. At the end of the novel when Azhar opens the door to Havers to discuss his past and his children, George writes, from Havers's perspective, "She could discover how he'd met Hadiyyah's mother and she could learn about the forces that had worked within him, making a lifetime of disjunction from his family worth the experience of loving a woman who had been deemed forbidden to him" (711). Havers then reflects on the struggle between passion and duty for Azhar, as George writes:

> She remembered once reading the seven-word excuse that a film director had used to explain the betrayal of his longtime love in favour of a girl thirty years his junior. "The heart wants what the heart wants," he had said. Barbara had long since wondered if what the heart wanted had, in reality, anything to do with the heart at all.
> Yet had Azhar not followed his heart — if that, indeed, had been the body part involved — Khalidah Hadiyyah would not have existed. And that would have doubled the tragedy of falling in love and walking away from love's possibility. So perhaps Azhar had acted for the best when he'd chosen passion over duty. But who could really say? [711–712].

While this passage arguably offers some, albeit minimal, hesitation on whether it really is best to adhere to passion over duty, much of the end of the novel is far less equivocal not only in privileging passion over duty but also, by extension, English culture over Pakistani culture. When Akram Malik has to decide between protecting Yumn at the end of the novel or letting police interrogate her, George writes, "He was so obviously caught in the middle, the human rope in a tug-of-war whose adversaries were duty and inclination. His cultural duty was to protect the women of his family. But his adopted inclination was English: to do what was proper, to accede to a reasonable request made to him by the authorities. Inclination won" (701–2). The language of this passage fascinatingly describes English culture as uniting passion and duty, inclination and rational propriety, as in following his "inclination," which finds expression in English culture, Akram also fulfills his duty to the nation by doing what is proper. One's "other" culture may be practiced in private but one is obliged finally to participate in a shared common culture, in this case English capitalist culture, rooted in a shared set of economic and social interests. And this public culture, moreover, is represented as finally superior in its ability to accommodate individual desires and to make those desires compatible with civic duty. Thus, again, while at times the novel strikes a sympathetic pose towards the repressive dictates of duty, of arranged marriage particularly, in Pakistani culture, finally the novel forgoes this cultural pluralist stance in valorizing English culture for its resilience in harmonizing liberty and duty, desire and propriety.

Additionally, what we see in the ending is that the novel does not finally support a full-fledged multiculturalism that recognizes the validity or equality of all cultures but rather concludes with a valorization of English capitalist culture. To further apply Mohanty's analytic model from above to the novel, we see that just as Mohanty argues that often while First World feminisms might take a tour through women's conditions in India, Indonesia, or West Africa finally "leaving the fundamental identity of the Euro-American feminist on her way to liberation untouched,"[18] we see that in this novel George represents Great Britain's First World culture and society not only as uninfluenced by Third World culture but also as unrelated to Third World culture, as if there is no conditioning dynamic between the two. Indeed, just as First World feminism, Mohanty argues, fails to redefine itself, or redefine the meaning of liberation taking into account the experiences of Third World women and recognizing that First World women benefit from and are complicit in the exploitation of the Third World, so George represents First and Third Worlds as largely unrelated and represents any exploitation in the Third World as an effect of internal Third World cultural values and socio-economic relationships. Indeed, sexual oppression and labor exploitation are represented in the novel as problems primarily occurring within Third World culture such that First World capitalist culture becomes, in George's vision, the solution to the backwards and repressive Pakistani culture.

The ideological significance of George's representation of First and Third World relations, or lack of relationship, becomes clear when we consider Mohanty's assertion that "no discussion of the contemporary contexts of Third World women's engagement with feminism could omit a sketch of the massive incorporation and proletarianization of these women in multinational factories."[19] While pointing out that numerous feminist scholars have in fact studied the exploitation of Third World women in multinational factories, she qualifies that "few studies have focused on women workers as subjects—as agents who make choices, have a critical perspective on their own situations, and think and organize collectively against their oppressors. Most studies of Third World women in multinationals locate them as victims of multinational capital as well as of their own 'traditional' sexist cultures."[20] Certainly, George represents Third World women as victims of their "traditional" sexist cultures and represents them as agents only insofar as they act against each other in murderous and exploitive ways. Like the scholars Mohanty critiques, George does not portray Yumn or Sahlah as having a critical perspective on their situation or contemplating collective organization. Indeed, this is largely so because George does not represent an exploited Third World labor force in the novel. First World multinationals do not appear as an exploitive force in the novel. In fact, the exploitation of Third World workers comes in the novel at the hands of the Third World capital class.

Interestingly, Yumn's own commitment to sexual oppression parallels the economic exploitation—indeed enslavement—of Third World migrant workers carried out by Muhannad. Again, the story is not about conflicts between First and Third Worlds, between Anglos and Pakistanis, but of the exploitive practices within Pakistani culture, of Pakistanis exploiting Pakistanis. Thus, it is not the British empire that is the source of exploitation but rather Third World militancy itself. Muhannad Malik heads a Pakistani organization in the novel that has as its objective the militant struggle for Pakistani rights against white racism. Of course, at the same time, Muhannad is effectively running a slave trade with Pakistani illegal immigrant labor, suggesting that so-called Third World liberation movements that seek liberation from empire are in fact the real source of exploitation whereas freedom is to be found at the heart of the capitalist world system, which has typically been figured as the belly of the beast by Third World liberation theorists. Thus, Muhannad's "playing the race card," of which he is accused throughout the novel, comes to be seen finally as a self-serving means of manipulating law enforcement, obfuscating the real exploitation taking place, and of masking the oppression of one's own people. In the terms of the novel, the quest for racial justice by people of color is unnecessary and a dead end. White racism and racial exploitation in the First World is not the problem, as the novel represents the situation; the problem lies within the Third World culture and slave economy. Indeed, the solution to exploitation is, in fact, to join the First World, culturally and economically.

This is not to say, of course, that English culture is represented as free of racism against Pakistanis in the novel. Not only do we see racist violence against Pakistanis in the novel, usually incidents between children or teens, but we see virulent expressions of "old" racist imperialist attitudes from leading citizens of the town. For example, Agatha Shaw — a real estate developer of old family and old money — repeatedly, while valorizing Englishness, speaks of the "damn coloureds" and laments that they do not know their proper places, which are "washing dishes, making beds, scrubbing floors ... [j]obs that 'll keep them in their places"(353). She insists that "[t]hey owe their lives to this country, and it damn well behooves them to keep that in mind"(353). The individual acts of racism, however, are seen as just that, individual acts that are not related to systemic values and racial structures and which the system in fact finally militates against, just as the economic system militates against Agatha's old imperalist racism. The new capitalism is represented by the likes of Theo Shaw, Agatha's grandson, a liberal-minded and warm-hearted character who had a secret affair with Sahlah Malik. He is overseeing the new development in Balford and repeatedly reminds his grandmother that racism and good business do not go hand in hand, that racist values serve the self-interest of no class, telling her that "unless the community is a place where future visitors don't have to be afraid of being accosted by someone with a grudge against the colour of their skin, any money we pour into redevelopment is money we might as well set up in flames" (97). Global capitalism, in Theo's mind and, I think, the ideology of the novel, no longer entails the racial exploitation of the old colonialist practices of the English empire. Rather, quite the opposite, global capitalism promotes anti-racism as serving the interests of all by creating larger consuming classes. Thus, characters such as Barbara Havers and Theo Shaw become for George representatives of the new culturally and racially sensitive socio-economic order, managing diversity to maintain law and order and retool capitalism to encompass the "united colors of Benetton."

## Conclusion: The Empire Just Keeps Writing Back

In our current context of global turmoil which persistently raises questions as to whether military interventions are continuous with that old-time imperialism (war for oil) or attempts to fight tyranny, spread democracy, and at the same time recognize the cultural autonomy and right to self-determination of all peoples, the narratives of detection spun by Corpi and George take on a charged significance as they tell conflicting stories about the conditions of racial justice in the multi-national corporate empires in the age of globalization. While, as I suggested earlier, the advent of the discourse now called (though variously defined) multi-

culturalism occurred in the 1960s with the Third World nationalist movements in the U.S. when people of color demanded representation in college curricula and the culture at large as well as liberation from what they
perceived to be colonial conditions of the U.S. racist state, George's multicultural narrative represents something of an imperial retort. The narrative in *Deception on His Mind* effectively retools the colonial discourse
that constructed and sought to subjugate cultural, racial, and religious
others. The new empire, on its best behavior, seeks to understand cultural
differences both to combat needless bigotry and to manage and police
more effectively the racial, religious, and cultural other. The empire will
still rule but will do so with sensitivity and understanding and without
the denigration of others' cultures that leads to exploitation.

Obviously, as I have discussed, Corpi's narratives tell a different story
about the prospects for a non-exploitive, culturally inclusive empire.
Corpi's multicultural vision challenges the normative vision and structure
of global capitalism and the concomitant epistemological and cultural
frameworks that are used to make sense of "other" cultures in developing
a putatively multicultural society. In critiquing the very institutions of
justice, criminality, and legality informing the Western narrative of reason and progress, Corpi's vision strikes at the foundations of the dominant culture, insisting that a genuine engagement with the other
encounters and is impacted by alternative ways of knowing and of imagining social relationships.

While Saddam Hussein and George W. Bush each point their fingers
at each other, declaring the other the criminal in international courts, people continue to suffer under the regimes created by each. Perhaps it is time
to find new ways of detecting crimes against humanity and to begin to
prosecute justice on behalf of the millions of unacknowledged others
suffering within cultures of exploitation. Hence, the stakes in how we
detect crime, how we define law and order, how we construct criminality
and, by extension, which narratives of detection we valorize become
increasingly clear.

## Notes

(I have an expanded discussion of Lucha Corpi's fiction in "Lucha Corpi and the
Politics of Detective Fiction" in *Multicultural Detective Fiction: Murder from the "Other"
Side*, Adrienne Johnson Gosselin, ed., New York and London: Garland, 1999, pp.61–81.)

1. Paul Gilroy, *"There Ain't No Black in the Union Jack": The Cultural Politics of Race
and Nation* (Chicago: The University of Chicago Press, 1987), p. 45.

2. Elizabeth George, *Deception on His Mind* (New York: Bantam Books, 1997), p.
91. All other citations from this work will be cited by page number, in text.

3. Gina Macdonald and Andrew Macdonald, "Ethnic Detectives in Popular Fiction:

New Directions for an American Genre" in *Diversity and Detective Fiction*, ed. Kathleen Gregory Klein (Bowling Green: Bowling Green University Press, 1999), p.95.

4. Kathleen Gregory Klein, ed. *Diversity and Detective Fiction* (Bowling Green: Bowling Green University Press, 1997), p. 1.

5. Klein, p.2.

6. Klein, p.2.

7. Andrew Pepper, "Bridges and Boundaries: Race, Ethnicity, and the Contemporary American Crime Novel" in *Diversity and Detective Fiction*, ed. Kathleen Gregory Klein (Bowling Green: Bowling Green State University Press, 1999), p. 241.

8. Lucha Corpi, *Eulogy for a Brown Angel* (Houston: Arte Publico Press, 1992), p. 28. All other references to this work will be cited by page number, in text.

9. Franco Moretti, *Signs Taken for Wonders: Essays in the Sociology of Literary Forms* (New York: Verso, 1983), p.14.

10. Lucha Corpi, *Cactus Blood* (Houston: Arte Publico Press, 1995), p. 173. All other references to this work will be cited by page number, in text.

11. Moretti, pp.139, 152.

12. Ernest Mandel, "A Marxist Interpretation of the Crime Story," in *Detective Fiction: A Collection of Critical Essays*, ed. Robin Winks (Vermont: The Countryman Press, 1980), p.210.

13. Michael Hardt and Antonio Negri, *Empire* (Cambridge: Harvard University Press, 2000), p.254.

14. Chandra Talpade Mohanty, *Feminism Without Borders: Decolonizing Theory, Practicing Solidarity* (Durham: Duke University Press, 2003), p. 240.

15. Mohanty, p.240.

16. Mohanty, p.240.

17. Mohanty, p.240.

18. Mohanty, p.240.

19. Mohanty, p. 72.

20. Mohanty, p. 20.

# 5

# Deliver Us to Evil: Religion as Abject Other in Elizabeth George's *A Great Deliverance*

### KATE KOPPELMAN

> It is death infecting life. Abject.
> — Julia Kristeva, *Powers of Horror*

John Foxe's 1563 *Acts and Monuments of These Latter and Perilous Days*, eventually referred to as *Foxe's Book of Martyrs*, describes the death of William Tyndale in the following dramatic way:

> Brought forth to the place of execution, he was tied to the stake, strangled by the hangman, and afterwards consumed with fire, at the town of Vilvorde, A.D. 1536; crying at the stake with a fervent zeal, and a loud voice, 'Lord! Open the King of England's eyes.'[1]

Tyndale, the Protestant reformer best known for his English translation of the Latin Bible, was apparently such a threat to the Catholic Church in Rome that he had to be both hanged and burnt. His death, fairly early in the process of English Reformation, demonstrates the depth of the anxiety and vitriol between Catholics and Protestants in England in the sixteenth century. It was not simply Tyndale's translation that marked him as heretical; it was also his vocal indictments of the corruption of the Catholic Church. Tyndale, and other equally strident Protestant reformers, saw the errors of the church as dangerous— threatening to the people of England through their potentially infectious teachings. Tyndale argues that

[B]ecause we be wrong taught, and corrupt with false opinions beforehand, and made heretics ere we come at the scripture, and have corrupt it, and it not us; as the taste of the sick maketh wholesome and well-seasoned meat bitter, wearish, and unsavoury.[2]

The "false opinions" voiced by representatives of the church have the power to spoil, decay, corrupt, and destroy. The language of spoliation and infection appears throughout sixteenth- and seventeenth-century reformist texts; all are directed at the church, its leaders, priests, and rituals.

A similar language of abjection appears throughout Elizabeth George's contemporary British detective novel, *A Great Deliverance.* For Julia Kristeva, the abject is a site of "aversion, repugnance ... [where] the clean and proper ... becomes filthy, the sought-after turns into the banished, fascination into shame."[3] George's novel asks readers to see religion as a whole, and the Catholic Church in England in particular, not only as abject, but also as both "other" and "Other." The first, lower case "o" other represents those that are different from the subject, objects and persons with which the subject competes and against which the subject compares him or herself. The second, capital "Other" represents what Jacques Lacan calls "the prehistoric Other that is impossible to forget ... something that is strange to me, although it is at the heart of me."[4] The Catholic Church represents difference, lower case "o" otherness—*not* reformed, *not* Anglican. At the same time, and more dangerously, it represents capital "O" Otherness— the source from which demands and expectations come. This particular combination makes the Catholic Church in George's novel the true criminal, the real danger, the impossible threat, what I will call the abject Other.[5]

*A Great Deliverance* opens with Father Hart, a Catholic priest, on the train from Yorkshire to London to plead the case of Roberta Teys, a young woman who has admitted to the brutal decapitation of her father by pronouncing: "'I did it. I'm not sorry.'"[6] We quickly learn that Father Hart has found both Roberta and the body — the body without a head, and Roberta slumped over it, covered in blood. The trip to London seems to be an attempt on the part of the priest to intercede on behalf of the soul he insists must be innocent. While he might, then, be seen as a mediator of mercy and forgiveness, a sign of the immaculate grace of the Catholic Church, George instead presents us with a "pitiful," "pathetic," "odd" man (3). Physically, he is grubby at best, contagious at worst. We first see him as infected and, potentially, infecting to those around him: "He sneezed loudly, wetly, and quite unforgivingly into the woman's face ... and after the act, to make matters worse, he immediately began to snuffle" (1). We soon learn that a nagging cold is only one of Father Hart's many physical frailties:

> [A] face with three separate nicks from a poor job at shaving; a crumb of morning toast embedded in the corner of his mouth; shiny black suit mended at elbows and cuffs; squashed hat rimmed with dust.... His nose continued to dribble until the slowing of the train announced that they were finally approaching their journey's end [3].

In describing the priest's meeting with Thomas Lynley and Barbara Havers, the detective team who will journey to Yorkshire to uncover the truth of the murder of William Teys, George remarks again upon the priest's bodily corruption: "Father Hart sucked eagerly at the cigarette. He looked at his fingers. The nicotine stains climbed past every joint" (41).

Father Hart is stained, cut, dusty, dripping, mended but clearly still fraying. As the novel progresses, we learn that the priest's decay is more than physical. In fact, it is decidedly spiritual in nature. The investigation of Lynley and Havers does, indeed, reveal the truth of the murder of William Teys; Roberta did kill her father, but she did so because he had been sexually abusing both her and her older sister, and he intended to continue that abuse with a young girl living in the village, Bridie Odell. What is more, Father Hart knew about the abuse and did nothing. The novel confuses the terms of detective fiction in multiple ways — not least of which is our understanding of the place of Father Hart in the crime of murder. Additionally, we are asked to suspect the place of the church that Father Hart represents in the crimes of incest, sodomy, and rape. George's novel presents a criminal who is to be judged innocent and a victim who is to be judged guilty. Most notably though, the novel presents a religious system, usually a site of solace and compassion, as a place of uncertainty, dread, and contagion.

The enactment of abject otherness by the Catholic Church in George's novel speaks both to the particularities of the characters involved in the mystery and to the past of both the Catholic and Protestant churches in England. By depicting Catholicism as an other, an infecting force, a decaying institution, George points to a specifically British history of conversion, reformation, and counter-reformation. In his study, *The Later Reformation in England, 1547–1603*, Diarmaid MacCulloch discusses "a Protestant Church which remained haunted by its Catholic past."[7] Indeed, many documents of the Reformation depict the Catholic Church as not only a failed, obsolete institution, but as a force of danger, evil, and contagion. The language of this early conflict resonates throughout George's modern novel as we see not only Father Hart, but also the physical markers of Catholicism (St. Catherine's Church and Keldale Abbey specifically) described as crumbling and, ultimately, dangerous to those around them. *A Great Deliverance* reminds readers of this dangerous and haunting past while maintaining that religious faith — of both a Catholic and a Protestant sort — is a potentially threatening other with which we might still have to struggle.

## Difference, Otherness, and Aggression

> Father Hart ... seemed to float between two distinct planes of existence.
> — Elizabeth George, *A Great Deliverance*

What does it mean to inhabit the place of the other? In his discussion of the formation of the subject, Jacques Lacan begins with the tale of the mirror stage. In this stage, the child, who has previously understood herself to be whole — a universe unto herself — is alerted to the fragility of such an understanding by a specular image.

> Unable as yet to walk, or even to stand up, and held tightly as he is by some support ... he nevertheless overcomes, in a flutter of jubilant activity, the obstructions of his support and, fixing his attitude in a slightly leaning-forward position, in order to hold it in his gaze, brings back an instantaneous aspect of the image.[8]

Lacan notes that this initial jubilation, this "illusion of autonomy," is soon replaced by confusion and aggressivity, particularly in relation to the other objects the child perceives both in the mirror and around her.[9] "This moment when the mirror-stage comes to an end ... decisively tips the whole of human knowledge into mediatization through the desire of the other."[10] For Lacan, at the primary stage of development, "the other" represents anything outside the child herself, those who are not her — her mother, her father, her siblings, even her own body as it appears in the mirror, as fragmented and out of control. Otherness, at this stage, is difference. It is also, as Lacan later explains, alienation and aggression. "[T]he alienating function of the I ... [releases] aggressivity ... in relation to the other."[11]

However, the child who becomes aggressive will soon learn that destroying the other is impossible and that, in fact, the maintenance of the child's identity is intimately connected to the relationship she will establish with that other. The child wants desperately to be recognized by the other (most immediately by the mother), to know what that other wants, how the child can make that other happy. However, such a desire to be always recognized is ultimately denied when the child realizes that the other's desires are not always clear and that the child may not always be the object of that other's attention. At this moment, the other the child loves becomes, simultaneously, the other that the child hates.

[I]t is by means of an identification with the other that he sees the whole gamut of reactions of bearing and display, whose structural ambivalence is clearly revealed in his behavior, the slave being identified with the despot, the actor with the spectator, the seduced with the seducer.[12]

Identification with the other produces an ambivalent subject who will constantly, Lacan argues, be "throwing back onto the world the disorder of which his being is composed."[13] The subject lives in a world populated by others from whom he desires love and to whom he most often displays hate, a world of difference that can confuse and, quite often, enrage.

Father Hart's status as a representative of otherness begins at the stage of difference, of lower-case "o" otherness. Lacan argues that the structure of the ego, the sense of self upon which identities are built, is based not upon sameness, but upon difference, indeed, upon "the *function of mécon-naissance* [misrecognition] that characterizes the ego in all its structures."[14] The experience of reality as an experience of misrecognition and confusion is dependent upon the presence of others: "[T]he subject's experience of satisfaction is entirely dependent on the other, on the one whom Freud designates in a beautiful expression ... the *Nebenmensch*."[15] The Nebenmensch, the neighbor, one beside you "expresses the idea of beside yet alike, separation and identity."[16] Lacan argues that the figure of beside yet alike "is initially isolated by the subject in his experience of the *Nebenmensch* as being by its very nature alien, *Fremde*."[17]

Our first experience of Father Hart is, as I have already suggested, an experience of difference of a very particular sort. The woman upon whom the priest sneezes during his train trip from Yorkshire to London reacts as she would to Freud's Nebenmensch: "And she stared. First at his Roman collar, then at his undeniably dripping nose" (1). Her aggression at the presence of Father Hart's difference ends with a statement that points again to the larger presence of Catholic otherness in the novel, while introducing the priest to a world of constant difference, London itself: "She stood and scourged him with a final look. 'At *last* I understand what you Catholics mean by purgatory,' she hissed and swept down the aisle to the door" (3). Hissing, as would a snake, the woman leads Father Hart to the streets of the city and we then learn that he has traveled "from Yorkshire" (3).

Now also a rural other, not only a religious one, the priest describes London: "Every race, every colour. It was all so different. He wasn't sure he could bear the noise and confusion" (4). Father Hart is surrounded with others who will, ultimately, see him as strange, as foreign, but not before he sees them as distinctly different as well:

> They were Pakistani, and although they spoke English, Father Hart found that he couldn't understand a single word beneath the obfuscation of their accents. The realization filled him with dread. What was he doing here in the nation's capital where the inhabitants were foreigners who looked at him with cloudy, hostile eyes and immigrant faces? [5].

Father Hart has entered a sea of otherness, a world of difference. Later, as he is trying to find Scotland Yard, the "dread" with which the priest has first marked London increases. Unknowingly, he has traveled to the city in the midst of a particularly terrifying crime spree, what the police are dubbing a new "ripper" case. Father Hart senses an uneasiness in the city, but does not realize that others see him not as a source of safety, but as a potential danger:

> 'All *kinds* is what I'm tellin' you, Pammy,' the younger of the two women declared to her companion. She shot a look of practiced, chilling contempt at the cleric. 'Disguised as *anything*, I hear.' Keeping her eyes on the confused priest, she dragged her withered friend to her feet, clung to the poles near the door, and urged her out loudly at the very next stop [7].

As the novel progresses, we come to see that the initial reaction on the part of women in the subway is actually quite apt. Father Hart, his church, and his religion, have effectively disguised themselves as givers of solace and mercy, but have actually been allowing, perhaps even encouraging, a crime far more horrible than the brutal killings in London that lurk in the background of George's novel. On the surface, the crimes could not be more different, but there is a sameness in their violence and hatred, and there is a similar sense that the work of the police must be to engage with both criminal forces— the "ripper" and the infected church.

    The journey Lynley and Havers must make out of London and into Yorkshire — the site of the crime, but also the site of historically Catholic resistance to reformation — duplicates the sense of confusion and disorientation that Father Hart experiences during his trip to London. The village of Keldale and its inhabitants confirm that George's novel is very much about the encounters of the subject with otherness. Before the two detectives leave the city for the rural countryside, we are informed of the fact that their pairing is itself a meeting of difference. Thomas Lynley, the sixth earl of Asherton, a member of the landed gentry who is handsome and gifted with impeccable taste, is paired with Barbara Havers, a working-class woman whose unfortunate physical attributes are only exacerbated by her wardrobe and her insistent self-loathing. "'*And think of it Barb: picture yourself in the presence of such greatness. What shall you do? Shall you swoon or vomit first?*'" (24). These two will be asked to leave their individual scenes of safety and sameness and enter a place of danger and difference, an area dominated by the looming presence of the true Other in George's novel: the Catholic Church in England.

## Otherness, Abjection, and Infection

In a later work, Lacan develops his sense of the other by introducing a slightly different term, the Other. The move from a lower-case to a capital "O" signifies that the ambivalence of subjectivity exists not only on the plane of materiality — others who are people, mothers, fathers, lovers, bosses, strangers on the street — but also extends to (and perhaps, actually originates in) a higher plane. The Other is, for Lacan, the place from which the subject gets her instructions about how to act. "[T]he human being has always to learn from scratch from the Other what he has to do, as man or as woman."[18] All of the capacity for aggressive ambivalence is just as present in the subject's relation to the Other as it was in her relation to multiple others. Though Lacan will develop his idea of the Other through an investigation of semiotics, he will, in even later work, follow Freud in seeing a model of Otherness in religion — most notably in Christianity. The Christian God reveals the signifying dependence of the subject on the Other. The multiple ways in which Christianity dictates behavior, from the ten commandments to the more detailed restrictions outlined in Leviticus and Deuteronomy (for Freud, the incest taboo — a taboo at the center of Elizabeth George's novel — is a dictate that Christianity shares with other religions), demonstrate the dependence of the subject upon the demands of the Other. However, these demands are themselves often contradictory.

> A lack is encountered by the subject in the Other, in the very intimation that the Other makes to him by his discourse. In the intervals of the discourse of the Other, there emerges in the experience of the child something that is radically mappable, namely, *He is saying this to me, but what does he want?*[19]

Again, for both Lacan and Freud, Christianity offers a model of the Other's potential for confusing the subject. The God of Christianity is "a God who introduces himself as an essentially hidden God," a God whose commandments are, at times, hard to understand.[20]

The kind of devotional ambivalence produced by such demands is presented in George's novel in specific physical ways — most notably, the Other of Catholicism is presented as decaying, physically repugnant, and potentially contagious; in Julia Kristeva's terms the Catholic Other is abject in the extreme. Christianity is a particularly suitable model of abjection because so much of the religion is based upon physical suffering, pain, and torture. Abjection is, for Kristeva, both "death infecting life" and "a sacred configuration."[21] Early in George's novel, Father Hart's Catholicism is not only marked repeatedly as different, it is also marked by its proximity to physical suffering. Father Hart has been the one to find the decapitated body of William Teys, and so the description of the murder scene is associated immediately with the priest himself and with his particular use of religious ritual:

> [William Teys'] head had rolled into a mound of sodden hay in a corner of the stall. And when [Father Hart had] seen it.... Oh God, the stealthy eyes of a barn rat glittered in the cavity — quite small, of course — but the quivering grey snout was brilliant with blood and the tiny paws dug! *Our Father, who art in heaven.... Our Father, who art in heaven.... Oh, there's more, there's more and I can't remember it now!* [40].

Unable to fully recall the words of the *Pater Noster*, Father Hart *is* able to recall the specifics of the grisly crime. As though aware of his spiritual shortcomings, the priest turns to the central image of faith for the Catholic Church, the suffering and tortured body of Christ:

> Father Hart made a determined effort to think clearly, chronologically, systematically for once. His fingers sought the rosary in his pocket. The cross dug into his thumb. He could feel the tiny corpus stretched out in agony [41].

The body in agony, in gross painful and physical excess, is a repeated sign of abjection throughout the novel.

Of course, in addition to reminding us of the murdered body of Christ, George's novel (and almost any detective novel) centers on the corpse, what Kristeva calls "the most sickening of wastes."[22] For Kristeva, murder is a site in which we see abjection because it reminds the living of the insistent and corruptive power of death.

> [R]efuse and corpses *show me* what I permanently thrust aside in order to live. These body fluids, this defilement, this shit are what life withstands, hardly and with difficulty, on the part of death. There, I am at the border of my condition as a living being.[23]

She further explains that the abject is not simply filth, it is a force of instability and confusion. A system that is meant to order but instead breeds disorder is a system of abjection. Equally, a relationship that is meant to offer safety and protection but instead offers threat and peril is abject.

> It is thus not lack of cleanliness or health that causes abjection but what disturbs identity, system, order. What does not respect borders, positions, rules. The in-between, the ambiguous, the composite .... Any crime, because it draws attention to the fragility of the law, is abject.... Abjection ... is immoral, sinister, scheming, and shady: a terror that dissembles, a hatred that smiles, a passion that uses the body for barter instead of inflaming it, a debtor who sells you us, a friend who stabs you.[24]

*A Great Deliverance* presents readers with abjection in almost all of its senses: the corpse, the decaying body, the corrupted relationship (of religion and also of family ties: father and daughter in particular), the perverse system. Each of these instances is equally threatening, just as all are both attractive and repellant.

For George, the corpse of William Teys, the body with no head, is the center of the mystery. However, George's novel is littered with other corpses as well — some of which specifically remind readers of the perversity of Catholicism. Found underneath the body of William Teys is the body of Whiskers, the beloved family dog. Whiskers' throat has been slit, and we later learn that Roberta's dress has soaked up much of the dog's blood, proving that she has been the one to murder her pet. Additionally, Lynley and Havers learn early in the novel that the corpses of two murdered children haunt Keldale — one, a legendary infant who was accidentally smothered by Keldale residents hiding from Oliver Cromwell's roundheads in 1644:

> They were desperate in terror that the dogs from the village would begin t'howl with the noise and Cromwell would find them. So they hushed the poor child. An' they *smothered* it! [74].

More recently, an abandoned infant was found dead at the abbey and was eventually buried by Father Hart in the church cemetery. We later learn that the second infant corpse was the child of Roberta and her father, a product of incest about which the priest not only knew, but helped to cover up. Clearly, the death of William Teys has been predicated by the fact that Father Hart knew of the abuse by William of his daughters, but did nothing to stop it. William is described throughout the novel as a devout Catholic. Tessa Teys, William's first wife, notes that Teys' devotion to the church was one of the reasons she left him: "The Bible, confession, daily communion. Within a year of our marriage, he became the backbone of St. Catherine's" (183). Father Hart also notes the man's fervent faith. "William is ... was our precentor. Such a wonderful basso profundo. He could make the church ring with sound.... The Teyses never miss Mass"

(41). In addition to his devoted attendance, William also visited Father Hart for confession, a detail that Lynley later uses to accuse the priest of specific wrongdoing.

Keldale's own church, St. Catherine's, is built upon a corpse, the body of St. Cedd. Father Hart proudly shows Lynley the burial place of the saint, "a damp and musty place, poorly lit and smelling of loam. Green mold clung to the walls" (240). Each of these corpses is uncovered during the course of the novel, each of them attracting Lynley and Havers while simultaneously repelling them with their sickening revelations. Again, Kristeva notes that the process of attraction and repulsion indicates abjection:

> Thus, fear having been bracketed, discourse will seem tenable only if it ceaselessly confronts that otherness, a burden both repellant and repelled, a deep well of memory that is unapproachable and intimate: the abject.[25]

Lynley himself describes this necessary confrontation and its results:

> Murder — its atavistic nature and ineffable consequences— was a hydra. Each head, ruthlessly cut off in an effort to reach the 'prodigious dog-like body' of culpability, left in its place two heads more venomous than the last. But unlike so many of his previous cases, in which mere rote sufficed to see him sear his way to the core of evil — stopping the flow of blood, allowing no further growth, and leaving him personally untouched by the encounter — this case spoke to him far more intimately. He knew instinctively that the death of William Teys was merely one of the heads of the serpent and the knowledge that eight others waited to do battle with him — and, more than that, that he had not even come to know the true nature of the evil he faced —filled him with a sense of trepidation [310–311].

Lynley's metaphor seems particularly apt — the "true nature of the evil" is slowly revealed to readers as intimate on a number of levels. Moreover, the spreading, infecting nature of that evil is revealed as particularly powerful.[26]

In addition to the corpses that are piled up throughout the novel, George shows us various decaying and corrupt bodies. Each of these crumbling bodies is, as many of the corpses are, intimately associated with the Catholic Church. Quite apart from the deterioration of Father Hart's body — runny nose, marred face, unkempt clothes— there are other bodies in the text that have, through their association with Catholicism, begun to fester. Most notably, the body of Roberta Teys is presented as abject.

> Her hair was filthy, foul-smelling. It was pulled back from her broad, moon-shaped face with an elastic band, but greasy tendrils had escaped imprison-

ment and hung forward stiffly, kissing on her neck the pockets of flesh that
encased in their folds the incongruous ornament of a single, slender gold
chain.... [W]hite, flabby thighs upon which the flesh, dotted by red pustules,
quivered when she rocked. There were hospital slippers on her feet, but they
were too small, and her sausage toes hung out, their uncut nails curling around
them [201–202].

Roberta's decay has begun as a reaction to her father's seemingly divinely
sanctioned abuse. Her literally intimate association with this man — a man
praised for his Christian faith — has turned her into "what is *abject* ... the
jettisoned object."[27] In fact, Roberta acts as the abject as well. According
to Kristeva, "from its place of banishment, the abject does not cease chal-
lenging its master ... it beseeches a discharge, a convulsion, a crying out."[28]
As a truly banished object, a victim of sexual abuse, imprisoned in a mental asylum, accused of killing her own father, Roberta has remained silent
until the abjection can no longer be hidden. "Roberta pressed her cracked
lips together as if to stop herself from speaking. The corners of her mouth
were spotted with blood. She gave a ragged cry and a flurry of words
escaped as if of their own volition" (393). In addition to her abject body,
Roberta's association with her father has caused her environment to dete-
riorate as well. When Havers and Lynley enter Roberta's bedroom and
begin searching for clues, they turn to the girl's mattress. Lynley asks for
Havers' help:

"Help me pull off the mattress."
She did so, covering her mouth and nose when the stench filled the room
and they saw what lay beneath the old mattress. The boxspring covering had
been cut away in the far corner of the bed, and resting within was a storehouse
of food. Rotting fruit, bread grey with mould, biscuits and candy, pastries half-
eaten, bags of crisps [143].

Later, the detectives return to Roberta's mattress and find breeding mice
among unwashed underwear — more signs of the power of the abject Other
to infect its surroundings with its wretchedness.[29]

The Catholic Church itself, not only its representatives and followers, is presented in George's novel as a decaying Other. St. Catherine's and
Keldale Abbey are both crumbling structures, their status as abject
confirmed as we see the material representations of Catholicism wasting
away. When Lynley and Havers first arrive in Keldale, they find the village
empty and soon realize that all its inhabitants are at church.

The ringing of St. Catherine's church bells told them immediately why there
was no sign of life in the village. Upon the cessation of what Lynley was begin-

ning to believe was surely Sayer's nine tailors, the church doors opened and the ancient building spewed forth its tiny congregation [110].

St. Catherine's is "a proud little church. Surrounded by trees and an ancient, crumbling graveyard," it serves as the center of the village, but also suffers from decay and potential destruction. Like others in the novel who will recoil from the abject, the church itself "spew[s] forth" those who have come to it for solace. Keldale abbey suffers even more from abject decay. Lynley describes the abbey as a "crumbling ruin ... a vestige of time dead, being devoured by time to come" (331). Its very design seems abject in terms of its lack of order: "Steps led to nowhere. Curving stairways that once had carried the devoted from cloister to parlour, from day room to court, now sank into moss-covered oblivion" (332). Even without Father Hart's own corruption, the danger of infection from decay is present in the very material markers of the Catholic faith.

## History and Salvation

Beyond pointing us towards the church and its supports as culpable in the crime of murder, George's novel alludes— at times in quite obvious ways— to the particular history of Catholicism in England. The decaying world of Father Hart has a past that confirms its potential status as abject Other —from the time of the Protestant Reformation, the Catholic Church and its faithful have been depicted as contagions, dangers to the health and safety of not only individual believers, but also entire nations. The rancor with which Protestant reformers attacked the hierarchy and structure of the church is duplicated in George's novel at various moments. By alluding to the history of this conflict in England, George's indictment of religious systems is even more far-reaching than simply a commentary on one particular priest, in one particular village, with one particularly dysfunctional family at its center. In fact, George's title, *A Great Deliverance*, alludes not only to the story of Joseph and his brothers, but also to the language used by the reformers in the sixteenth and seventeenth centuries.[30] In his recounting of the details of the English Reformation, J.J. Scarisbrick quotes Thomas Becon, the sixteenth-century Protestant divine, as saying the following about his previously Catholic life and faith:

> What confidence we had to be delivered out of the pope's pinfold [i.e., Purgatory] after our departure, though we lived never so ungodly, through the popish prattling of monstrous monks and the mumbling masses of those lazy soul-carriers.[31]

Besides hoping for deliverance — a word that means the "fact of being set free, of or from confinement, danger, or evil" — Becon depicts the Catholic Church as monstrous, mumbling, lazy, as what I have been calling an abject Other.[32] Scarisbrick also notes that during the English Reformation "there were plenty of occasions for that form of anticlericalism which is really disappointment at clergy who have failed to live up to their ideals and exasperation with authorities who tolerate endemic mediocrity" and that "anticlericalism of that deeper and more serious kind which generates bitterness and bloodshed could have festered."[33]

The history of the Protestant Reformation in England is a long and complicated one. Beginning, in simple terms, with Henry VIII's acrimonious split from the Roman Catholic Church in 1533 — over the Pope's unwillingness to grant Henry a divorce from Catherine of Aragon, along with Henry's particular sense of an English King's right to rule both spiritually and temporally — the Reformation most clearly starts in England with the establishment of the Anglican Church and ends (if, indeed, it has ended at all) with the restoration of Charles II to the throne in 1660.[34] MacCulloch notes, in fact, that "the story of Anglicanism ... is a result of the fact that this tension between Catholic structure and Protestant theology was never resolved."[35] One of the key elements of this tension is the geographical split in alliances during the sixteenth and seventeenth centuries. The rise and support for Protestant reform came primarily from London and other southern cities. Again, MacCulloch notes that "Protestant advance in northern England was ... hesitant and patchy."[36] Christopher Haigh specifies the sites of lagging Protestant reforms:

> [E]specially in the countryside, the reformist breakthrough came much later. In Cambridgeshire, Cornwall, Gloucestershire, Lancashire, Lincolnshire, Norfalk, Suffolk, Sussex and Yorkshire, the Protestant Reformation was an Elizabethan (and often mid–Elizabethan) event.[37]

MacCulloch further notes, "Anecdotal evidence from the conservative Yorkshire priest Robert Parkyn suggests that throughout Edward's reign, the north lagged behind the south in carrying out official orders to alter ceremonies and purge Church furnishings."[38]

George's depiction of the village of Keldale, most securely and obviously located in Yorkshire, reminds readers of this specific history and the particular ways in which Catholic resistance to the spiritual, legal, and eventually military efforts of reformers was recorded and remembered. MacCulloch argues, "The Catholic community was increasingly introverted and cut off from the mainstream of English political life."[39] Indeed, the village of Keldale is isolated, introverted, secretive, and often actively resistant to the representation of "mainstream English political life" in George's novel — the two Scotland Yard detectives from London, Thomas Lynley and Barbara Havers. When she first describes Yorkshire to us, George points out that "[t]here were contradictions everywhere," and Lynley reacts by proclaiming, "'I still love Yorkshire. I think it's the loneliness here. The complete desolation'" (108, 109). Though he initially sees this loneliness and desolation as somehow charming, Lynley comes to see it as troublesome and dangerous. In commenting on a painting of Keldale Abbey, Lynley calls "the crumbling ruin ... a vestige of time dead, being devoured by time to come" (331). Yorkshire, Keldale, and most notably, the Catholic Church's remains in those places, are, for the inhabitants of the village and for those who come into that place from the outside, devoured and devouring; Lynley and Havers are confronted by the history of that isolated church and the power that isolation has to infect those who come into contact with it.

The anger and skepticism with which Father Hart is initially met — and which Lynley and Havers both eventually adopt in their perceptions of the priest and his faith — are echoes of the language used by Protestant reformers against the Catholic Church during the later sixteenth century. Like William Tyndale in his comment about the corrupting power of the Catholic Church ("as the taste of the sick maketh wholesome and well-seasoned meat bitter, wearish, and unsavoury"), both John Jewel and John Foxe describe that church as abject Other, as a corrosive and dangerous force of difference.[40] Jewel, in his 1561 "An Apologie of the Church of England," asks about Catholics:

> [W]hat manner of men be they, and how is it meet to call them, which fear the judgement of God himself and do prefer before them their own dreams, and full of cold inventions; and, to maintain their own traditions, have defaced and corrupted now these many hundred years, the ordinances of Christ and of the apostles?[41]

These are unknown "others" for Jewel — different from him and from the system of religion he endorses. However, they are also "Others," dangerous because of their power (and tendency) to direct and control the actions of those who follow them. They are vandals and corrupters, and Jewel's form of questioning implies, as his later argument confirms, that these O/others are not men at all, not truly human but instead abject threats to the faithful reformers. Jewel calls the Bishop of Rome "the king of pride ... Lucifer ... the forerunner of Antichrist."[42] His followers are described as "parasites," "the infection of naughty persons and hypocrites," they "lurk ... and beguile silly creatures with their vain glozing."[43] Their faith is "a mockery" which has "defiled," "mangle[d]," "decayed," and "spoiled and disannulled almost all, not only ordinances, but even the doctrine of the primitive Church."[44] Jewel's text is not only an "apologie," it is also a warning against those who might be deceived by the language of faith and devotion used by the Catholic Church.

> Thus with a gay and jolly shew deceive they the simple, and seek to choke us with the very name of the Church. Much like as if a thief, when he hath gotten into another man's house, and by violence either hath thrust out or slain the owner, should afterward assign the same house to himself, casting forth of possession the right inheritor; or if Antichrist, after he hath once entered into the temple of God, should afterward say, This house is mine own; and Christ hath nothing to do withal.[45]

For Jewel, the language of the Catholic Church is dangerous because it might infect those who are deceived by it. Jewel hopes that, through language of his own, he might warn others of this linguistic and spiritual threat.

Clearly, Jewel's sense of deception through language is also a central element in the "crime" of the church in George's novel. Father Hart's inaction has been sanctioned by the language of faith that he recalls at certain points in the novel. When Lynley returns to St. Catherine's to confront Father Hart about his culpability in both the murder of William Teys and the child of William and Roberta, Father Hart's voice, "insubstantial, disembodied, wavering ... came out of nowhere, tremulous and uncertain, and it hovered mistily in the frigid air" (356). He quotes scripture to Lynley: "'Evil-doers shall be cut off; But those that wait upon the Lord, they shall inherit the earth. For yet a little while and the wicked shall not be'" (356).[46] Likewise, William Teys has used the language of faith to authorize his abuse. His choice of readings from the Bible, the story of Lot and his daughters, is what Gillian Teys cites as one reason that she submitted to her father's cruelty: "'He came to my room. It was late. He said it was time to become Lot's daughter, the real way, the way the Bible said, and he took off his clothes'" (386). Roberta Teys borrows the same strategy when she uses the story of Joseph to justify the brutal killing of her father: "'The Pharaoh put a chain on his neck and dressed him in fine linen and he ruled over Egypt and Joseph's brothers came to see him and Joseph said I am supposed to save your lives by a great deliverance'" (393). Father Hart and Lynley both cite auricular confession, a particular and sacred feature of the Catholic Church, as the most damning evidence of the priest's complicity in William Teys' sins:

'He came to you here,' Lynley said. 'This was the place where he confessed his sins. Did you absolve him, Father? Did you make some sort of mystical configuration in the air that told William Teys he was free of the sin of abusing his children? What did you tell him? Did you give him your blessing? Did you release him from the confessional, his soul purged once more, to go home to his farm and begin it again?' [404].

Jewel also criticizes Catholicism's failure in the confessional, noting that even Christ's own disciples did not receive the authority to "hear private confessions of the people, and listen to their shiperings, and the common massing priests do everywhere nowadays."[47]

Just as Jewel does, John Foxe also hopes to warn Protestant reformers "[o]f such stinging wasps and buzzing drones" that populate the Catholic Church in the sixteenth century in England.[48] Foxe, the English reformer most known for his *Acts and Monuments*, or *Foxe's Book of Martyrs*, talks of "this catholic corruption" in his 1563 "To the True and Faithfull Congregation of Christ's Universal Church."[49] His critique, like Jewel's, depicts the followers of Catholicism as less than human, as others with the capacity to infect and decay those to whom they preach:

> But to carp where no cause is; to spy in other straws, and to leap over their own blocks, to swallow camels, and to strain gnats; to oppress truth with lies, and to set up lies for truth.... Such barking curs, if they were well served, would be made a while to stoop. But with these brawling spirits I intend not at this time much to wrestle.[50]

Foxe calls the actions of Catholic priests and Bishops "necromancy and sorcery ... hypocricy... corruption ... [and] treachery."[51] Unlike Jewel, however, Foxe hopes to push his critique farther back into the history of the Catholic Church in England.

> And thus the Church of Rome, albeit it began then to decline apace from God.... Then riches begot ambition, ambition destroyed religion, so that all came to ruin. Out of this corruption sprang forth here in England, as did in other places more, another romish kind of monkery, worse than other before, being much more drowned in superstition and ceremonies, which was about the year of our Lord, 980. Of this swarm was Egbert ... Cedda ... Lanfranc, Anselm, and such others.[52]

George's novel points directly to this history in its depiction of the details of St. Catherine's and Keldale Abbey.

One of the points of pride for Father Hart is the location of the tomb of St. Cedd (St. Cedda in Foxe's text), the seventh-century Bishop who founded numerous monasteries and died of the plague in 664. Father Hart boasts to Lynley, "If they'd built the abbey here, where the remains of St. Cedd are, it would have been destroyed in the time of Henry VIII. Can you imagine destroying the very church where St. Cedd lay buried?" (240). The priest continues his praise for the early saint and in doing so, points to the particular otherness of the Catholic Church in the north of England. Father Hart says to Lynley, "'I speak to him [St. Cedd] daily ... because we owe him everything.... He saved us. The village, the church, the life of Catholicism here in Keldale'" (241). He cites Cedd with the survival of a faith that reformers in the sixteenth century saw as corrosive and threatening.

> He gave them the courage to keep their faith, Inspector, to remain true to Rome during the terrible days of the Reformation. The priests hid *here* then. The stairway was covered with a false floor, and the village priests remained in hiding for years. But the saint was with them all the time, and St. Catherine's *never* fell to the Protestants.... I'm not sure you could understand [241].

George's novel points specifically to a history about which Lynley and Havers, as English citizens, likely have a good sense. However, the particularities of that history, its own relation to images of abjection and O/otherness that are present in George's twentieth-century England, remain, for much of the novel, distinctly foreign to the two detectives from London. However, that distance, that difference, does not protect either of them from the infecting force about which reformers like Tyndale, Jewel, and Foxe were concerned four centuries earlier.

Certainly, Lynley cannot understand the particular details of the Catholic history in Keldale. Not simply because, as he tells Father Hart, "'I'm not a Catholic,'" but because the murder case and its revelations about the culpability of the church in multiple crimes have made him feel that Catholicism, and perhaps religion in general, has failed him. As Lynley begins to understand the details of the Teys case, he turns to St. Catherine's for solace but is met with perfidy. "He felt immediately as if the church had betrayed him with its early promise of comfort and peace" (234). The church's status as abject and infecting force violently affects both Lynley and Havers. On hearing Gillian tell her story of abuse, Lynley reacts with repulsion and a sense of corruption: "He had never known such rage, such sickness. He felt Gillian's anguish overcome him like a disease" (387). Similarly, the infectious power of the abject touches Havers during the final confessions by both Gillian and Roberta:

> Barbara crashed into the lavatory, fell blindly into a stall, and began to vomit. The room swam around her. She was so ragingly hot that she was sure she would faint, but she continued, instead, to vomit [395].

As Kristeva has noted, the abject is "death infecting life," but her description of that abjection should also remind us of the precise reactions we see in both Lynley and Havers. Kristeva notes that "[t]he spasms and vomiting ... protect me. The repugnance, the retching that thrusts me to the side and turns me away from defilement, sewage, and muck. The shame of compromise, of being in the middle of treachery."[53] By the end of the novel, Lynley and Havers are both well aware of their place "in the middle of treachery." However, George's novel does not provide a convenient escape from either the current details of the Teys murder, or the past history of the violent and dangerous clash between Catholicism and Protestantism in England.

Thus, although the Catholic Church is clearly the main site for criminal and abject Otherness, religion as a whole occupies a place of ambivalence and abjection in George's novel. In his book *The Gift of Death*, Jacques Derrida calls all religion "the wholly and infinite other that sees without being seen."[54] While Derrida does not capitalize his "other," the definition he offers of the power of religion matches that offered by Lacan in reference to the "Other" in that Derrida's "other" is "an absolute being who transfixes me, takes possession of me, holds me in its hand and in its gaze (even though through this dissymmetry I don't see it; it is essential that I don't see it). This supreme being, this infinite other."[55] For Derrida, our engagement with such an O/other produces a terror and dread that both attracts and repels us: "[R]eligious faith [is] a form of involvement with the other that is a venture into absolute risk, beyond knowledge and certainty."[56] Further, "We fear and tremble before the inaccessible secret of a God who decides for us although we remain responsible, that is, free to decide, to work, to assume our life and our death."[57]

Elizabeth George's novel is about uncertainty, risk, and Otherness in Catholicism, but perhaps also in all religious faith — the faith of William and Roberta Teys, the faith of Father Hart, and the faith of both Thomas Lynley and Barbara Havers (neither of whom, we should note, is a pronounced Catholic). While the primary Other seems clearly to be the Catholic Church (Father Hart is a Catholic priest; the village of Keldale is an historic Catholic village; William Teys is identified multiple times as a devout Catholic; Lynley rails against the failures of Catholicism from the position of self-identified Protestant), the kind of Otherness described by Lacan and ("otherness" by) Derrida — an Otherness that produces ambivalence, risk, and terror — manifests itself in George's depictions of almost all religious ritual and practice. Kristeva writes, "Abjection accompanies all religious structurings and reappears, to be worked out in a new guise, at the time of their collapse."[58] We can see such larger abject Otherness in two main places in George's novel: the use of scripture to authorize criminal behavior, and the figure of Jonah Clarence, the Protestant minister.

William Teys' own particular abjection is uncovered through the revelations about Teys' textual devotion to the Bible. Beyond the willingness of Father Hart to overlook Teys' abuse, we learn that William himself has used the Bible to not only excuse his behavior, but to sanction it. When Lynley and Havers enter the Teys house, one of the first things they notice is the "immense, illuminated Bible" upon a stand in the center of the living room (137). We learn that William read from many sections of the Bible, but the story with which he spent the most time was the story of Lot's daughters. Gillian Teys, Roberta's sister who had previously been abused by William and who ran away from home, recites a part of that story when she recalls the abuse she suffered at the hands of her father:

> She called his name Moab, father of Moabites unto this day. She called his name Ben-ammi, father of the children of Ammon unto this day. The smoke of the country went up as the smoke of a furnace. They went up out of Zoar and dwelled in the mountain. For they were afraid [339].

The story is about willful incest — incest instigated by the daughters of Lot in order to save a tribe, a family name, all of humanity. William Teys uses the threat of total destruction, of damnation, in order to demand and sanction his abuse. The demands of the Other as father (this time, the Other who is a literal father) are sanctioned by the demands of the Other as church. The first and central corpse reminds readers not only of the death "that has encroached upon everything," but also of the demands of the unknowable Other — demands that seem unthinkable, but that are legitimized by promises of salvation and threats of damnation.[59] When Lynley realizes this particular connection, the effect it has on him is visceral:

> In the darkened observation room, the terrible realization cut like a sword's swath down Lynley's spine. The knowledge had been there before him all along. A nine-year-old girl being schooled in the Bible, being read the Old Testament, learning the lessons of Lot's daughters [393].

The abjection of the religious, not strictly Catholic, text points us to the various presences of the abject throughout the rest of George's novel.

Additionally, the primary Protestant representative in the novel does not offer a very bright alternative to the dangers and confusions of Catholicism. When Havers finds Gillian Teys, Gillian has changed her name to Nell and is living with a Protestant minister, Jonah Clarence. We are told that Jonah's love for Gillian has imagined no infecting past or future.

> It was her purity he so admired, the purity which allowed her to lead a new
> life, unaffected by personal animosities in a world where she had simply decided
> that such ugliness would never exist. Then it was her devotion to God — not
> the breastbeating, ostentatious piety of the religious reborn but a calm accept-
> ance of a power greater than her own — that touched him [369].

But clearly, when Gillian's past reaches back and claims her — when Barbara
Havers finds her and tells her the news of her father's death and her sister's
confession — the pure woman of Jonah's world is destroyed, violently rent
apart by her own past and very Catholic faith. As a result, Gillian locks herself in her bathroom and proceeds to tear her naked body with metal brushes.
In the midst of her self-destruction she, like Father Hart, William Teys, and
Roberta before her, reveals her particular intimacy with the stained Catholic
Church in this novel. Gillian's prayers are not exact, but they signal to Jonah
that her purity has already, and irrevocably, been infected.

> Bless me father. I have sinned. Understand and forgive. Brushes digging,
> brushes digging, brushes *dig* to make me clean.... One last chance before Lot
> finds me. One last chance to make me clean [340–341].

Jonah's reaction to Gillian's revelation is initially to remember his quite
fervent and religiously inspired attitude towards her when they first met.
"Like a crusader, he had set on a quest, and Nell [Gillian] was his Grail.
No one else would do" (350). But his love for Gillian, a love based on an
ideal of perfection, is immediately corrupted and destroyed. "The sight of
her in the bath — mindlessly lacerating her flesh, staining the water with
her blood — had demolished that carefully constructed façade in two short
minutes" (351). Finally, the agent of the reformed church in England flees
from the site of abjection, never to be heard from again.

The desire to flee when faced with the abject other is, for Lacan and
Kristeva, paired with the desire to speak to that other, to be heard and so
validated by him, her, it. The "subject who manifests himself as such to
the intention of the other" reveals what Lacan calls "the very bipolar structure of all subjectivity."[60] The action of manifesting oneself to the other,
perhaps paradoxically, secures the subject's very being. To flee entirely and
not confront would create a subject that was void — vanished as is Jonah
Clarence in George's novel. The confrontations between Catholic and
Protestant in the novel (and in the history of England) have threatened
destruction of one or the other but have simultaneously guaranteed the
survival of both. For Kristeva, engagement with the abject is both productive and destructive. It must be both and it must be located in the intimate encounter between the subject and the abject.

> Speech addressed to the other, not sinful speech but the speech of faith, is pain; this is what locates the act of true communication, the act of avowal, within the register of persecution and victimization. Communication brings my most intimate subjectivity into being for the other, and this act of judgment and supreme freedom, if it authenticates me, also delivers me over to death.[61]

When Lynley, after his final confrontation with Father Hart, escapes the claustrophobic interior of St. Catherine's, he does so in a manner that suggests the pain of the speech of faith, the encounter with the abject Other: "Scarcely able to breathe, Lynley flung open the church door and stepped out into the air" (406). However, though the abject is infectious, dangerous, not fully knowable, it is also, in its position as a border-dweller, the guarantee of existence at all. "On the edge of non-existence and hallucination, of a reality that, if I acknowledge it, annihilates me. There, abject and abjection are my safeguards. The primers of my culture."[62]

For almost all of the characters in George's novel (Lynley, Havers, Roberta, Gillian, even Tessa Teys) the abject Other — the corruption of the Catholic Church in Keldale — has, indeed, safeguarded their culture at the same time it has threatened it with total annihilation. In fact, the novel ends with Lynley redefining his particular form of faith, a form that foregoes all traditional and institutional supports, in a way that creates a sense of wholeness where only fragmentation had previously existed. "He had never thought of himself much as a praying man, but as he sat in the car in the growing darkness and the minutes passed, he knew what it was to pray. It was to will goodness out of evil, hope out of despair, life out of death" (413). The abject Other can and must connect life and death, life through death — thus, as George's novel defines the Catholic Church as criminal, as dangerous difference, it also sets it up as the occasion for at least tentative reunification and healing. Without the Other, no subject can exist.

## Notes

1. John Foxe, *Foxe's Book of Martyrs: A History of the Lives, Sufferings and Triumphant Deaths of the Early Christian and the Protestant Martyrs*, ed. William Byron Forbush, D.D. (Philadelphia: The John C. Winston Co., 1926), p. 134.

2. William Tyndale, "The Fyrst Epistle of Seynt Jhon," *The Library of Christian Classics, Volume XXVI: English Reformers*, ed. T.H.L Parker (Philadelphia: Westminster Press, 1966), p. 104.

3. Julia Kristeva, *Powers of Horror: An Essay on Abjection*, trans. Leon S. Roudiez (New York: Columbia University Press, 1982), p. 8.

4. Jacques Lacan, *The Ethics of Psychoanalysis, 1959–1960*, ed. Jacques-Alain Miller, trans. Dennis Potter (New York: W.W. Norton, 1992), p. 71.

5. Henceforward, "other" is meant to refer simply to difference — objects that demonstrate to the subject that she is distinct from those around her. The capitalized "Other" refers to an often enigmatic, demanding force — in this case, the church — from which the subject gets instructions on how to act.

6. Elizabeth George, *A Great Deliverance* (New York: Bantam, 1989), p. 39. All subsequent references will be in parentheses within the text.

7. Diarmaid MacCulloch, *The Later Reformation in England, 1547–1603* (Hampshire: Palgrave, 2001), p. 5.

8. Jacques Lacan, "The Mirror Stage as Formative of the Function of the I as Revealed in Psychoanalytic Experience," *Écrits: A Selection*, trans. Alan Sheridan (New York: W.W. Norton & Co., 1977) pp. 1–2.

9. Lacan, "Mirror Stage," p. 6.

10. Lacan, "Mirror Stage," p. 5.

11. Lacan, "Mirror Stage," p. 6.

12. Jacques Lacan, "Aggressivity in Psychoanalysis," *Écrits: A Selection*, trans. Alan Sheridan (New York: W.W. Norton, 1977), p. 19.

13. Lacan, "Aggressivity," p. 20.

14. Lacan, "Mirror Stage," p. 6.

15. Lacan, *Ethics*, p. 39.

16. Lacan, *Ethics*, p. 51.

17. Lacan, *Ethics*, p. 52.

18. Lacan, "The Subject and Other: Alienation," *The Four Fundamental Concepts of Psycho-Analysis*, ed. Jacques-Alain Miller, trans. Alan Sheridan (New York: W.W. Norton, 1977), p. 204.

19. Lacan, "The Subject and Other," p. 214.

20. Lacan, *Ethics*, p. 173.

21. Kristeva, p. 6.

22. Kristeva, p. 3.

23. Kristeva, p. 3.

24. Kristeva, p. 4.

25. Kristeva, p. 6.

26. There are other corpses throughout the novel as well — not all of which are associated specifically with the Catholic Church. The London that Lynley and Havers are leaving is being terrorized by the ruthless murders of the "ripper," and we learn quite late in the novel that one of the victims of the killing spree is the new husband of Tessa Teys, Roberta's mother. Additionally, we learn that Barbara Havers lives with the memory of the dying body of her younger brother — to whom she has built a shrine in the home of her father and mother.

27. Kristeva, p. 2.

28. Kristeva, p. 2.

29. Other aspects of the novel also speak to this contagious power. When Lynley and Havers go to visit Richard Gibson, Roberta's uncle who is also Catholic, they note, "Somewhere, a glass of milk had been left too long in the room, for its sour smell overcame even the other odours of poorly cooked food and plumbing gone bad" (George, 124).

30. When Lynley first turns to the large Bible in the Teys' living room, he finds the book open to the following passage: "I am Joseph your brother, whom ye sold into Egypt.... Now therefore be not grieved, nor angry with yourselves, that ye sold me hither. For God did send me before you to preserve life. For these two years hath the famine been in the land: and yet there are five years, in the which there shall neither be earning nor harvest. And God sent me before you to preserve you a posterity in the earth, and to save your lives by a great deliverance" (George, 137).

31. J.J. Scarisbrick, *The Reformation and the English People* (Oxford: Basil Black-well, 1984), p. 56.

32. "deliverance," *Oxford English Dictionary*, s.v. def. 1.

33. Scarisbrick, p. 56.

34. Clearly, this is an over-simplification. The Reformation begins sooner on the continent and undergoes multiple forms through the next century at least. In 1521, Henry VIII had been named "Defender of the Faith" by Pope Leo X, and ten years later, Henry named himself "Supreme Head of the Church in England." He was officially excommunicated by the pope in 1533, the same year that Thomas Cranmer, Arch-bishop of Canterbury, declared the marriage between Henry and Catherine void and Henry's marriage to Anne Boleyn lawful. It should also be noted that Henry's Church itself became the object of attack from later, seventeenth-century reformers such as Oliver Cromwell's Puritan roundheads. For my purposes here, however, it is enough to note that in the eyes of Henry and those English monarchs who immediately suc-ceeded him — Edward, Mary, and Elizabeth most notably — the split was between Catholic and Protestant, in relatively clear binary terms.

35. MacCulloch, p. 29.

36. MacCulloch, p. 108.

37. Christopher Haigh, "The Church of England, the Catholics and the People," *The Impact of the English Reformation, 1500–1640*, ed. Peter Marshall (London: Arnold, 1997), p. 236.

38. MacCulloch, p. 110.

39. MacCulloch, p. 124.

40. Tyndale, p. 104.

41. John Jewel, "An Apologie of the Church of England," *The Library of Christian Classics, Volume XXVI: English Reformers*, ed. T.H.L. Parker (Philadelphia: Westmin-ster Press, 1966), p. 19.

42. Jewel, p. 23.

43. Jewel, pp. 24, 33, 44.

44. Jewel, pp. 30, 31, 43, 46, 48, 47.

45. Jewel, p. 34.

46. This quote is from Psalms 37: 9–10.

47. Jewel, p. 24.

48. John Foxe, "To the True and Faithfull Congregation of Christ's Universal Church," *The Library of Christian Classics, Volume XXVI: English Reformers*, ed. T.H.L Parker (Philadelphia: Westminster Press, 1966), p. 73.

49. Foxe, p. 77.

50. Foxe, p. 73.

51. Foxe, p. 76.

52. Foxe, p. 80.

53. Kristeva, p. 2.

54. Jacques Derrida, *The Gift of Death*, trans. David Wills (Chicago: University of Chicago Press, 1995), p. 2.

55. Derrida, p. 32.

56. Derrida, p. 5.

57. Derrida, p. 56.

58. Kristeva, p. 17.

59. Kristeva, p. 3.

60. Lacan, "Aggressivity," pp. 9, 10.

61. Kristeva, p. 129.

62. Kristeva, p. 2.

# 6

# Missing Persons and Multicultural Identity: The Case of Philip Kerr's *Berlin Noir*

## JOHN SCAGGS

Detective fiction is a narrative of missing persons. While one perception of detective fiction is that a dead body marks the beginning of such narratives, it is often the disappearance of a close friend or relative that prompts a client to approach the detective. The themes that will be examined in Philip Kerr's *Berlin Noir* trilogy center around the paradoxically absent figure of the missing person in hard-boiled detective fiction, and include the instability of the idea of identity and the self, and the disappearance of the human subject in modern multicultural society. The analysis will focus on the idea of missing persons as those people who are socially, culturally, legally, and politically marginalized in society according to "issues of 'difference' stemming from gender, class, culture, or race."[1] The term multicultural, therefore, as it is employed in this study, considers subcultures based on gender and sexuality, and class, alongside the more central focus of those communities whose identity is based on race and ethnicity.[2] Furthermore, the historical framework of Kerr's trilogy, which is set in Germany in the years immediately before and after World War Two, can still allow significant commentary on the present moment, as the past is, and always will be, the legacy of the present. Consideration of the trilogy as historical fiction will provide the opportunity to discuss the role of social and cultural memory in the formation of identity, as well as historical memory, and to consider notions of otherness in modern Britain from a historical perspective, as well as a contemporary one.

## Hard-Boiled Fiction and the Body in Hiding

The novels of Raymond Chandler are a clear model for Philip Kerr's *Berlin Noir* trilogy, and this is evident in every aspect of Kerr's trilogy, such as the characteristic hard-boiled tone, the first-person narrative structure, the tough and cynical façade of its narrator and detective hero, Bernhard Gunther, disguising a romantic and honorable identity, and, of course, a narrative and thematic centre of crime and violence. In Kerr's trilogy, however, this crime and violence is institutionalized in the fascist ideology of the Third Reich, transforming Gunther's personal investigations into a broader social, cultural, and political struggle. In addition, just as the Nazis are representative of immoral criminality in the novels, their victims are invariably ethnic, social, cultural, and gender others, in particular the Jewish community, whose ultimate fate as missing persons in Nazi Germany has been historically documented. In a less disconcerting and more straightforward manner, a missing persons case also features in all of Chandler's novels, either as the P.I. Philip Marlowe's central case, or arising from his investigations. Vivian Sternwood, in *The Big Sleep* (1939), believes that her father has hired Marlowe to find her husband Rusty Regan. Sylvia Lennox, in *The Long Good-Bye* (1953), approaches Marlowe to ask about the whereabouts of her husband, who has left her and gone to Las Vegas. In *The Little Sister* (1949), Orfamay Quest hires Marlowe to find her brother, Orrin, who came to Los Angeles but has subsequently disappeared. In *The Lady in the Lake* (1944), Marlowe is hired by Derace Kingsley to find his wife, Crystal, who has gone to their cabin on Little Fawn Lake, but has not returned. *Farewell, My Lovely* (1940) opens with Marlowe searching for one Dimitrios Aleidis, whose wife "said she was willing to spend a little money to have him come home."[3] This missing persons case, which Marlowe never solves, or even mentions again, is a precursor to the case that he then follows for Moose Molloy. Moose hires Marlowe to find Little Velma, the girlfriend from whom he has heard no word since going to prison eight years before. Furthermore, the case of Dimitrios Aleidis suggests a definition of a missing person that is central to detective fiction.

A missing person, in the detective fiction in which he or she paradoxically plays a central role, is a person who loses his or her place in society. The missing person falls out of the socio-economic system of family, friends, work, home, and obligations. A missing person, in this way, is a person who is positioned outside society.[4] Dimitrios Aleidis, by leaving his wife and his home, becomes just such a missing person. Richard Swope observes, however, that "[c]onventional detectives themselves are essentially 'outsiders.'"[5] As Stephen Knight observes of Marlowe:

> He lives alone, in rented flats of houses. He works alone, in a cheap, comfortless office. He drinks and smokes a lot: a single, masculine lifestyle. He is choosy about his work, never showing much interest in money. In general, he has dropped right out of the normal family and financial patterns of modern culture.[6]

Bernhard Gunther's similarities in this regard are made clear from the opening of the first novel in Kerr's trilogy, *March Violets* (1989). Marlowe is widower, who lives alone. With the marriage of his secretary to a pilot in the National Socialist Flying Corps at the opening of the novel, Gunther also works alone. He smokes a lot, and drinks, but only, as he jokingly tells his secretary's father, because he uses alcohol as mouthwash and is "too damned lazy to spit the stuff out."[7] Just as his secretary's new husband, in his capacity as a representative of National Socialism, frowns on Gunther's profession as a private investigator, Marlowe's profession is frowned upon by conventional society, and is often associated with the criminal element. Both Marlowe and Gunther are characteristically hostile to authority, and to the forces of law and order, which serves to heighten the negative response that they can provoke in others. But despite this, their job is to find missing persons, and to return them to the socio-economic order which they have left: the socio-economic order of which the detective himself is typically not a part.

There are two possible scenarios in a missing persons case. In the first, the search for the missing person uncovers a corpse, and the case becomes a murder investigation. In this scenario, "[t]he detective story is set in motion by the problem of the identity of the body and the questions of how and why death occurred.[8]" Even after the discovery of the body of the missing person, however, until the detective has determined how and why death occurred, and the case is solved, the murder victim is still, in a crucial sense, missing. Their identity, and their place in both the socio-economic order and the narrative order of the novel, is always in question. In the second scenario, the person is missing because he or she is *hiding*, and does not want to be found. In this situation, the detective examines the traces left by the missing body, either dead or alive, in order to establish its identity, and its whereabouts. In the case of murder, "[t]he mystery is solved when the missing body is recovered, its identity established, the murderer named, and his motives explained."[9] The case of the body in hiding, however, is more problematic since the object of the detective's search seeks an erasure of identity, and the creation of a new identity to take the place of the one discarded. This act of erasure and replacement can be material, consisting of anything from a basic disguise or a change of clothes to extensive plastic surgery. It can be verbal, encompassing the use of role-playing, of aliases, the adoption of different speech patterns, and even the use of a different language. It can even be mental. The detective himself employs many of the same techniques in the course of his investigations, adopting aliases and attempting to put himself in the shoes of the person he searches for. In this way the figure of the detective is also a missing person, who suffers from an erasure of self-identity in his search to see beneath the masks worn by the characters that he encounters, and to reveal their true identities.

In this self-erasure of the missing person, and of the detective who searches for the missing person, can be seen both the basic structuring device of detective fiction, and the mechanism of its own deconstruction. According to Mark Taylor, "[w]hen nothing remains ... the body is deprived of its substance and appears to be on the verge of disappearing. The missing body sets in motion the detective story—in all of its (dis)guises."[10] Simultaneously, the missing body of the detective sets in motion the deconstruction of his or her own narrative. In this way, the missing body of the detective is symptomatic of a more profound occurrence examined in critical theory—the disappearance of the human subject. According to Michel Foucault, "it is possible to have access to him [the human subject] only through his words."[11] and such a claim is echoed by Jacques Lacan, who, speaking for the subject, states, "I identify myself through language."[12]

The human subject (dubbed the "speaking subject" by Lacan), is created in, and through, language, and the central importance of language in establishing personal, social, and cultural identity is clear in hard-boiled detective fiction. In this way one of the central concerns of hard-boiled fiction, specifically, the relationship between language and identity, has clear parallels with the foundational importance of language in the creation of identity in a multicultural society. The Germany of *Berlin Noir* is one such multicultural society, albeit one in which minority cultures are subjugated by the dominant ideology of the Third Reich, a subjugation reflected in a less violent, but no less pervasive, way in contemporary multicultural societies in the marginalization of the languages of social minorities by the official language of a state. Denying an individual the language necessary for the creation of a sense of self rooted in a particular culture or ethnicity creates entire communities of missing persons, and in the same way the detective who disguises himself through language is not only a missing person, but since his identity will always be somehow absent, he also highlights the impossibility of ever being found. This erasure of human subjectivity in this way extends beyond the personal to include the social and the cultural as well.

## Social Minorities and Missing Persons in Berlin Noir

While hard-boiled detective fiction is typically identified as a characteristically American genre, British crime writers have appropriated this genre, and a certain multicultural perspective evident in American fiction, to comment on the multicultural world of post–1980s Britain. Philip Kerr is one such author, and his *Berlin Noir* trilogy (1993) is a collection of three historical detective novels set in Berlin around World War Two and featuring the private investigator Bernhard (Bernie) Gunther. *March Violets*, the first of the novels, is set against the backdrop of the 1936 Berlin Olympics, and the plot centres upon a murder, and the recovery of a diamond necklace. Gunther is hired by a rich industrialist, Hermann Six, to recover a necklace that has been stolen from his daughter, Greta Pfarr. During the robbery Greta and her husband, Paul Pfarr, are murdered, and the couple and their apartment burned. Six reasons that by finding the necklace, Gunther will also find the murderer, but what begins as an insurance investigation quickly becomes a missing persons case when Gunther discovers that the body burned in the fire is not that of Greta Pfarr. The second of the novels, *The Pale Criminal* (1990), takes place two years after the events in *March Violets*. Gunther is persuaded to rejoin Kripo (the Berlin Kriminal Polizei) in order to find a serial killer who is murdering teenage girls in Berlin. The victims all conform to the blonde Aryan stereotype, and soon the Jews are being blamed for the murders. However, Gunther's investigations reveal that the murders are an attempt by a division in the SS to stir up anti–Semite aggression and to start a pogrom. The final novel in the series, *A German Requiem* (1991), takes place in 1947, in Berlin and Vienna, and recounts Gunther's efforts to prove the innocence of a pre-war colleague who has been accused of the murder of an American officer. The murder, however, is merely one episode in a further-reaching plot involving a group of Nazi war criminals who are faking their own deaths and creating new identities for themselves in order to escape going to trial for the war-crimes of which they are guilty.

The relationship between the past and the present is foregrounded in *A German Requiem*, as it is, in various ways, in much historical crime fiction. According to Ray Browne and Lawrence Kreiser, in one of the few academic studies of the genre, "[h]istorical crime fiction registers the actions of the people of the past, recording how they influenced, both good and bad, their future — and our present,"[13] and in this way the spatial and temporal setting of *Berlin Noir* is significant. It allows Kerr's novels to reflect, and critique, both the social and historical context in which they were written, as well as the social and historical context in which they are set. In particular it is the physically fragmented cities of Berlin and Vienna in *A German Requiem* that reflect the social disintegration of postwar Europe that is still evident in the early twenty-first-century. This social disintegration is reflected in the divisive topographical effect that is the result of rigidly demarcated cultural communities in the twenty-first-century urban environment, and the fragmentation is evident in *A German Requiem* in the partition of Berlin and Vienna among the Four Powers. There are clear parallels in the partition of the cities of Berlin and Vienna in what is termed the "colour bar" in modern Britain.

The color bar is evident in the "invisible" discrimination that functions in the gaps and fissures of often inadequate or unevenly implemented legislation. As Benjamin Bowling notes, the Race Relations Acts of 1965, 1968, and 1976 did not dissolve the color bar, vestiges of which "are still evident to this day."[14] According to Bowling, "individual black people have had to learn where they could or could not work, what pubs and clubs it was safe to attend and where it was safe and unsafe to live."[15] In this way, Kerr's focus on urban modernity and the modern city as a cultural melting-pot in postwar Europe is a direct reflection of discrimination evident in the contemporary urban centres of modern Britain. Specifically, Kerr uses his series detective, Bernie Gunther, to directly comment on, and look behind, the façades of social and cultural identity in the modern world. As Gunther observes of a Berlin left in ruins by Allied bombing, "you needed a lot of nerve to find your way along facsimile streets on which only the fronts of shops and hotels remained standing unsteadily like some abandoned film-set" (537). The physical destruction of the city has exposed a chasm between inner and outer, between surface and depth, and it is Gunther's job as a detective to look beyond the social and cultural markers of race, gender, ethnicity, political allegiance, and religion.

In this respect, Bernhard Gunther's conformity, and paradoxically his own marginalized status, are evident in his background, which, in its more general characteristics, is typical of the hard-boiled detective. He has a war record, and an Iron Cross, having fought on the Turkish front in the First World War. After the war, he joined *Kripo*, or the Berlin Kriminal Polizei, reaching the rank of Kriminalinspektor. However, Gunther resigned his rank when National Socialism began to make its presence felt in the German police forces. After working for a spell as the house detective at the Adlon Hotel, Gunther then became a private investigator. The shift from a position in the military and the hierarchical police system to that of self-employed "private" investigator, and from his conformity to (and decoration for bravery by) the dominant ideology, to that of an outspoken critic of the National Socialist regime, marks Gunther as an out-

sider. His cynicism towards, and hostility to, National Socialism is a political manifestation of the characteristic attitude of the private detective to
the public forces of authority. Gunther remarks on the irony of this in
*March Violets* as follows: "I have to admit that I am naturally disposed to
be obstructive to authority. I suppose you would say that it's an odd attitude for an ex-policeman" (242). Gunther's hostility to National Socialism situates him on the margins of the National Socialist regime, and by
belonging to a community whose way of life, history and values, in this
way, "differ from those of the so-called mainstream, [the detective's] story
inadvertently ... turns into a comment on the challenges of everyday life
in a 'multicultural' society."[16] Such commentary invariably touches on the
politicisation of race, and on the corresponding responses of racial and
ethnic minorities to personal, social, and institutionalized discrimination.

We can read in Gunther's actions and attitudes, therefore, a direct
commentary on contemporary multicultural Britain. Significantly for this
study, *Berlin Noir* is full of missing persons, Gunther's specialty. In *March
Violets*, these include Gerhard Von Greis, Kurt Mutschmann, and Inge
Lorenz, an ex-reporter who assists Gunther in his investigations, but disappears just as he comes close to solving the case. He is still searching for
her two years later when *The Pale Criminal* begins. *The Pale Criminal*
focuses on the disappearances, and subsequent murders, of eight teenage
girls, while the plot of the final novel in the trilogy, *A German Requiem*,
concerns the attempts of a group of Nazi war criminals to become missing persons by faking their own deaths, and recreating their identities.
They approach Gunther to find one of their own, a dentist by the name of
Dr. Karl Heim, whose body Gunther has ironically helped to dispose of
earlier in the novel. But the most prevalent group of missing persons in
the three novels are those of the Jews, and this includes "Jewish U-Boats"
(27)—or Jews in hiding—as well as others who are less fortunate. Early
in *March Violets*, Gunther reflects on the fate of the Jews as missing persons in National Socialist Germany:

> It's true that a lot of my clients are Jews. Their business is very profitable
> (they pay on the nail), and it's always the same—Missing Persons. The results
> are pretty much the same too: a body dumped in the Landwehr canal cour-
> tesy of the Gestapo or the SA; a lonely suicide in a rowboat on the Wannsee;
> or a name on a police list of convicts sent to a KZ, a Concentration Camp [10].

Jews, in such a society, are doubly missing. Besides disappearing physically, in any of the ways described by Gunther, they are also missing in
that they are removed from the dominant socio-economic order. Later in
the same novel, Gunther goes to a Jewish pawnbroker to follow a lead, and

here he discovers one of these restrictions. As Weizmann, the pawn-broker, tells Gunther, "'The Nuremberg Laws ... forbid a Jew to sell books. Even secondhand ones'" (38). Such restrictions brand Jews as outsiders, in the same way (although to a far greater degree) that the detective is marked as an outsider. By being socially, culturally, legally, and politically marginalized, they become "missing persons," and as such they are denied any part in the processes and procedures of social and political power.

The social, cultural, economic, and political disappearance of the Jews outlined by Kerr in *Berlin Noir* allows a comparison to be drawn with similar disappearances in contemporary Britain, as racial, ethnic, and social prejudices similarly marginalize large portions of the modern British population. Furthermore, Kerr's examination of the postwar social order in *A German Requiem* is a useful barometer by which to measure postwar immigration in Britain, and its contemporary legacy. From 1939 to 1950 the number of aliens resident in Britain almost doubled, from 239,000 to 429,329,[17] while in the period from 1966 to 1976, a total of 2,275,000 immigrants, not including a significant number of immigrants from the Republic of Ireland, came to Britain.[18] A new Race Relations Act in 1976, dealing with racial and ethnic discrimination in employment, education, housing, and the provision of goods, facilities, and services, was a clear reflection of how the majority of this large immigrant population were, like the Jews in Kerr's trilogy, "missing persons," excluded from the dominant socio-economic order, and from the democratic process upon which that order was founded.

Like banned books, the Jews in Kerr's trilogy are both metaphorically and literally erased from National Socialist society. As missing persons, they are like the signifier, defined by their absence. "[I]n the world of the sign, where one thing can stand for another," a world which Colin MacCabe calls "the world of absence,"[19] the subject is a sign that will always and only represent its absence. If language can operate only by assigning a word to an object in its absence, subjectivity functions in a similar way by assigning an identity to the subject in his or her absence. In this way, presence signifies absence. By being both present and absent the missing person is a ghost, and in the same way that the ghosts of early modern revenge tragedy are often allied with the figure of the revenger, missing persons find a kind of champion in the figure of the detective. By "standing for" missing persons, both in the sense of standing up for, or championing, them, and in the sense of taking their place, the presence of the detective signifies their absence. By taking their cases, Gunther assumes a political role by standing for the victim in both the sense described, and the racial, ethnic, and gender appropriation of hard-boiled detective fiction is clearly an attempt to create detectives capable of standing for particular minorities. Sara Paretsky's V.I. Warshawski and Sue Grafton's Kinsey Millhone are stand-ins for the missing women of contemporary society, while Walter Mosley's Easy Rawlins is a black stand-in for the black community rendered missing by racial prejudice in the United States in the years after the Second World War. The detective, furthermore, works against the forces that cause the disappearance of the people that he or she tries to find. "Traditionally," according to Ralph Willett, "the hard-boiled detective has been a kind of people's champion," working to expose and redress the betrayals of the forces of authority.[20] In *Berlin Noir*, this aspect of the detective becomes more pronounced as the betrayals by the forces of the authority become more obvious.

## Black Angels and Blonde Bombshells: Institutionalized Discrimination and Erased Identity

Gunther explains his work as a private investigator to his secretary's husband at their wedding in *March Violets*, and his explanation is also the first suggestion of the irony that permeates the three novels. In the majority of the cases that he investigates, it is not merely the failure of the police and military to find the missing persons that prompts Gunther's clients to seek out a private investigator. As Gunther is aware, in many cases it is the forces of law and order that are responsible for those people's disappearance, and such a situation is an ironic reflection of a modern Britain in which political authority is frequently implicated in the socio-economic disappearance of large portions of the population as a result of racial, ethnic, gender, class, and age-related discrimination and prejudices. As John Solomos notes, the continued emphasis for tighter immigration control under the Thatcher and Major administrations implicitly blamed conflicts and social strain on the black and ethnic minority communities, thus allowing for an identification of these minorities as an enemy within, threatening social stability.[21] The *Berlin Noir* trilogy, and particularly *March Violets*, reinforces this point, as Gunther tells his secretary's husband, who, as an officer in the German Flying Corps, is a representative of these forces of authority:

> These days I do anything from insurance investigations to guarding wedding presents to finding missing persons—that's the ones the police don't already know about, as well as the ones they do. Yes, that's one area of my business that's seen a real improvement since the National Socialists took power [5–6].

In *March Violets*, an insurance investigation becomes a murder investigation, which in turn becomes a missing persons case. Besides discovering that Greta Pfarr did not in fact die along with her husband, Gunther discovers that Paul Pfarr was a Hauptsturmführer, or captain, in the SS: a Black Angel in charge of his own department "investigating corruption among servants of the Reich" (93). This further emphasizes the idea of an enemy within, but neatly inverts it to point the finger not at the Jews, as the National Socialist regime attempted to do, but at the National Socialist regime itself. The discovery of Paul Pfarr's secret identity as a Black Angel prompts Gunther to speak to the chief pathologist at Kripo about his murder.

Gunther's reflections on death as he enters the pathologist's lab identify the most common scenario in a missing persons case, where "the trail of a missing person so often led to the morgue at St. Gertrauden, Berlin's largest hospital" (52). The body that Dr. Illmann is working on when Gunther meets him conflates the two categories of missing person. It is the body of a man who has been murdered, and has then had his head burned with acid in an attempt to hide his identity. In *March Violets*, the attempt to hide the identity of a murder victim is mirrored in the death of Greta Pfarr. "Inasmuch as the outer is an expression of the inner," Taylor notes, "the body is a sign that can be deciphered by those who know the code."[22] As a forensic pathologist, Illman, in *March Violets*, knows the codes of the body, and therefore his autopsy reveals a gap between the inner and the outer in the case of Greta Pfarr as he tells Gunther that she was eight weeks pregnant. When Gunther informs Herr Six of this, a gulf opens between the outer (the body of Greta Pfarr), and the inner (the body's true identity), which is symptomatic of the disappearance of the human subject. According to Six, Greta could not have children, and so the identification of the body as being that of Greta Pfarr is impossible. Greta Pfarr is alive, and the investigation into her death becomes an investigation into her disappearance.

This missing persons case is echoed in the novel by a second missing persons case. In this instance Gunther is hired by Hermann Goering, former head of the Gestapo before it was taken over by his rival, Heinrich Himmler. The job is to track down one Gerhard Von Greis, who has confidential information that Goering does not want to fall into Himmler's hands. When Gunther does find Von Greis, he identifies the body by the imperial German eagle tattoo on its right arm. Here, "[t]he skin … is a text that can be read if one knows the subtext or decoded if one knows the code,"[23] but as with any code, misinterpretation is equally possible, and is often deliberate, as much racial prejudice clearly indicates. Gunther's reading of the tattoo extends to encompass a wider statement regarding identification and control in National Socialist Germany. As Gunther observes, "it makes identifying someone relatively straightforward, and it occurred to me that it wouldn't be very long before every German citizen was the subject of compulsory tattooing" (149).

In *A German Requiem*, Gunther has been subjected to such compulsory tattooing, and by bearing the text of his identity on his body, his bodily text, like the bodily texts of those people discriminated against on the basis of the color of their skin, can be misinterpreted. At the outbreak of the war, as a Kriminalkommissar in the Reich Main Security Office, Gunther was automatically ranked as an Obersturmführer (Lieutenant) in the SS. Like every other Black Angel, he has an SS tattoo under his arm, and Taylor observes that "one of the functions of tattooing is to mark membership in a group that can be as inclusive as the entire society, or as exclusive as a small gang."[24] Membership in the SS, once as desirable in Nazi Germany as a low party number (indicating a membership in the party from an early date), in postwar Europe has become a mark of criminality, like the tattoo that marks Gunther as a former Black Angel. Like the Black Angels that he finds himself investigating, he has removed the tattoo; in Gunther's case, with the muzzle-flash of an automatic pistol fired under his arm. He removes his SS tattoo out of the fear of misinterpretation, but such hiding, through the erasure and re-creation of identity, carries with it the possibility of the final disappearance of the subject, for, as Taylor observes, "*[t]attooing represents the effort to mark the body at the very moment it is disappearing.*"[25] Gunther, despite this danger (or perhaps because of it), has altered the text of the body that can identify him as a possible war criminal, in the same way that the war criminals he is investigating further rewrite the texts of their bodies by having their teeth removed and replaced with dentures as part of their new identities. Such reinvention and rewriting of the text of the body reinforces the point that personal identity, like social identity, is not fixed and prescribed according to outer appearance, such as skin color or tattooing. It is fluid and changing, and subject to interpretation, misinterpretation, and even erasure.

Altered identities are common in detective fiction, and, like Chandler, Kerr employs the motif of the movie industry to emphasize the theme. Appropriately, it is to Orson Welles' *The Third Man* (1949) that *A German Requiem* most frequently refers, but references to film are prevalent throughout all three novels. A meeting of the SS officers responsible for the murders in *The Pale Criminal* takes place in an old schoolhouse "with rather more of the horror film about it than was entirely comfortable a proposition for the intendant [sic] trespasser" (506). The face of the porter in the building where Gunther has his office in *March Violets* has "something about it that always reminded [Gunther] of Max Schreck's screen portrayal of Nosferatu" (26). In addition to these references to film, references to detective fiction are also common in the novels. Gunther observes of the evidence that he discovers at a dentist's office in *A German Requiem* that none of it "was enough for Conan Doyle to have made into a short story" (722), and Hermann Goering, in *March Violets*, asks Gunther if he has ever read "'any of Dashiell Hammett's detective stories'" (132).

This narrative self-awareness extends to a self-awareness on Gunther's part of his own conformity to the image of the detective, and also, as will be discussed later, to the image of the Aryan ideal. Heydrich, in *March Violets*, describes the image of the private detective to Gunther as follows: "'The shoddy little man in the barely furnished office, who drinks like a suicide who's lost his nerve, and who comes to the assistance of the beautiful but mysterious woman in black'" (220). Colonel Poroshin, at the conclusion of *A German Requiem*, describes Gunther as "'a strong and valiant knight'" (829), in accordance with the view of the hard-boiled detective as a kind of questing knight. Gunther is aware of such an image of the detective in hard-boiled fiction, even though he denies that he conforms to it. "I'm no knight in shining armour," he says in *The Pale Criminal*, "just a weather-beaten man in a crumpled overcoat on a street corner with only a grey idea of something you might as well go ahead and call Morality" (487). The terms of his denial, however, are significant, as they reinforce the idea of hiding in the division between inner identity and outer appearance, identifying him as being in hiding in the same way as the war-criminals that he searches for in *A German Requiem*.

The war criminals of *A German Requiem* are bodies in hiding, attempting to bury their past identities, and to create new identities in the present. The process of resurrection is one that is common in Chandler's novels, and Kerr borrows the motif. A character fakes his or her death, and creates a new identity in the present, and this reinvention of the self is the focus of *A German Requiem*. Arthur Nebe, supposedly executed in early 1945 for his part in a plot to kill Hitler, is resurrected (in Gunther's words) as Arthur Nolde, a vintner. Gestapo Heinrich Müller is reborn as Dr. Heinrich Moltke, and one Max Abs is reborn as Martin Albers. Abs, however, is a "'sentimental kind of man,'" as Nebe describes him (794), and cannot pretend to be dead without erecting a headstone for himself, and this reinforces the theme of resurrection in the novel. Gunther discusses the headstone with an American intelligence officer called Belinsky, appropriately enough, in The Renaissance Bar (643). Belinsky, it later transpires, is a double agent working for the Russians. At the close of the novel Colonel Poroshin, the Russian who contacted Gunther about the job in Vienna, meets Gunther in the Imperial Crypt, which Gunther, with a new sense of purpose, later leaves "with as much spring in [his] step as Lazarus" (834).

While such resurrection offers the possibility of a new life in the present, as Nebe is well aware, the problem with creating a new identity is that it has no past. Without the foundation of the past, present identity, be it personal, social, or cultural, is unstable, and the importance of the past in a multicultural society is clearly reflected in the adherence to social and cultural traditions, including language. Tony Kushner discusses the role of memory in the relationship between the past and the present in terms of the anti–Semitic disturbances that occurred in many British towns in the first week of August 1947, but which have been largely forgotten by both history and the British Jewish community.[26] Kushner suggests that the "collective forgetting" of these riots stems from a desire to "emphasise the rootedness of Jews in the host society."[27] Prohibiting access to, or abandoning, the past, however, results in the fragmentation of identity, and in *March Violets*, Gunther notices that all the clothes in Frau Teichmüller's suitcase are new, that she is "'like a woman with no past'" (144). Frau Teichmüller is the new identity of Greta Pfarr, and, as such, Gunther is correct. She has no past. In *A German Requiem*, in order to survive in the present, Nebe, Abs, Müller, and the others need a past, and so the creation of a new identity depends on the creation and legitimation of a *false* past, as Kushner argues about the collective forgetting of British Jewry regarding the 1947 anti–Semitic riots. In an inversion of this, in *A German Requiem*, entire war records, less incriminating than the Gestapo officers' real ones, are created, complete with personal files and even dental records, and it is these dental records that provide a physical link between an artificial identity on paper, and an actual corporeal identity. Like their tattoos, their teeth can also function as a sign of their true identities, and must be removed. According to Taylor, "[f]or the canny detective, surfaces harbour clues of depths that render seemingly senseless appearances surprisingly intelligible."[28] He also observes, however, in reference to the relationship between surface and depth, that "masks never simply mask. To screen can be either to hide or to display. If hides hide nothing ... nothing but other hides, then hiding is actually a complex display."[29]

Gunther identifies the relationship between hiding and display when asked by Frau Lange in *The Pale Criminal* to describe the people of Berlin:

They buy expensive Biedermeier cabinets as solid as blockhouses, and then hang little curtains on the insides of the glass doors to hide what they've got in there. It's a typically idiosyncratic mixture of the ostentatious and the private [268].

Such a description parallels that of the private detective, and Gunther identifies the same relationship between "the ostentatious and the private" in Vienna in *A German Requiem*. According to Gunther, "the omnipresent combination of [public and private] embodies everything that was phoney about Vienna, like the syrupy sentiment and the affected politeness" (691). In this artificiality, Berlin and Vienna become "unreal cities," in which any secure relationship between surface and depth, between signifier and signified, has been disrupted. One metaphor for such disruption is the changing identity of both cities. In Vienna, such change is topographical, and is a result of the destruction that occurred during the war. In Berlin before the war, as described in *March Violets*, the change is semantic. The street names are changed under the National Socialist Regime, and Budapester Strasse becomes Ebertstrasse, which then becomes Hermann Goering Strasse, "'or whatever the hell the party calls it now'" (41). As texts to be read, the codes needed to decipher the two cities have been changed so much as to make such reading impossible. As Gunther observes of Berlin after the destruction of the war, "a street map would have been of little more use than a window-cleaner's leather" (536), and in a similar way the color bar in contemporary Britain alters British cities for minority groups to such an extent that, like a street map of Vienna after the war, a conventional map would be equally unhelpful.

If identity, as it is inscribed on the body, or in a map, is a text that can be read, then in the absence of the compulsory tattooing to which Gunther is subjected, it is possible for Greta Pfarr, in *March Violets*, to fake her death and create a new identity for herself in the same way as Nebe and his colleagues in *A German Requiem*. Such doubling springs from a *division* of subjectivity, through which Greta and her lover, Haupthändler, reinvent themselves as Herr and Frau Teichmüller. This creates in *March Violets* the appearance of one case, when in fact, as Gunther eventually realizes, there have been two separate cases all along. The first case revolves around Paul Pfarr's investigations into the corruption of servants of the Reich, which have unearthed evidence of corrupt activities in the business dealings of his father-in-law, Hermann Six. Six, terrified at what might happen to him now that the information is in the hands of Paul Pfarr and the Black Angels, arranges to have the papers stolen. By chance, on the same evening on which the robbery has taken place, Greta Pfarr arrives home to find her husband in bed with his mistress. In a fit of rage, she shoots them dead. She turns to Haupthändler, her lover, who decides to burn the bodies and make it look as if Paul and Greta have been murdered during a bungled robbery. To this end, he takes Greta's wedding ring and puts it on the finger of the dead woman. He also takes the diamond necklace from the safe for them to start a new life together, later obtaining forged identification in the name of Herr and Frau Teichmüller. There are two robberies, and thus two separate cases, but Six, like Gunther, assumes that there is only one, and that the man hired to steal the papers saw the diamond necklace and seized the opportunity. He therefore hires Gunther, reasoning that if Gunther finds the man who stole the diamonds, he will also find the incriminating papers.

Stephen Knight identifies the existence of such "double plots" in Chandler's novels,[30] and Taylor observes that the "strategy of doubling"[31] is a common one in detective fiction, and is used to generate the narrative.[32] The strategy manifests itself in many ways in detective fiction, but it is the duality of the detective, both in language and identity, that is most significant. This duality, which Knight identifies in the division of Marlowe's voice between his insightful and ironic narrative voice, and the terse and aggressive voice he employs in dialogue with other characters,[33] also characterizes Gunther's voice in *Berlin Noir*. Furthermore, this duality is linked to the division between the private *eye* and the private "I" in detective fiction, the division between seeing and being seen. This division is a form of split personality, in which the detective's true identity is hidden behind a tough-talking mask. Obergruppenführer Heydrich, another Black Angel, who admits that he has "'a passion for detective stories'" (220), remarks on this division in Gunther in *March Violets*: "'The ability to talk as toughly as your fictional counterpart is one thing, Herr Gunther,' he said. 'Being it is quite another'" (221).

Before Gunther realizes that there are two separate cases, he uses the metaphor of a jigsaw puzzle in an attempt to understand the problems with the case. "There's no logic to anything, none at all," he tells Inge Lorenz. "It's like trying to make up a jigsaw, with not one but two sets of pieces" (170–1). In such a jigsaw, missing persons become missing pieces, and when a person, like Greta Pfarr in *March Violets*, is both a corpse *and* a missing person, a puzzle becomes a mystery, for, as Gunther explains to Six's wife in *March Violets*:

> A mystery is something that is beyond human knowledge and comprehension, which means that I would be wasting my time in even trying to investigate it. No, this case is nothing more than a puzzle, and I happen to like puzzles [65].

However, since the detective is himself a kind of missing person, he too can become a missing piece in the case that he is investigating. When this happens, "the condition of the possibility of disguising turns out to be the condition of the impossibility of detection,"[34] as the detective becomes both the investigating subject, and the object of investigation. This, in part, explains the limited success of the detective, and the small, local victories that are all that he achieves.

## Double Agency and Divided Identity

The erosion of the division between the subject and the object of the detective's investigations occurs because the detective lives in a world in which "signifiers have divorced themselves from signifieds, while the distinction between self and other has conflated,"[35] and it is this conflation that marks the detective as a double agent. Gunther's role as a double agent is evident in *March Violets* when Heydrich sends him to a KZ, or concentration camp. This foregrounds Gunther's role-reversal by placing him in the same position as many of the Jews that he searches for as a private investigator. The fictional detective depends on a relationship of difference and similarity in order to solve cases and find missing persons, and in this case it is Gunther's similarity as an outsider, or a missing person, that is foregrounded. However, he is sent to a concentration camp to work for Heydrich and to find Kurt Mutshmann, the man who has the papers that incriminate Hermann Six. Mutschmann has avoided arrest for his theft of the papers by being arrested for socialist activities, and in order to follow him Gunther is given a new identity, Willy Krause, and a file that identifies him as a black-marketeer. To further aid his disguise, he is given a thorough beating by the SS. In the same way that his cut and bruised skin can be read as a bodily text that identifies him as a criminal, so too is Mutschmann's body a text that can be decoded, if Gunther knows the correct code. He is told that Mutschmann has a ganglion on his right wrist, and this ganglion, like Von Greis's tattoo earlier in the novel, is the code to his true identity.

In *The Pale Criminal*, as in *March Violets*, Gunther must both decipher the text of the body and play roles in order to solve the case. The novel is structured around an inversion of the detective's method of reading the body — both dead and alive — in order to solve the crime. Here, it is the killer who reads the bodies of the girls in order to commit the crime, by selecting only those girls who conform to the Aryan stereotype. There are parallels here with racially motivated violence in multicultural societies, in which the body is read as a text of otherness in order to attempt to justify racial violence, but the formula of racial violence is inverted in *The Pale Criminal* as Gunther discovers that it is a group within the SS that is responsible for the murders as part of an attempt to stir up anti–Semitic aggression. The forces of National Socialist law and order, of which Gunther, as a Kriminalkommissar, is now a part, are responsible for the murders that he is investigating. As Illmann, the pathologist who is assisting in the case, observes in *March Violets*, "[h]alf the time I find myself presenting the forensic evidence of a homicide to the very people who committed it. It's an upside down world we live in" (55).

It is the upside down nature of the world that allows one girl to narrowly escape death at the hands of the killer. In appearance, Sarah Hirsch conforms to the blond Aryan stereotype. This initially draws the killer to her, but she ironically escapes death by virtue of the fact that she is Jewish. Her conformity to the Aryan stereotype is an unwitting kind of role-playing, but Gunther wryly remarks "that for once Sarah's race had been to her advantage — that being Jewish had probably saved her life" (407). In a similar way to Sarah Hirsch, Gunther also unwittingly plays roles. In appearance, he conforms to the Aryan ideal, with "blond hair and blue eyes" (68), but he is hostile to the National Socialist regime which promotes the ideal. However, his role-playing is also intentional at times, and he even depends on his appearance, as when he poses as the husband of Hildegard Steininger, the mother of one of the girls who has disappeared, in order to follow a lead. The extent of Gunther's role-playing is indicated by the fact that he moves into Hildegard's apartment for a short while, and even becomes her lover. The inversion suggested by such role-playing, in which the man investigating a murder becomes, temporarily at least, the father of the victim, is almost total. Furthermore, the clue that Gunther is following leads him to another private detective, Rolf Vogelmann, who has been hired by the parents of at least two of the other missing girls. In this way, Vogelmann's investigative methods are themselves subjected to investigation (442). Despite the extent of this inversion, however, and despite Gunther's rank in Kripo and his conformity to the Aryan stereotype, by the end of the novel Hildegard has replaced him with a young SS major who "could have been something straight out of one of Irma Hanke's racial theory classes: pale blond hair, blue eyes and a jaw that looked like it had been set in concrete" (522).

Gunther, in contrast, lacks such solidity, and the division of identity that is characteristic of the figure of the detective becomes a fragmentation of the subject that reflects a broader social fragmentation, particularly in the modern multicultural environment. At the conclusion of *A German Requiem*, this fragmentation is corporeal. Gunther suffers a fractured skull, a broken collar bone, a broken arm, and several broken ribs (816). In addition, on first being admitted to hospital, he is also diagnosed as having gonorrhoea (824), and this social disease is a further indication of how Gunther's fragmentation of subjectivity mirrors a broader social fragmentation In *The Pale Criminal*, despite the fact that Gunther solves the case, the pogrom that the SS were seeking still occurs, and the fragmentation of the figure of the detective is more profound. Gunther walks through a city that, like the British towns that experienced anti–Semitic riots in August 1947, is being torn apart. The destruction of the city reflects the fragmentation of the self that the figure of the detective suffers, and which is emblematic of a broader social and cultural fragmentation which mirrors that of multicultural post–1980s Britain:

> Further on, at the corner of Kurfürstendamm, I came across an enormous mirror that lay in a hundred pieces, presenting shattered images of myself that ground and cracked underfoot as I picked my way along the street [519].

Gunther is a "disunified subject," who acknowledges in a direct reference to *Hamlet* at the end of *March Violets* that he has "grown used to living in a world that is out of joint" (245–6). The detective's quest is a quest to restore order to a disjointed world that has been put out of joint by racism, sexism, class and religious prejudices, and an intolerance of difference and otherness.

## Notes

1. A. Johnson Gosselin, "Multicultural Detective Fiction: Murder with a Message," in A. Johnson Gosselin, ed., *Multicultural Detective Fiction: Murder from the "Other" Side* (New York & London: Garland, 1999) pp. 3–14, p. 5.
2. Gosselin, 'Multicultural Detective Fiction," p. 6.
3. R. Chandler, *Farewell, My Lovely*, in *Raymond Chandler: Three Novels* (Harmondsworth: Penguin, 1993), p. 167.
4. R. Swope, "Approaching the Threshold(s) in Postmodern Detective Fiction: Hawthorne's 'Wakefield' and Other Missing Persons," in *Critiques: Studies in Contemporary Fiction*, Vol. 39:3, 1998, pp. 207–227, p. 211.
5. Swope, "Approaching the Threshold(s)," p. 211.
6. S. Knight, "'A Hard Cheerfulness': An Introduction to Raymond Chandler," in Brian Docherty, ed., *American Crime Fiction: Studies in the Genre* (London: Macmillan, 1988), pp. 71–87, p. 78.
7. P. Kerr, *March Violets*, in *Berlin Noir* (Harmondsworth: Penguin, 1993), p. 6. Further references to the novels will be incorporated in the text.
8. M. Taylor, *Hiding* (London: University of Chicago Press, 1997), p. 27.
9. Taylor, *Hiding*, p. 28.
10. Taylor, *Hiding*, p. 12.
11. M. Foucault, *The Order of Things: An Archaeology of the Human Sciences* (London: Tavistock, 1977), p. 313.

12. J. Lacan, *Écrits: A Selection,* trans. Alan Sheridan, (London: Tavistock, 1977), p. 86.

13. R.B. Browne and L.A. Kreiser, eds., *The Detective as Historian: History and Art in Historical Crime Fiction* (Bowling Green, OH: Bowling Green State University Popular Press, 2000), p. 2.

14. B. Bowling, "The Emergence of Violent Racism as a Public Issue in Britain, 1945–81," in P. Panayi, ed., *Racial Violence in Britain in the Nineteenth and Twentieth Centuries,* revised edition (London: Leicester University Press, 1996), pp. 185–220, p. 209.

15. Bowling, "The Emergence of Violent Racism," p. 209.

16. P. Freese, *The Ethnic Detective: Chester Himes, Harry Kemelman, Tony Hillerman* (Essen: Die Blaue Eule, 1992), pp. 9–10.

17. D. Childs, *Britain Since 1939: Progress and Decline* (Basingstoke: Macmillan, 1995), p. 96.

18. Childs, *Britain Since 1939,* p. 188.

19. C. MacCabe, *Theoretical Essays: Film, Linguistics, Literature* (Manchester: Manchester University Press, 1985), p. 89.

20. R.Willett, *Hard-Boiled Detective Fiction* (Staffordshire: British Association for American Studies, 1992), p. 7.

21. J. Solomos, *Race and Racism in Britain,* third edition (Basingstoke: Palgrave Macmillan, 2003), pp. 65–6.

22. Taylor, *Hiding,* p. 15.

23. Taylor, *Hiding,* p. 83.

24. Taylor, *Hiding,* p. 123.

25. Taylor, *Hiding,* p. 129.

26. T. Kushner, "Anti-Semitism and Austerity: The August 1947 Riots in Britain," in P. Panayi, ed., *Racial Violence in Britain,* pp. 150–170, p. 150.

27. Kushner, "Anti-Semitism and Austerity," p. 165.

28. Taylor, *Hiding,* p. 15.

29. Taylor, *Hiding,* p. 39.

30. Knight, "'A Hard Cheerfulness,'" pp. 82–83.

31. Taylor, *Hiding,* p. 48.

32. Taylor, *Hiding,* p. 48.

33. Knight, "'A Hard Cheerfulness,'" p. 81.

34. Taylor, *Hiding,* p. 17.

35. Swope, "Approaching the Threshold(s)," p. 211.

# 7

# "At the Threshold of Eternity": Religious Inversion in Peter Ackroyd's *Hawksmoor*

### ANDREW HOCK-SOON NG

Recently, the term "metaphysical detective fiction" has been used to define a type of detective narrative that foregrounds problems rather than solutions.[1] According to critics Patricia Merivale and Susan Elizabeth Sweeney, the metaphysical detective narrative is distinguished from its traditional counterpart by "the profound questions that it raises about narrative, interpretation, subjectivity, the nature of reality, and the limits of knowledge."[2] They go on to demonstrate that this subgenre also

> parodies or subverts traditional detective-story conventions— such as narrative closure and the detective's role as surrogate reader — with the intention, or at least the effect, of asking questions about mysteries of being and knowing which transcends the mere machinations of the mystery plot. Metaphysical detective stories often emphasize this transcendence, moreover, by becoming self-reflexive (that is, by representing allegorically the text's own process of composition).[3]

These critics consider Peter Ackroyd's *Hawksmoor* (1988) as an example of a metaphysical detective narrative — without, however, going into any details. This chapter is an attempt at situating Ackroyd's novel within this new fictive form. Several critics on Peter Ackroyd's *Hawksmoor* (1988) have noted the novel's ludic form, and read it as a game which the author is playing with the reader.[4] Without discounting the ludic nature of the narrative, my emphasis is on the metaphysical questions it poses with regards to time, death, and religion. I am of the opinion that *Hawksmoor* as a post-modern detective novel is not merely playful, but embodies in both theme and form a deep philosophical awareness. In traditional detective narratives, an all-knowing detective sets out to solve an initially unsolvable crime; this privileges the modernist self who is rational and logical, and who is able to reduce aspects of the supernatural to mere artifice (*The Hound of the Baskervilles* is a classic example). In the case of Ackroyd's novel, however, the narrative is not ultimately about deviance and crime-solving. It is about interpretation and the nature of reality; and finally it is about transcendence — not only in Merivale's and Sweeney's term, which is the transcendence of the "mere machination of the mystery plot," but the transcendence of subjectivity above constructed reality to encounter an otherness that is mysterious. Religion offers a glimpse into this profundity but, in the end, remains a veil which confounds any philosophical, textual or ideological closures.

For the benefit of those who are unfamiliar with the narrative, a brief synopsis will be offered here. *Hawksmoor* fictively recreates the life of the eighteenth-century architect Nicholas Dyer, whose main achievement was the reconstruction of the churches which were destroyed in the Great Fire of London (1666). Ackroyd, however, gives Dyer a sinister quality. Inspired by another literary work on London, *Lud Heat* by Iain Sinclair,[5] Ackroyd depicts this figure as someone who is repulsed by death and who practices an occult system which he hopes will free him from the inevitability of dying. Among some of the beliefs within this cult is the necessity for human sacrifice in order to avert death of oneself. The novel alternates between the eighteenth and the twentieth century, and, in the latter, Dyer is "reincarnated" as the detective Hawksmoor, who is on a mission to solve several mysterious deaths which have occurred within the churches that Dyer had built hundreds of years ago. Hawksmoor, of course, becomes increasingly frustrated in his hunt, only to, in the end, come face-to-face with his centuries-old double in one of the most enigmatic denouements in postmodern detective fiction.

The fundamental premise of my argument is that in *Hawksmoor*, religion itself is configured as an otherness. It is not merely the marginality of Dyer's occult belief that situates it as an "other" from the established religion of his time, which he systematically undermines; it is also the fact that religion cannot be confined within any form of human control — be it rationalistic principles, empirical surety (as in eighteenth-century philosophy), or diabolical reconstitution (Dyer). Religion is a site of *aporia*, and to confront it (to explain God or faith, for example) is to become silenced by it. Religion can only, in other words, be known by admitting its unknowingness— what Derrida would term "negative theology." Dyer's desire to redefine for himself a unique faith that is dependent on, and deconstructive of, the established religion can be seen as an attempt to control religion, only to realize that in the end, religion both escapes and entraps him — an entrapment that persists all the way into the twentieth century through his reincarnated self (or selves). Religion, therefore, is always already an other, and any form of establishing it is only a symbolic attempt at reining in something which ultimately escapes human comprehension. As a postmodern novel, *Hawksmoor* is able to address this fundamental mystery of religion by rehearsing several forms of human endeavors to institutionalize religion to serve its ends, only to have religion thwarting those very attempts in the end. My argument is not that religion is another Lyotardian metanarrative which this postmodern text deconstructs; instead, I argue that the narrative reveals that religion is ultimately enigmatic and necessarily escapes all forms of theorizing, including postmodern ones.

## Varieties of Religious Experiences in Eighteenth-Century England

"Eighteenth-century England," according to literary historian James Sambrook, "was a Christian country."[6] But he then goes on to explain the complex state of Christianity which has largely shaped the way the religion is viewed hitherto. With the Enlightenment, and beginning with Descartes, the supernatural elements of the religion were slowly being eroded and replaced with a more scientific, or mathematical and rationalistic, outlook. Newton, Locke and Addison were the new prophets who preached a brand of Christianity that eschewed irrational doctrinal matters such as miracles, the virgin birth, and original sin (among others). But as Sambrook points out, "Newton's new philosophy, at first a defence of Christianity, as Newton intended, became a means of attack upon it: Locke's new philosophy suffered a similar fate."[7] This is because this new brand of Christianity, in proposing a mathematical God and a mechanistic universe, also paved the way for free thinking.[8] If the world before Descartes was governed by a structure that was permanent and sacred, and which had inherent values, the world of the Enlightenment and after is "an event within knowledge. Knowledge validates the world, and is independent of it. In a society which in the last analysis is built on and wholly dependent on the growth of knowledge, knowledge is not treated as sacred, and also confers no social authority."[9] In this new world where existence is validated by knowledge — or more precisely, rational and mathematical precision — religion's truth must also be empirically measured and approved. Yet this would mean that much of the system of Christian belief must be disregarded as well.

Fundamental doctrinal matters concerning the divinity of Christ and the figure of the Trinity, for example, by the very fact that they do not conform to empirical categories, are to be treated as inaccurate at best, and absurd at worst. It is then evident that more and more Christian truths were being questioned, prompting many dissenters to look elsewhere for verification of the Deity's reality. One group turned to natural religion as evidence of God's presence on earth. But this subsequently led to a brand of pantheism which, according to its most important proponent, John Toland (1670–1722), was an esoteric form of religion revealed only to the enlightened few.[10] Toland's religious conviction was also decidedly Socinian.[11] Others, like David Hume, saw monotheistic religions as an evolution from polytheistic ones, thus jettisoning the belief that Christianity is as old as creation. He further argued that monotheism encourages the "monkish virtues of mortification, penance, humility and passive suffering,"[12] which then led to oppression and subjection by one group over another through religious justification. England in the eighteenth century was a Christian country not because of a unified belief system, but because of a struggle for what constitutes as truth by the increasingly diverging factions of the faith.

It is within this religious atmosphere that Nicholas Dyer lives. Dyer's patron is the architect Christopher Wren, who in the novel is portrayed as someone who adheres to the new religion propounded by Locke and Newton. As he says to Dyer in one conversation, "Of all nations we were most us'd to order our Affairs by Omens and Praedictions, until we reached this Enlightened Age: for it is now the fittest season for Experiments to arise, to teach us the New Science which springs from Observation and Demonstration and Reason and Method, to shake off the Shaddowes and to scatter the Mists which fill the Minds of Men with a vain Consternation."[13] But these "Observation and Demonstration and Reason and Method" have not solved some of the great mysteries and terrors of existence, such as death, with which Dyer is profoundly acquainted. For the demise of both his parents in the plague that swept London in 1665 has indelibly inscribed death in his consciousness. For the rest of his life, Dyer's *modus operandi* is largely influenced by his powerful aversion to, and desire to escape from, death. His religious convictions (and later, architectural endeavors) are largely motivated by this need to elude death forever. To do this, he follows a cult which performs various inversions of the Christian faith. Within this system, known as the *Scientia Umbrarum* (9), is a synthesis of "esoteric doctrines, syncretic mixture of the world's mythologies, refutation of established religion and morality, and veneration of ancient architectural monuments as expressions of [a] menacing worldview,"[14] all of which is heavily reliant on the established religion of eighteenth-century England. I want to examine some of the ways Dyer's occult faith inverts Christianity. It is important, however, to first and briefly trace Dyer's initiation into the occult arts. After the death of his parents, and while being looked after by an aunt, Dyer meets the mysterious Mirabilis, who subsequently disciples him. Dyer explains why he follows this man:

> And thus I began my strange Destiny. I rested with Mirabilis seven dayes, and if any Reader should inquire why I did so I will answer: Firstly, I was a mere poor Boy and had seen my Mother in his Glass; Secondly, the teachings of Mirabilis are trew ones, as I shall explain further hereafter; Thirdly, the most wonderful thing in the Plague Year was that his intire Assembly had been preserv'd from Contagion by his Practises and his Prophesying; Fourth, I was curious about all these Matters and Hunger and Thirst are no Appetites more vehement or more hard [20].

Mirabilis is able to show Dyer an image of his mother in a looking glass, which is his first attraction to this cult. What is more telling however, is the third reason which is probably the strongest initial motivation for Dyer's trust in Mirabilis. As I have mentioned, Dyer's encounter with horrific death of his parents has aroused within him a great fear of death. Witnessing the incredible preservation of Mirabilis's followers during the Plague Year certainly crystallizes Dyer's faith in this man.

Mirabilis's "trew" teaching which whets Dyer's "Appetites" is intermittently explained throughout the novel; for instance, one of the most sustained explication of this belief is during a conversation Dyer has with his assistant Walter early in the novel:

> 1) That it was Cain who built the first City, 2) That there is a true Science in the World called *Scientia Umbrarum* which, as to the publick teaching of it, has been suppressed but which the proper Artificer must comprehend, 3) That Architecture aims at Eternity and must contain the Eternal Powers: not only our Altars and Sacrifices, but the Forms of our Temples, must be mysticall, 4) That the miseries of the present Life, and the Barbarities of Mankind, the fatall disadvantages we are all under and the Hazard we run of being eternally Undone, lead the True Architect not to Harmony of Rationall Beauty but to quite another Game. Why, do we not believe that the very Infants to be the Heirs of Hell and the Children of the Devil as soon as they are disclos'd to the World? I declare that I build my Churches firmly this Dunghill Earth and with a full Conception of Degenarated Nature [9].

Laying aside for the moment the significance of Cain and the role of architecture, I will draw some conclusions as to how the religious milieu in eighteenth-century England has contributed to Dyer's arcana. Its interrogation of the ultimate truth about God and faith enables a reassessment of the whole religious foundation upon which England stands.

Christianity, which has enjoyed an unchallenged position in Europe, is now coming apart at its seams even as the very reality of God is put in doubt. Like Toland who views the established, public religion as repressive of the esoteric version, Dyer views his *Scientia Umbrarum* as similar to that form of religious mysticism which has been repressed by the dominant public religion but with which pure adherents will identify. His pronouncement of the "very Infants to be the Heirs of Hell and Children of the Devil" is at once an affirmation of the doctrine of original sin,[15] as well as a parodic inversion of it. For Dyer also believes "that Sathan is the God of this World and fit to be worshipp'd" (21). If this is the case, original sin then is not something from which one should wish to be delivered, but which, in Dyer's conviction, is precisely the preferred condition. Here, one can see how the "scientific" religion proposed variously by Locke and Newton has been deviously integrated by Dyer in his occult system in an ironic manner. For if this new religion discredits original sin, then Dyer's religion reclaims it but makes it the original condition of humankind, so as to say that there *is* no original sin in the first place whatsoever. This is further reinforced by Dyer's own proclamation of his belonging to an "older faith" (20), which among its creeds includes the following:

> He who made the World is also author of Death, nor can we but by doing Evil avoid the rage of evil Spirit. Out of the imperfections of this Creator are procreated divers Evils: as Darknesse from his Feare, shaddowes from his Ignorance, and out of his Teares come forth the Waters of this World. Adam after his Fall was never restor'd to Mercy, and all men are Damned. Sin is a Substance and not a Quality, and it is communicated from parents to children: men's Souls are corporeal and have their being by Propagation or Traduction, and Life is an inveterate Mortal Contagion. We baptize in the name of the Father unknown, for he is truly an unknown God; Christ was the Serpent who deceiv'd Eve, and in the form of a Serpent entered the Virgin's womb; he feigned to die and rise again, but it was the Devil who truly was crucified [21].

The inversion of Christianity in the passage above is unmistakable. Indeed, each credo is a parasitical reversal of, or a negative extension of, or a direct challenge to the host faith. If the Christian God is the author of life, then Dyer's God is the author of death. If Christianity preaches acts of goodness as being favorable in God's eyes, Dyer's religion requires that its adherents practice evil in order to find favor with evil (and thus, prevent evil to oneself). If the Christian God is knowable and perfect, Dyer's God is imperfect and unknown. In the Christian faith, sin is a quality that can be reversed through conversion and repentance; but Dyer's religion gives sin the permanence of substance. In Dyer's faith, the Christ figure is a deceiver and the original harbinger of sin. He is not the Son of God, but of the Devil, and it is not he who is crucified but the Devil, thus reinforcing the latter's deity.

However, Dyer submits to the Christian theological view that Adam is not restored to mercy (in the sense of reversing the condition of sin back to the original state of innocence and holiness) and that "all men are Damned" through the communication of sin from parents to children. Yet, as mentioned, in Dyer's religion, sin is not seen as an effect of the Fall, but the original condition of mankind. His statement about the soul challenges the traditional view that the soul is incorporeal and eternal, and echoes an argument that will be later popularized by Hume. In his *A Treatise on Human Nature*, Hume argues that the Self is "nothing but a bundle or collection of different perceptions, which succeed each other with an inconceivable rapidity, and are in a perpetual flux and movement."[16] Jonathan Dollimore argues that for Hume, "there is absolutely nothing within us which remains unalterably the same through flux and change — certainly not a soul, and not even an unchanging self."[17] Hence, Hume's opinion of the self's mutability is extended to the soul as well, subverting the orthodox Christian view that the soul is unchanging and everlasting. This view also problematizes the belief in the existence of the soul beyond death, for if the soul is inextricably conjoined to the corporeal, and that the soul has its beginning at birth, then the physical body's cessation would also suggest the soul's end. Dyer, it could be argued, perhaps subscribes to this understanding as well, and attempts to ameliorate his mortality through architecture which he hopes to employ to extend his existence indefinitely. If the Christian faith at crisis does not guarantee an eternal life, perhaps his service to evil and his architectural endeavors can prevent the evil — and this includes death — from overwhelming him.

It is not difficult to see how the religious debates in eighteenth-century England have partly contributed to Dyer's occult beliefs. The entire traditional Christian foundation is being subjected to a critical assessment that largely denies any inherent supernatural elements. Anything that cannot be empirically verified — original sin, the soul, the virgin birth, the deity of Christ and others — is placed in doubt and is either given a rational explanation or rejected. But Dyer is not conforming to the new religion proposed by the empiricists and the rationalists. Although he appropriates their criticism against established religion, he does not eschew the supernatural from his occult system. In an ironic way, it can be said that Dyer actually resituates the supernatural into religion after its steady removal from the metaphysical debate in the eighteenth century. Once more, the Devil takes prominence, and sin and evil have powerful roles to play in the lives of humankind.

## Architecture as the Reproduction of the Cosmogonic Act

Dyer's inversion of the established religion would of course entail a rejection of its moral law as well, which explains Dyer's performance of evil — especially murder and instigation of suicide. His stance could be viewed as subscribing to, in historian David Frankfurter's term, "antinomian libertinism": here, to transcend the basic laws (of the established religion)

> would require acts of systematic inversion of those laws. These acts would be performed deliberately, secretly, and only by select coteries of adepts, and they would either anticipate a "postnomian" paradisical world to come or repeat a "prenomian" *paradise in illo empore*. As such … antinomian libertinism suggests a theory of ritual as the performative capacity to invert morality for ideological purposes.[18]

Frankfurter is, in this context, discussing a branch of Jewish mysticism that advocates "redemption through sin," and I find this view relevant to my reading of *Hawksmoor*. Dyer is inverting the moral law laid down by the established faith in order to repeat a prenomian experience: that is, the original creation — one where death has yet to infiltrate — must be refigured in order for him avert death. According to Susana Onega, Dyer believes that the "world is created by Satan and is controlled by innumerable demons that keep man on earth, suffering the horrors of history. The only hope man has of getting out of this *mundus tenebrosus* is to abolish linear time by a reproduction of the cosmogonic act itself."[19] Here, it becomes evident that there are two distinct worldviews in Dyer's occult system. Firstly, in order to prevent evil from the self, one must perform evil. Secondly, in order to escape evil, one must reproduce the act of creation, and thus align oneself with the god (Satan) who made the world and death. By creating, the adherent of this mystical cult becomes one with the original creator, and thus stands beyond the threat of death, for he is now greater than death. The act of salvation, in this sense, is no longer dependent of god, but on self acting as god.[20] This is where Dyer's architecture comes into significance, for in architecture, both these convictions can be realized.

Dyer is commissioned to rebuild seven churches in London, but he has an agenda of his own with regards to these buildings. He plans to turn his churches into a talismanic inscription in stone[21] to harness the power of evil so as to house death. As I have already discussed the nature of Dyer's architecture as serving the paradox of housing death and entombing its creator elsewhere,[22] here I will discuss only the churches in relation to Dyer's attempt at inverting the established Christian faith. As he announces, the seven churches form an everlasting order which will ultimately help him attain eternity (186). His decision to turn churches into places of infernal powers is not merely another example of his inversion of the Christian belief but involves certain strategic reasons as well. On the surface, his commitment to the building of the churches represents him as a pious Christian whose task it is to reconstruct places of worship. But his real intention is to gather the dead in one place. In fact, the sites which he has chosen for his churches were once upon a time either vast burial grounds or close to one. His church at Limehouse, for example, is built near "a great Fen or Morass which has been a burying-place of Saxon times," which Dyer believes to be "a massive Necropolis [that] has Power still withinne it, for the ancient Dead emit a certain Material Vertue that will come to inhere the Fabrick of the new Edifice" (62). Dyer's essential belief is that "when there are many Persons dead, only being buryed and laid in the Earth, there is an Assembling of Powers" (24), and it will be such places that will serve as his "Pillars and [his] Foundations" (24). Dyer desires to contain the "Assembling of Power" in his churches to achieve "an everlasting order which would permit his crossing the planetary orbs that separate the material from the spiritual world."[23] He is seeking eternal life, but not in the Christian sense of an eternal life which is dependent on faith in God. Dyer's god is the Devil, whom he serves in fear and knowledge that this god cannot save him; salvation must be engineered by himself by aligning with the Devil in the act of creation. In this sense, Dyer actually occupies a dual position of being both believer and "god" himself.

Each of the churches that Dyer erects is consecrated with the blood of a (human) victim. The church in Spittle-Fields, for example, is consecrated by the blood of the mason's son, who, in performing the traditional custom of laying the highest and last stone on top of a finished building, falls to his death. This tragedy, for Dyer, integrates the church into his cultic beliefs, for to be initiated into the cult of Mirabilis, adherents "must be washed and consecrated by the Sacrifice, and that in our Eucharist the

Bread must be mingled with the Blood of an Infant" (20). Hence, the future patrons of the church are unknowingly already assimilated into Dyer's demonic system because the Eucharistic rite in *Scientia Umbrarum* has already been performed. This is also the entrapment of which Dyer speaks with regards to the labyrinthine structure of his church. Dyer takes the Eucharistic rite of blood sacrifice literally and criticizes that "ridiculous Maxim that *The Church loves not Blood*," arguing instead that the "Eucharist must be mingled with Blood" (25, emphasis in original). This indirectly echoes René Girard's argument that this kind of violence "is the heart and secret soul of the sacred."[24] Dyer targets mainly children or tramps, again reasserting by inversion a biblical principle that children and the poor are valued individuals in the kingdom of God (see Matthew 18: 2–4 and Luke 6:20 respectively). But in the case of the poor, the inversion goes further. For Dyer, their "place is by my Church: they are the Pattern of Humane Life, for others are but one Step away from their Condition, and they acknowledge that the beginning and the end of all Flesh is but Torment and Shaddowe. They are in the Pitte also, where they see the true Face of God which is like unto their own" (63). In Dyer's system, the poor have already inherited the kingdom of their god. Symbolically dead and acquainted with the sufferings of hell in their daily struggle, they certainly qualify.

Unsurprisingly, Dyer's first victim is a tramp named Ned whom he "helps" to commit suicide. But sacrifice also powerfully binds murderer to victim. Killing involves an intimacy that dissolves, in Joel Black's view, any "illusion of individual identity."[25] It is "both an act of knowing and an act of creating because it is fundamental, originating act. But its originating potential is inseparable from its violent, destructive, excessive character."[26] Appropriating Black's reading of murder to Dyer's situation, several interpretations can be deduced. Firstly, it reiterates the architect's demonic intention of reproducing the act of creation in order to escape death. To kill is an act of creative reversal, which fits in very neatly with Dyer's belief system. Secondly, his victim also becomes his substitute in the event, in that another's death enables *his* escape from death. In this way, Dyer is performing exactly what Girard says about any society which practices sacrifice in order to deflect violence away from itself.[27] Finally, murder is also his way of identifying with the victim and turning the latter's suffering into his own. This may seem a contradiction, but it is actually related to Dyer's profound connectedness with death and his powerful desire to elude it. Suffering entails knowledge, which is a necessary step to overcoming. This follows a strange logic in which the victim's pain is introjected by the perpetrator in order that the latter can become one with the former in the shared suffering. In this way, the perpetrator "knows" suffering, but because he does not directly experience it, he escapes it at the same time. Hence, suffering-through-knowing equals knowing-to-escape. This explains why, directly after Ned's death, Dyer is seized with sudden elation. He meets a "Band of Rogues" who are "Bawling and Calling to one another"; in this midst of confusion, he "ran towards them with outstretch'd Arms and cried, Do you remember me? I will never leave thee! I will never, never leave thee!" (66–67). This, in my view, suggests a consummation of Dyer's identification with his victim. And this too, is another act of inversion; in the Christian faith, God, who desires to identify with His creation, becomes manifest as a human being to undergo suffering and death in order to redeem humankind from damnation and grant everlasting life. In Dyer's faith, *he acts as a god who desires the death of others in order to know everlasting life.* Christ is the ultimate scapegoat who sets the sinners free, but Dyer scapegoats others to set himself free.

In Girard's theory, sacrifice is an important ritual to protect the society from its own violence. It is "a deliberate act of collective substitution performed at the expense of the victim and absorbing all the internal tensions, feuds, and rivalries pent up within the community."[28] The sacrificed victim functions as a scapegoat who bears the burden of societal conflict which can only be purged by violence and the spilling of blood. It is, in this sense, an act of violence to mitigate a greater violence. This, according to Girard, is what religion also entails. In its broadest sense religion "must be another term for that obscurity that surrounds man's efforts to defend himself by curative or preventive means against his own violence.... Religion shelters us from violence just as violence seeks shelter in religion."[29] But Girard also points out that the institution of sacrifice necessarily involves a certain degree of misunderstanding. He goes on to explain:

> Its vitality as an institution depends on its ability to conceal the displacement upon which the rite is based. It must never lose sight entirely, however, of the original object, or cease to be aware of the act of transference from that object to the surrogate victim; without that awareness no substitution can take place and the sacrifice loses all efficacy.[30]

This notion of misunderstanding involves a paradox: sacrifice simultaneously effaces the "original object" of violence, which is the self/society itself, *and heightens* it by the very act of transference from self to scapegoat.

Richard Kearney also points out this essential problem in the Girardian view of scapegoating, which he believes will ultimately fail because a "society can only pretend to believe in the lie because it is that same society which is lying to itself! Hence the ultimately self-defeating nature of ideological persecution. This is borne out in need for constant renewal of the sacrificial act."[31] In Dyer's case, sacrificing others in his stead merely postpones the inevitable (the death of self) and does not ultimately rescue the self from violence. Another way out of this ideological dilemma must be sought. Kearney argues that the Christian faith provides a solution in the figure of Christ, "who underwent death on the Cross in order to expose the sacrificial lie for once and for all by revealing the innocence of the victim. The sacrifice to end all sacrifice."[32] According to Ulrich Simon:

> this predetermination settles the understanding of all Christians, who also begin to see their own destiny as providential in its climax of death. The appalling 'The Son of Man must suffer and be killed' is met by a divine will which not only assents to, but wills, the death. In this transcendental understanding death becomes sacrifice.[33]

Christ's death reclaims the victim of sacrifice and exposes the "original object" of violence. No longer now do adherents of the faith need a scapegoat to purge their own violence, because by identifying with Christ in His death, they too have undergone symbolic death and hence have overcome violence.

In the same process of identifying with the Christ for Christians, Nicholas Dyer must also identify with his god in order to overcome death. If his cosmogonic reproductive act through architecture is one example of how he identifies with his god, his final act of identification is his self-sacrifice at the church at Little St. Hugh, the last of the seven churches[34]:

> The Church was above me now and, tho' I was plunged into Shaddowe, I did not move but waited until my Eyes had cleared a little. Then I opened the Door and crossed the Threshold. I walked forward saying, *From my first Years Thy Horrour have I endured with a troubled Mind*, and I stood in the Aisle looking upwards till I could look no more: I had run to the end of my Time and I was at Peace. I knelt down in front of the Light, and my Shaddowe stretched over the World [209, emphasis in original].

Self-sacrifice achieves a very interesting resolution to the problem of self-preservation. In fact, in Derrida's interpretation, the two are mutual. According to him, what is at stake in sacrifice is the "absolute price" of human life; that is, what must be kept safe at all cost is this life — "the price of what ought to inspire respect, modesty, reticence, this price is priceless. It corresponds to what Kant calls the dignity (*Würdigkeit*) of the end in itself."[35] But Derrida goes to demonstrate:

> This dignity of life can only subsist beyond the present living being. Whence, transcendence, fetishism and spectrality; whence, religiosity of religion. This excess above and beyond the living, whose life only has absolute value by being worth more than life, more than itself — this, in short, is what opens the space of death.... [The] salvation of the safe, the humble respect of that which is sacrosanct (*heilig,* holy) *both requires and excludes sacrifice,* which is to say the indemnification of the unscathed, the price of immunity. Hence: auto-immunisation and the sacrifice of sacrifice.... Violence of sacrifice in the name of non-violence. Absolute respect enjoins first and foremost sacrifice of self, of one's most precious interest.[36]

If the preservation of the self is the ultimate reason for sacrifice, the best way to protect the self is to place the self beyond the reach of violence once and for all. Life is most valuable when it is worth more than itself, and the only way to ensure this is by sacrificing the original object of sacrifice through an act of auto-immunization. When Dyer finally stretches his 'Shaddowe ... over the World," he is performing exactly this auto-immunization to elude death. He does this by merging with his final architecture, immortalizing himself in stone (an art which he has learned from an obscure architect-mystic, Hermes Trismegistus [205]). There is an earlier episode in the novel when Dyer visits Stonehenge, and there, for the first time, realizes the profound relationship between architecture and his demonic god (57–60). Read in the light of this revelation, the amalgamation of man and stone would then rehearse Dyer's belief that this will identify him with his god once and for all. He will, in other words, become the Daemon whom "our Ancestors worship ... in the form of great Stones" (57).

The serial killings, however, persist into the twentieth century. Children and tramps who die mysteriously continue to turn up at the churches once built by Dyer. Dyer's death, which is an inversion of the death of Christ, selfishly guarantees eternal life only to himself. In Christ's death, adherents can project their own violence and death onto his body; Christ's sacrifice is also the symbolic sacrificial act participated by Christians. Adherents need not perform the act literally anymore because it has been sublimated once and for all by and in Christ. Dyer's self-sacrifice, on the other hand, only further implicates his victims. In the twentieth century, when Dyer's belief system has become the stuff of obscurity and forgotten legend, it seems that the only way to signify its presence is by leaving behind a body count. If before, Dyer kills to substitute his death with another, now he "kills" to substitute his *presence* with another's absence-in-presence. The dead becomes his mark of immortality, signaling to others that he is still here. More important, however, is the need for Dyer, who is reincarnated as Hawksmoor in the twentieth century, to preserve his self from his own obscurity. For Hawksmoor has become the extreme other to his eighteenth-century double, and this must be ameliorated somehow to prevent a final death through forgetting. In other words, the detective must be "awakened" to who he really is by his double (and hence, preserve the self), and this is achieved once more through victims of sacrifice.

## The Double and Eluding Death

It is only inevitable that Dyer will be replicated as Hawksmoor to conform to the novel's theme of time as non-linear but an eternal cycle.[37] As Dyer reflects, "Time is a vast Denful of Horrour, round about which a Serpent winds and in the winding bites itself by the Tail. Now, now is the Hour, every Hour, every part of an Hour, every Moment, which in its end does begin again and never ceases to end: a beginning continuing, always ending" (62). This pronouncement will prove horribly prophetic in his reincarnation as Hawksmoor, which carries an ironic twist (see below). Not only is Dyer replicated, but his victims are as well, resulting in a series of deaths in the London churches which prompt an investigation by Hawksmoor. In this sense, the murderer is now the detective who must solve his own crime. Ackroyd deploys a very familiar Gothic motif in a highly original way to suggest a collapse of historical linearity. In Gothic literature, the double:

> is a second self, or *alter ego*, which appears as a distinct and separate being apprehensible by the physical senses ... but exists in a dependent relation to the original. By 'dependent' we do not mean 'subordinate'. For often the double comes to dominate, control, and usurp the functions of the subject; but rather that, *qua* double, it has its *raison d'etre* in its relation to the original.[38]

One can see how *Hawksmoor* confirms to and extends this standard use of the double. Hawksmoor, who is not aware of his historical double, is nevertheless profoundly drawn to him through his investigation of the mysterious deaths. In this sense, his existence *is* dependent on the original, although he may not register this initially. But if in Gothic literature the double is usually the unconscious, repressed self which "comes to dominate, control, and usurp the functions of the subject," finally dissolving both self and double because of absolute irreconcilability, in Ackroyd's novel, the double is completely subordinated to the subject to the extent that he cannot resist the strange pull towards a final meeting and reconciliation with the original other. More and more, Hawksmoor is so drawn to his double that despite numerous false leads and dead ends, he is ever surer that the killer is near (198). One other difference demonstrates *Hawksmoor*'s unique deployment of this motif: In traditional Gothic narratives, an individual gradually separates into self and double; *Hawksmoor* deliberately reverses the process by implying the possibility of the double motif throughout the narrative, only to confirm it at the very end. Hence, while traditional Gothic splits the subject into two diametrically opposed entities, *Hawksmoor* remerges the split selves back to a single subject once more.

The double has also a religious dimension which is important in my reading of the novel as an inversion of the established version of Christianity. Literary historian John Herdman demonstrates that the double motif is symptomatic of western Christianity because of the religion's emphasis on the will of man which is ambivalently situated between good and evil. Various Christian cults have developed diverging explanations as to the presence and persistence of evil despite the supposition that God is purely good; one of the most extreme is Gnosticism, which claims that the material world is not created by the Supreme God, but by an evil demiurge to prevent men and women from realizing their true nature as spiritual beings. The flesh is a prison conferred upon humankind by this alien creator.[39] The literary culmination of this theological concern of the nature of man is Christopher Marlowe's *Doctor Faustus*. According to Herdman, *Doctor Faustus* is "a work which is seminal to the later development of the theme of the double, in relation to both form and content."[40] The play reiterates the story of the Fall of man who, in his pride, is tempted and deceived by the serpent, represented in the play by Mephistopheles. Faustus can therefore be seen as a text which attempts an inversion of the established faith, but with tragic consequence. It is therefore telling that in *Hawksmoor*, one of the first "occult" books which fascinated Dyer was *Doctor Faustus* (12). And when he later meets Mirabilis, it was "Faustus" that he gave when asked his name (18). In many ways, Dyer desires to emulate Faustus in his defiance of his allotted limitations. Dyer too seeks forbidden knowledge and aspires to be like his deity. But if Faustus in the end is dragged to hell because he has forfeited his soul, Dyer becomes eternally petrified in time because he has forfeited death. Dyer can only be doubled indefinitely without hope of ever escaping permanence. This is perhaps the most paradoxical aspect of all in a novel ridden with paradoxes.

However, the religious dimension of the double in *Hawksmoor* also has a more direct reference to the Bible. To demonstrate this, I need to make references once more to Girard's theory of the sacrificial victim. Earlier in this chapter, I quoted a passage from the novel in which Dyer claims that Cain is the first architect. This is interesting because, biblically, Cain is also the first murderer. By making Cain his patron saint of architecture, Dyer is merging the builder and the murderer in a single figure whom he will subsequently follow. But the Cain motif has further implications in *Hawkmoor*. Girard reads the Cain and Abel story as one which highlights the necessity of sacrifice to deflect violence from self. It is Cain who murders because unlike his brother, he "does not have the violence-outlet of animal sacrifice at his disposal."[41] But this reading curiously implies that in the final analysis, there is really no difference between the two siblings at all with regards to violence and sacrifice. Both are, in a sense, murderers, but only one type of murder is sanctioned by divinity. This would then imply that Cain and Abel are another instance of doubles. Girard goes on to argue that this familiar motif of sibling rivalry in both the Old Testament and Greek myth involves a "fatal penchant for violence [that] can only be diverted by the intervention of a third party, the sacrificial victim of victims."[42] The ritual of sacrifice is precisely to dispel the ambiguity and blurring between self and (br)other that is resulted from a pursuance of an object of desire by both subject and rival.[43] In *Hawksmoor*, Nicholas Dyer, in his embodiment of both Cain and Abel, highlights his own propensity for doubling, which will culminate, at least within the scope of the narrative, in detective Hawksmoor. His victims are the violence-outlet that enables a deflection of violence away from himself (hence, his affinity with Abel), but he chooses the way of Cain in his ritualistic acts. His murders are also divinely sanctioned (according to the *Scientia Umbrarum*, that is), thus further suggesting his alignment with Abel, but his eternal dwelling in perpetuity through endless replication reinforces his affinity with Cain (for Cain is also the Wandering Jew). If Dyer already evinces a split personality, then Hawksmoor is just another extension of that schizophrenia (Dyer is a man of the supernatural, while Hawksmoor is a man of logic and scientific rationality; Dyer acts against the law, while Hawksmoor serves the law) which underlies the character of the architect. For someone whose belief system at once depends on and inverts the host religion, it is not illogical that doubling would make up part of his personhood.

## Religion and Postmodernity

I will discuss the nature of religious otherness with regards to Dyer's reincarnated self as Hawksmoor through a detailed analysis of the last pages of the narrative in which two selves meet and culminate in an enigmatic ending which is not a closure. But to do this, I need to briefly discuss postmodernity and its relation to time and religion. The religious dimension of *Hawksmoor* is decidedly Christian, and much of the strategies of inversion have to do with overturning established beliefs within that faith. The religion that Dyer practices can thus be construed as the "other" of eighteenth-century religiosity. In this section, I want to position my reading of the novel's metaphysical preoccupation within a postmodern framework. It is very significant that Ackroyd situates his novel within two very crucial historical moments with regards to the dominant religion in Europe. I have already pointed out the paradigmatic shifts in culture and philosophy which occurred in the eighteenth century and how they have fundamentally influenced and transformed the way Christianity was viewed and practiced. A rational outlook on religion inherited from Newtonian physics finally relegated God to nothing more than a "clockmaker" deity because "a God who created a natural order only to violate it was repugnant to many Enlightenment thinkers."[44] Zygmunt Bauman, who reads the Enlightenment as coterminous with modernity and humanism, argues that this period heralded

> the collapse of the old order and the emergence of a new one — differing from the one it was about to replace by being understood from the start as something which needed to be *constructed* and *designed*— not found and protected. In the absence of any *given* order of things, it was clear that there would be as much sense and order in the world as its human inhabitants managed to insert into it; and that the ordering work at the top must be replicated by the work at the bottom — each individual having to shape and direct his or her own life, which otherwise would remain shapeless and bereft of purpose.[45]

Bauman demonstrates that the mechanization of religion led to an increasing centering on the self as the ultimate meaning. The self must now define its own destiny; there is no longer a sacred, given order conferred by a divine Being, and men and women must now construct and design their world as they go along.

Bauman also elucidates the humanistic emphasis on human potential in the now, which means that the traditional eschatological concerns with death and the afterlife have become drastically downplayed:

> Modernity undid what the long rule of Christianity had done — rebuffed the obsession with afterlife, focussed attention on the life 'here and now', redeployed life activities around different narratives with earthly targets and values, and all-in-all, attempted to defuse the horror of death. The toning down of the impact of the awareness of mortality and — more seminally yet — the detachment of it from religious significance, thus followed.[46]

In the postmodern era, this optimistic humanist view is rigorously questioned and debunked. It is an era which has revealed "the insufficiency of man and the vanity of dreams to take human fate under human control."[47] Postmodernism, in its rejection of neat categories, clear-cut divisions, and rigid boundaries, actually reclaims (and even celebrates) belief systems which focus on the numinous, the indefinable and the ambiguous. Hence, *Hawksmoor*, in being situated in these two crucial historical periods, is decidedly antimodern in its religious preoccupation, and encompasses both premodern and postmodern versions of religiosity. As I have argued earlier, Dyer's inversion of Christianity is actually a resistance towards the "enlightened" view of religion which eschews dimensions such as the supernatural and the afterlife. It is therefore unclear if Dyer is upending the established religion, or is really "protecting" the more esoteric aspects of the religion by, ironically, inverting it. Clearly, if read in this way, the "otherness" of religion in *Hawksmoor* becomes dispersed through a series of inversion, irony, and reclamation. The detective Hawksmoor, in his initial reluctance to admit the impenetrable mystery of the murders, is decisively modernist in outlook (114); but he is Dyer's double, which means that he will inevitably be drawn once more into that premodern and postmodern religiosity in which some things, such as death and the afterlife, are beyond explanation.

## Time and the Eternal Return

Having discussed the strategy of juxtaposing these two cultural paradigms in the novel, I must carefully deliberate upon the whole notion of time as problematized by the novel. If postmodernity reclaims, to an extent, the mystery of religion, does it necessarily entail a promise of an escape from historical time? Is not postmodernism, in its suspicion of history, itself antithetical towards the Christian faith which posits a world of determined causality that leads ultimately to the apocalypse? And if this is the case, would not postmodernism be unwilling to entertain the notion of eternity as postulated by the Christian faith,[48] but instead suggest an alternative? It is my view that this alternative, which celebrates time as cyclic and fragmentary, is already in place within postmodern considerations, and it is one which is largely informed by Nietzsche's important concept of the eternal return (or recurrence).[49] But *Hawksmoor*, despite pitting linear time against the cyclic one, questions both in the end. Its deconstruction of time as a linear progression on the level of form is complemented by its thematic interrogation of the limits of cyclic time. To demonstrate this, I will look at the final paragraphs of the narrative in which Hawksmoor and Dyer finally encounter each other.

It is difficult to discuss the notion of religion once the novel shifts its focus to the twentieth century, because there is a significant de-emphasizing of religiosity. But I want to argue that religion, rather than becoming effaced, is actually carefully merged with other aspects of the mysterious such as time and death. Religion, in other words, is no longer represented as a set of rituals or a belief system, but has become seamlessly converged into these other mysteries. The final paragraphs profoundly stage this: Here, the Nietzschean concept of the eternal return (time), the postmodern reconfiguration of the double motif (self), and the mystery of religious otherness are wonderfully collapsed into each other. Here, in the darkness of the church of Little St. Hugh, Hawksmoor comes face to face with his original other:

> And his own Image was sitting beside him, pondering deeply and sighing, and when he put out his hand and touched him he shuddered. But do not say that he touched him, say that they touched him. And when they looked at the space between them, they wept.... And when they spoke they spoke with one voice: ... And I must have slept, for all these figures greeted me as if they were in a dream....
>
> And then in my dream I looked at myself and saw in what rags I stood; and I am a child again, begging on the threshold of eternity [216–217].

This enigmatic conclusion has variously been interpreted as the author's textual play to frustrate the reader, a metaphor for the waste land of twentieth-century London,[50] and a final dissolution of separate selves in which "time and space, personal identity and language and vision" are no longer meaningful grids with which one identifies oneself.[51] Susana Onega reads this passage as Dyer/Hawksmoor finally freeing "himself from the shackles of time, [wiping] out the memory of his 'fall into history' and in a word, [situating] himself in eternity."[52] But I disagree because the tragic tone suggested in these passages precludes such a happy resolution.

In Dyer's occult logic of contradiction, building and killing are ways to evade death. These passages evince his survival of time's passing and his discovery by his twentieth-century double. But the shifts in pronouns—from "him" to "they" and finally, to "I"—create a sense of dislocation of the self. Earlier, I quoted a section from the novel in which Dyer depicts time as a Serpent biting its tail (62) to suggest time's eternal repetition of itself. In the passages above, the meeting of Hawksmoor and Dyer rehearses this serpentine quality of time, trapping both men within its cycle. Dyer may have overcome death, but he must relive his affinity with death again and again. Killing prevents him from dying, but it also binds him intimately to his victim and causes him to identify indefinitely with death itself. When Dyer and Hawksmoor speak, they "spoke with one voice," but the gap between paragraphs indicate that there can be no dialogue. In the penultimate paragraph, the two selves collapse into an "I," waiting to rehearse once more another lifetime (suggested by the child figure). The "I" is also the tramp — the intimate victim who awaits being murdered all over again, thus once more inextricably binding murderer and victim in this eternal cycle (or eternal return). The last sentence brilliantly captures Dyer's eternal dilemma. He has eluded death only to keep on *living and dying forever*; he is simultaneously freed from, and bound to, death eternally. This is the novel's ultimate paradox.

According to Gilles Deleuze, the most sophisticated reader of Nietzsche's concept:

> Eternal return cannot mean the return of the Identical because it presupposes a world (that of the will to power) in which all previous identities have been abolished and dissolved. Returning is being, but only the being of becoming. The eternal return does not bring back 'the same', but returning constitutes the only Same of that which becomes. Returning is the becoming-identical of becoming itself. Returning is thus the only identity, but identity as a secondary power; the identity of difference, the identical which belongs to the different, or turns around the different. Such an identity, produced by difference, is determined as 'repetition'. Repetition in the eternal return, therefore, consists in conceiving the same on the basis of the different.... Only the extreme, the excessive, returns; that which passes into something else and becomes identical.[53]

It is not difficult to see how *Hawksmoor* fits into this Nietzschean temporal model; Hawksmoor is the recurrence of Dyer. He complies with Deleuze's interpretation of the eternal return in that he is not identical to the original; in fact, he is the extreme other of Dyer (Dyer kills, while his double investigates killings), thus abolishing and dissolving all traces of the original. And in his temporality to be again renewed as a child in the next return, Hawksmoor also fulfils the notion of becoming which is a fundamental condition of that which returns. He is but one of the many successive recurrences of Nicholas Dyer. All Dyer's subsequent returns, if Hawksmoor can be taken as a case in point, will be totally dissimilar from him ("identity of difference"), with only the act of returning as being eternally the same. In this way, Dyer achieves an "afterlife," but this is not the same as the Christian notion of eternity. In Christianity, eternity has a sense of escape *from* time. Dyer succeeds in eluding linear time, but he is still trapped *in* time. Although he boasts, "I cannot change the Thing call'd Time, but I can alter its Posture" (11), he is unable to transcend it altogether. Dyer, in his desire to alter time to escape death, is in the end unable to escape both. He may never die (because he will return eternally), but he will also never attain eternity, existing merely, as the novel's conclusion suggests, "on the *threshold* of eternity" (217, emphasis added).

The Nietzschean eternal recurrence heralds a positive looping of history, in which only novel differences return in an act of a will-to-becoming. The same cannot be constitutive of the eternal return for the very fact that it resists a newness of being. Reading the text in this light, it is difficult to decide what Dyer's eternal recurrence suggests. On the one hand, his return is always new in that each becoming takes a dissimilar form of embodiment. But, as this discussion has shown, each of his selves is basically a replication of his first self, rehearsing over and over again that first self's act of origination. Hawksmoor may not be doing the killing, but the fact that he is investigating himself demonstrates his inability to escape being eternally implicated in the original crime. More importantly, Dyer's negative eternal return reveals his ultimate failure in trying to confine the mystery of religion within his unique system of religious practice. If eighteenth-century Christianity is a version of limited religiosity sanctioned by an ideologically motivated religious establishment, Dyer's subversive religion is not, in the final analysis, any different. He too is trying to construct, or establish, a distinct method of religiosity, thus confining his belief within a very strict, even diabolical, system of practices. And as I have shown, his endeavors ultimately fail when he finds that instead of escaping death through his religious adherence, he becomes eternally entrapped. This irony of Ackroyd's narrative as a detective genre is not missed by David Richter, who writes that "[e]verywhere the theme of postmodern mystery is the impossibility of solving mysteries, the nausea-provoking contrariness of objects and clues, the emotional dead-end of aporias."[54] This is largely because the mysteries of religion — the mysteries of God, time, eternity, death — are ultimately inscrutable, and to question or control them will only leave one "begging at the threshold of eternity." Dyer and Hawksmoor are, in various ways, endeavoring to understand and contain these mysteries, only to be met with defeat and silence in the end.

## Conclusion

In my conclusion I want to briefly look at Ackroyd's novel as an example of a novel with twentieth-century religious concerns. Despite its de-emphasizing of the religious angle when the novel enters the twentieth century (largely due to the privileging of the detection theme), *Hawksmoor* remains a powerful work about the otherness of religion from all ideological closures. No doubt religion is often adulterated by ideological agendas which privilege the powerful against the weak, but the novel seems to suggests that there are fundamental aspects of religion which are beyond human understanding. Philosophy may very well try to comprehend such profundities, but in the end, they escape any form of categorization and explanation. In this sense, the celebration of the ambiguous in postmodernity is gainfully deployed to retrieve the mystery of religion. But the novel is also suspicious of the postmodern agenda of resituating grand metanarratives in a different guise. In the case of *Hawksmoor*, my view is that there is an implicit criticism of the cyclic time which postmodernism privileges and often sets up as another totalizing theory of how late capitalism should read and comprehend time. Despite the fact that there is a recurrence in characters, the fundamental site of origination which is religious in orientation remains irresolvable, and thus subjecting each recurrence to a sameness-in-difference. Read in this way, there is a subtle juxtaposition of religion and the postmodern ideology of the late twentieth century which, on the surface, are supposed to be happy complements, but in the novel, are revealed to be deeply problematic in their relationship. Religion is, in the end, an *aporia* which even postmodernism cannot realign or reclaim in its alleged pluralistic celebration. As Derrida astutely acknowledges, an *aporia* is the end of a problem, not because a solution has been reached (like the solution as presented in postmodernism) but because it is now beyond the obvious question-answer dialectic.[55] Religion (and its associated dimensions of death and the sublime) is such an *aporia*, at least as suggested in my reading of Ackroyd's novel. Belief and death, which Dyer and Hawksmoor endeavor to submit to familiar systems of knowledge (be it defined religion or scientific rationalism), ultimately escape, and persist in their return to haunt and deconstruct whoever that desires their constraints. Hence, despite the fact that the novel celebrates the postmodern reclamation of the unexplainable, it is also suspicious of certain postmodern claims.

Religion remains vitally elusive as something which compels and repels at the same time. Despite its surface coherence within institutionalized practices of religion, "religious and sacred identitites," as Richard H. Roberts contends, "are not uniform, nor do they function in a way reducible to a single mode of reductive explanation."[56] This view corresponds with my argument about the way *Hawksmoor* subverts any form of reducing religion to a particular representation. In this way, despite the de-emphasis of the religious angle when the narrative enters the twentieth century, *Hawksmoor* retains sight of its religious concerns by proposing, in a rather ludic and abstract but effective manner, the enigmatic and impenetrable nature of religion.

## Notes

1. In her essay on Felipe Alfau's novel *Locos*, Susan Elizabeth Sweeney identifies the beginnings of the metaphysical detective fiction in the works of Nabokov, Borges, and Flann O'Brien ("Aliens, Aliases, and Alibis: Alfau's *Locos* as a Metaphysical Detective Story," in *Review of Contemporary Literature* 13:1 [1993], 207–214). But the term "metaphysical detective fiction" is nevertheless relatively new.

2. Patricia Merivale and Susan Elizabeth Sweeney, "The Game's Afoot," 1.

3. Merivale and Sweeney, "The Game's Afoot," 2.

4. See for example Edward J. Ahearn, "The Modern English Visionary," 353 – 369; Susana Onega, "The Mythical Impulse in British Historiographic Metafiction," 184 – 204; Susana Onega, *Metafiction and Myth in the Novels of Peter Ackroyd* (1999); and Jeremy Gibson and Julian Wolfrey, *Peter Ackroyd: The Ludic and the Labyrinthine Text* (2000).

5. See Iain Sinclair, "Lud Heat" (1975).

6. James Sambrook, *The Eighteenth Century*, 25.

7. Sambrook, *The Eighteenth Century*, 30.

8. Free thinking in the eighteenth century does not have the connotation of atheism. Instead, it covers a wide range of dissenting views of Christianity that ranged from Deism to Christian pantheism.

9. Ernest Gellner, *Plough Sword and Book,* 118. Gellner roughly divides human history into the Platonic world and the Cartesian one.

10. James Sambrook, *The Eighteenth Century,* 31. The word "pantheist" first appeared in the English language as part of the title of one of Toland's tracts entitled *Socinianism ... Recommended by a Pantheist to an Orthodox Friend* (1705).

11. The Socinians deny the pre-existence of Christ.

12. David Hume, *Natural History of Religion and Dialogues Concerning Natural Religion*, 32.

13. Peter Ackroyd, *Hawksmoor* (1985), 145. All subsequent references are to this edition.

14. Ahearn, 'The Modern English Visionary," 454 – 455.

15. The doctrine of original sin posits that because Adam, the first man, disobeyed God and therefore brought sin into the world, mankind will subsequently be born in sin.

16. David Hume, *A Treatise on Human Nature*, 301.

17. Jonathan Dollimore, *Death, Desire and Loss in Western Culture*, 93.

18. David Frankfurter, "Ritual as Accusation and Atrocity: Satanic Ritual Abuse, Gnostic Libertinism and Primal Murders," 369, 371.

19. Susana Onega, "The Mythical Impulse in British Historiographic Metafiction," 200.

20. This confirms another existing dissenting Christian view in the eighteenth century, championed by, among others, Viscount Bolingbroke (1678–1751). According to him, "God does not interpose himself into the workings of his great machine. The universe continues distinct from the workman, like any human work" (Sambrook, *The Eighteenth Century*, 33).

21. This observation is made by Susana Onega in *Metafiction and Myth in the Novels of Peter Ackroyd*, 53.

22. See my *Dimensions of Monstrosity in Contemporary Narratives*, chapter one.

23. Onega, *Metafiction and Myth*, 52.

24. René Girard, *Violence and the Sacred*, 31.

25. Joel Black, *The Aesthetics of Murder*, 129.

26. Black, *The Aesthetics of Murder*, 130–131.

27. Girard, *Violence and the Sacred*, 4.
28. Girard, *Violence and the Sacred*, 7.
29. Girard, *Violence and the Sacred*, 23, 24.
30. René Girard, *Violence and the Sacred*, 5.
31. Richard Kearney, *Strangers, Gods and Monsters*, 39.
32. Kearney, *Strangers, Gods and Monsters*, 39.
33. Ulrich Simon, *Pity and Terror: Christianity and Tragedy*, 45.
34. The narrative is decidedly vague with regards to Dyer's strange end; however, in light of the fact that Dyer consecrates his churches with blood, it is not incorrect to surmise that it is his own blood which he spills to sanctify the church at Little St. Hugh.
35. Jacques Derrida, "Faith and Knowledge," 87.
36. Derrida, "Faith and Knowledge," 87, 88, emphasis in original.
37. There are already many suggestions in the novel which indicate that Hawksmoor is Dyer's potential double. For example, a madman tells Dyer that "one Hawksmoor will this day terribly shake you" (100); later, Dyer meets his own "Apparition" in the street, "with Habit, Wigg, and everything as in a Looking-glass" (205). Of course, the structure of the novel in which certain episodes in the odd (past time) and even (present time) numbered chapters are repeated also points to a potential doubling at work.
38. John Herdman, *The Double in Nineteenth-Century Fiction*, 14.
39. See Herdman, *The Double in Nineteenth-Century Fiction*, chapter 1.
40. Herdman, *The Double in Nineteenth-Century Fiction*, 9.
41. Girard, *Violence and the Sacred*, 4.
42. Girard, *Violence and the Sacred*, 4.
43. See Girard, *Violence and the Sacred*, 145 and 159—160.
44. Gregory R. Peterson, "God, Determinism, and Action," 883.
45. Zygmunt Bauman, "Postmodern Religion?" 62, emphasis in the original.
46. Bauman, "Postmodern Religion?" 64.
47. Zygmunt Bauman, "Postmodern Religion?" 72.
48. This is the suggestive take which Jacques Derrida seems to consider in his deconstructive theory; for an elaboration, see John Caputo's *The Prayers and Tears of Jacques Derrida*.
49. Nietzsche introduces the eternal return in *Thus Spake Zarathustra: A Book for None and All*, but his exploration of this concept remains a subject of contention amongst his critics because of its deliberate ambiguity.
50. The first is by Luc Herman in "The Relevance of History," while the second is David Richter's in "Murder in Jest."
51. Ahearn, "The Modern English Visionary," 467.
52. Onega, "The Mythical Impulse in British Historiographic Metafiction," 201.
53. Gilles Deleuze, *Difference and Repetition*, 41.
54. Richter, "Murder in Jest," 108.
55. Derrida, *Aporias*, 12.
56. Richard H. Robert, "Space, Time and the Sacred in Modernity/Postmodernity," 350.

## Works Cited

Ackroyd, Peter. *Hawksmoor* (1985). Harmondsworth: Penguin, 1993.
Ahearn, Edward J. "The Modern English Visionary: Peter Ackroyd's *Hawksmoor* and Angela Carter's *The Passion of New Eve*." *Twentieth-Century Fiction* 46:4 (Winter, 2000): 353–369.

Bauman, Zygmunt. "Postmodern Religion?" *Religion, Modernity and Postmodernity.* Ed. Paul Heelas with the asst. of David Martin and Paul Morris. Oxford/Malden: Blackwell, 1998. 55–78.

Black, Joel. *The Aesthetics of Murder: A Study in Romantic Literature and Contemporary Culture.* Baltimore and London: Johns Hopkins University Press, 1991.

Caputo, John. *The Prayers and Tears of Jacques Derrida: Religion without Religion.* Bloomington: Indiana University Press, 1997.

Deleuze, Gilles. *Difference and Repetition.* Trans. Paul Patton. New York: Columbia University Press, 1994.

Derrida, Jacques. *Aporias.* Trans. Thomas Dutoit. Stanford: Stanford University Press, 1993.

_____. "Faith and Knowledge: The Two Sources of 'Religion' at the Limits of Reason Alone." Trans. Samuel Weber. *Acts of Religion.* Ed. and intro. Gil Anidjar. London and New York: Routledge, 2002. 40–101.

Dollimore, Jonathan. *Death, Desire and Loss in Western Culture.* Harmondsworth: Penguin, 1998.

Frankfurter, David. "Ritual as Accusation and Atrocity: Satanic Ritual Abuse, Gnostic Libertinism, and Primal Murders." *History of Religions* 40:4 (May 2001): 352–380.

Gellner, Ernest. *Plough Sword and Book: The Structure of Human History.* Chicago and London: University of Chicago Press, 1988.

Gibson, Jeremy, and Julian Wolfreys. *Peter Ackroyd: The Ludic and the Labyrinthine Text.* London: Macmillan, 2000.

Girard, René. *Violence and the Sacred.* Trans. Patrick Gregory. Baltimore and London: Johns Hopkins University Press, 1977.

Herdman, John. *The Double in Nineteenth-Century Fiction.* London: Macmillan, 1990.

Herman, Luc. "The Relevance of History: *Der Zauberbaum* (1985) by Peter Sloterdijk and *Hawksmoor* (1985) by Peter Ackroyd." *History and Post-War Writing.* Eds. Theo D'haen and Hans Bertens. Amsterdam: Rodopi, 1990. 107–124.

Hume, David. *Natural History of Religion and Dialogues Concerning Natural Religion.* Eds. A. W. Colver and J. V. Price. Oxford: Oxford University Press, 1976.

_____. *A Treatise on Human Nature* (1739–1740). Ed. and intro. Ernest C. Mossner. Harmondsworth: Penguin, 1969.

Kearney, Richard. *Strangers, Gods and Monsters.* London and New York: Routledge, 2003.

Merivale, Patricia, and Susan Elizabeth Sweeney. "The Game's Afoot: On the Trail of the Metaphysical Detective Story." *Detecting Texts: The Metaphysical Detective Story from Poe to Postmodernism.* Eds. Patricia Merivale and Susan Elizabeth Sweeney. Philadelphia: University of Pennsylvania Press, 1999. 1–24.

Ng, Andrew Hock-soon. *Dimensions of Monstrosity in Contemporary Narratives: Theory, Psychoanalysis, Postmodernism.* Basingstoke and New York: Palgrave-Macmillan, 2004.

Nietzsche, Friedrich. *Thus Spake Zarathustra: A Book for None and All.* Trans. Walter Kaufmann. Harmondsworth: Penguin, 1954.

Onega, Susana. *Metafiction and Myth in the Novels of Peter Ackroyd.* Columbia: Camden House, 1999.

_____. "The Mythical Impulse in British Historiographic Metafiction." *European Journal of English Studies* 1:2 (1997): 184–204.

Peterson, Gregory R. "God, Determinism, and Action: Perspectives from Physics." *Zygon: Journal of Religion and Science* 35:4 (Dec. 2000): 881–890.

Richter, David. "Murder in Jest: Serial Killing in the Post-Modern Detective Story." *The Journal of Narrative Technique* 19:1 (1989): 106–115.

Roberts, Richard H. "Space, Time and the Sacred in Modernity/Postmodernity." *International Review of Sociology* 11:3 (2001): 331–355.

Sambrook, James. *The Eighteenth Century: The Intellectual and Cultural Context of English Literature, 1700–1789*. Essex: Longman, 1986.

Simon, Ulrich. *Pity and Terror: Christianity and Tragedy*. Houndsmill and London: Macmillan, 1989.

Sinclair, Ian. "Lud Heat: A Book of Dead Hamlets" (1975). *Lud Heat and Suicide Bridge*. London: Granta, 1998.

Sweeney, Susan Elizabeth. "Aliens, Aliases, and Alibis: Alfau's *Locos* as a Metaphysical Detective Story." *Review of Contemporary Literature* 13:1 (1993): 207–214.

# 8

# Ian Rankin and the God of the Scots

## BRIAN DIEMERT

"If you are going to take it seriously," Graham Greene wrote, "murder ... is essentially a religious subject,"[1] and there's little doubt Ian Rankin agrees, for as a quick glance at many of Rankin's titles will attest, spiritual themes and motifs are never far from his vision.[2] The author of many novels and stories, Rankin is best known for those featuring John Rebus, an Edinburgh CID officer and one of the most irascible of fictional detectives. Haunted by his past, Rebus finds shelter in alcohol and meditates on the deeper problems of evil in the world and his own spiritual destiny. Indeed, one of the first things we learn about him is that he is explicitly identified as a Christian.[3] As a detective, of course, Rebus works to uncover the mysteries behind a crime, but in Rankin's series finding the solution is just the most basic problem: Edinburgh, Scotland, the self, and the cosmos all have their mysteries, and Rebus usually grapples with all of them. This may be a grand claim to make for a best-selling series of detective novels, yet in Rankin's case it is wholly apt: As he says, "The real mystery in these books isn't the crime.... [U]nderneath, the real mystery is Rebus coming to terms with Edinburgh."[4] Rankin and his reviewers often remark on Edinburgh's importance in the novels—likening the city to a character[5]—but it is not the only "real" mystery. Rankin's breakthrough novel, *Black and Blue*, continues to be one of his favorites because with it he discovered he could write about larger questions affecting Scotland.[6] And as for investigating the self, Rankin's and Rebus's frequent references to Robert Louis Stevenson's *Jekyll and Hyde* leave little doubt that *that* mystery is basic to Rankin's books. And then there is a further metaphysical probing that takes him into the heart of Scottish Calvinism and beyond.

In some ways, as Greene implies, the spiritual is always a part of the detective story. René Girard noted long ago that "violence and the sacred are inseparable,"[7] and David Grossvogel, perhaps taking his cue from Dorothy Sayers,[8] suggested that the detective story allegorizes "the mystery of what lies beyond consciousness"[9] by establishing a "false boundary" that invites a "mock penetration of the unknown through an active participation (that of the initiatory ritual) or a speculative one (through the 'rehearsive' nature of art or myth)."[10] John G. Cawelti offers comparable insight:

> one key to the literature of mystery is this strange ambiguity and tension between mystery as supernatural and religious and the use of mystery to denote secular secrets accessible to rational solution…. There is a strong modern fascination with the intersection between larger mysteries and lesser mysteries, those that are beyond human understanding, and those that can be solved or at least resolved through human reason and action…. [T]he literature of mystery … addresses in secular terms the concerns and themes that were once dealt with in religious myth and ritual. [It] developed out of the need for a narrative form capable of exploring the boundaries between the new secular world of man, society and nature and the traditional world of the supernatural and mythical.[11]

In this context, Rankin's statement that the "real" mystery is not the mystery of the crime gains added significance because Rankin repeatedly shows Rebus working within a spiritual context he struggles to understand; for Rebus, the world is often at odds with his inherited religious tradition: "He hated congregational religion. He hated the smiles and the manners of the Sunday-dressed Scottish Protestant, the emphasis on a communion not with God but with your neighbours. He had tried seven churches of varying denominations in Edinburgh, and had found none to be to his liking. He had tried sitting for two hours at home of a Sunday, reading the Bible and saying a prayer, but somehow that did not work either. He was caught, a believer without his belief. Was a personal faith good enough for God? Perhaps, but not *his* personal faith" (*Knots* 71).[12] Similarly, in *Hide and Seek* we read, "He was a Christian, after all. He might not attend church often … but that didn't mean he didn't believe in that small, dark personal God of his. Everyone had a God tagging along with them. And the God of the Scots was as ominous as He came."[13] Indeed, the very form Rankin uses is steeped in a theological rhetoric that reflects a fundamentally gnostic vision of the world: To explore the self, to hear the voice of conscience, and then to sense a deeper presence within are crucial tasks for Rebus as he moves, like Theseus "threading his way further into the maze" (*Hide* 30), through Edinburgh's labyrinthian underworld.[14]

## The Gothic and Calvinism

That Rankin's brand of hard-boiled fiction should align itself with gnosticism is not surprising when we consider that crime and detective fiction have a great deal in common with gothic fiction, a form already "demonstrably theological in character."[15] Rankin has often remarked, "In Scotland the tradition I was coming from was the Gothic novel,"[16] which is marked by "a great supernatural strain"[17]; he adds elsewhere, "there's something of the gothic in John Rebus's Edinburgh."[18] *Knots and Crosses*, his first Rebus novel, was not intended to be a crime novel, but rather "an update on *Jekyll and Hyde*, a serious literary novel, a psychological gothic novel. I'd never read any crime fiction. I was horrified.... I was doing a Ph.D. on Muriel Spark. I was going to be a Professor of English...."[19] On the surface, Rankin appears to separate crime fiction from the more "literary" work of Spark or Stevenson, yet he also finds Spark is a writer who "learned how to combine her profundity with a great level of 'entertainment', so that her books appear less serious in intent than in fact they are"[20]— an observation that resonates in any consideration of Rankin's own fiction. As for his claim that he had "never read any crime fiction," that surely must be viewed with skepticism, especially if we remember his acknowledgment elsewhere that he was or is strongly influenced by American crime fiction or his admission that he came to crime fiction "by reading a lot of criticism, like Umberto Eco's books on literary theory, in which he was fascinated by James Bond and by Sherlock Holmes."[21] (Rankin's admirable gloss on many of *Knots and Crosses'* particular puns and puzzles clearly demonstrates his academic background.[22]) Granted that some of these comments might reflect his reading after *Knots and Crosses*, it remains difficult to believe Rankin was ignorant of crime fiction, especially if he was "reading a lot of criticism, like Umberto Eco's books of literary theory."[23] Even his explicit identification of *Knots and Crosses* with the gothic tradition is telling because, as anyone who has read Poe, Collins, or LeFanu, for instance, will acknowledge, crime fiction grows out of the tradition of gothic fiction, with Poe being the obvious hinge between the gothic and the modern detective story. Rankin deftly reinforces the link between the two in *Tooth and Nail* by having Rebus notice that the criminology section is next to books on the occult and witchcraft in Dillon's Bookshop in London: "Rebus smiled at the curious marriage: police work and hocus pocus" (155). Significantly, one of the books he buys and begins to read is Peter Ackroyd's *Hawksmoor* (161), a metaphysical detective story that exploits occultist lore surrounding Nicholas Hawksmoor's seven churches in London. If we accept Victor Sage's reading in *Horror Fiction in the Protestant Tradition*, we can see that this same tradition must also have informed the development of crime fiction. Hence, what is true of gothic fiction may be equally true of crime fiction, and this includes the gothic's supernatural concerns as well. As Stefano Tani reminds us, all detective fiction has an irrational strain in it that is part of the gothic's legacy,[24] and never wholly "exorcized" from the genre no matter how analytical the story.[25] Indeed, in many postmodern detective stories, such as *Hawksmoor*, the irrational and the fantastic are fully embraced.

Victor Sage's study of horror fiction offers numerous insights that can help us in a discussion of detective fiction. Sage emphasizes the place of religious conflict in British literature from the Reformation to the mid-twentieth century, and he is particularly good at showing how a legacy of anti–Catholic propaganda fed the gothic tradition and especially horror fiction. However, two points emerge in Sage's book that have clear co-relations to detective fiction and Rankin's work. The first involves the notion of conscience which, though paradoxical in its application, allows one to defy established authority on the grounds of inner conviction. Sage notes that the idea of an internalized conscience, derived from Luther's separation of the office and the person,[26] is "a badge of identity in English culture."[27] This same notion, however, also works to isolate individuals and can in many circumstances place them in conflict with political and ecclesiastical communities. That is, the concept provides glue for Protestant sects opposed to Catholicism, but the degrees to which one accepts the authority of individual conscience separate Protestant sects from each other.[28] Surely the hard-boiled detective's difficulties with the mundane authority of supervisors, clients, politicians, or in many cases, the police represent a kind of antinominism and can be attributed to conscience.

The second relevant point Sage emphasizes has to do with the belief in resurrection. Horror fiction, he argues, frequently plays on the fear that spiritual resurrection, to say nothing of bodily resurrection, may not occur.[29] Often regarded as a spiritual event in the Protestant tradition, resurrection in the Catholic tradition is also corporeal, and this idea is often implicitly critiqued through horror's focus on physical corruption, monstrosity, and the undead. Of course, the horror of physical decay can also be evoked to expose the necessity for atonement in order to retain the hope of salvation and spiritual resurrection. Sage enumerates several ways in which horror fiction reflects the protestant tradition, but Rankin's novels can be read through a similar lens. We can, for example, see the grisly scenes of murder, such as those that open *Hide and Seek* and *Mortal Causes*, the vivid descriptions of physical mutilation, as in *Tooth and Nail*, and the macabre humor of the coroner Curt in Rankin's books emphasizing the body's fragility and taking the place of horror fiction's ghastly deformities and semi-decayed corpses. Even the "ghosts" Rebus sees, though seldom an explicit presence in the narratives, hint at the problematic aspects of resurrection that are a continuing theme in the Rebus series.

Since W. H. Auden's classic essay "The Guilty Vicarage," analytical detective fiction of the Christie, Sayers, S. S. Van Dine variety has often been read in a religious context that emphasizes its structure as Judeo-Christian allegory: The garden is polluted by the crime of murder and the detective's work is redemptive.[30] Auden saw thrillers, such as the hard-boiled work of Americans Hammett and Chandler, however, as lacking this allegorical depth, and so he appreciated them less.[31] Yet hard-boiled fiction is, arguably, just as "religious," although Auden's tradition of sin and redemption through the agency of the detective is seldom the religion of hard-boiled fiction. If in Conan Doyle's, Christie's, or Sayers' stories, for example, the detective restores grace to "the great good place,"[32] in Hammett's, Chandler's or Rankin's stories the possibilities for redemption are narrower and certainly less obvious. But as their many references to spiritual matters show, Rankin's novels are never without a religious context.

In the Rebus books, Rankin emphasizes the pervasive Calvinism of the Scottish milieu. As filtered through Knox, Calvin's pessimism leaves Rebus cold. His habit of reading the Bible (*Knots* 149; *Tooth* 5)[33] well reflects his Protestantism in its emphasis on a personal search for a religious truth that accords with his experience, but the fact is that religious and spiritual elements in the Rebus novels spread beyond the bounds of Christianity. From the outset, Rankin's series shows us a world permeated with complex systems of belief. Within a dozen pages of *Knots and Crosses*, we learn Rebus's brother Michael is a hypnotist whose hypnotically induced narratives of a client's past lives are chilling. Rebus responds dismissively, "It's a nice story, Mickey" (10), but then we read, "*Past lives ... Yes, he believed in some things ... In God, certainly ... But past lives....* Without warning a face screamed up at him from the carpet, trapped in its cell. He dropped his glass" (11, Rankin's italics). Here, Rebus's open skepticism masks a deep uncertainty that is further complicated by the apparition Rebus sees. In *Hide and Seek* occultist symbols at a murder scene lead Rebus to explore elements of esoteric belief that bring him into contact with Matthew Vanderhyde, a blind self-declared occultist (the parallels with Tiresius are obvious—"that's because I *know*, Inspector" [153]), who recurs as a minor figure in several later novels. In *Hide and Seek* the occultist elements underscore the gothic that Rankin sees as so important to Scottish fiction, but in terms of the actual murder case, they are largely irrelevant: "[B]y candlelight they hadn't seen the pentagram on the wall, and they hadn't meant anything by placing the body the way they had. Rebus had made the mistake of reading too much into the situation, all along" (245). *Tooth and Nail*, the third Rebus book, continues the gothic strain insofar as there is considerable talk about the "Wolfman" and "silver bullets" (17). One could extend this catalogue through all of the Rebus novels, and, of course, argue its presence is due to Rankin's interest in the gothic, which we recognize as intimately connected to the development of detective fiction, and so such an argument is wholly justified. Yet the gothic elements when considered in light of Rankin's other spiritual referencing points us toward a world that is as much myth as grit. Edinburgh may be a favorite tourist destination, but as the novels frequently note, it is "a very repressed city, a very Calvinist Presbyterian place."[34] Rebus's concern is with the "hidden city" behind or even beneath the city as it appears (see, for example, *Hide* 52).[35] And in this respect it is worth remembering that Edinburgh is the home of John Knox, that Presbyterian reformer who for many commentators erased the Scottish past to create a new nation:

> Gray stamped his foot on the pavement. "This is everything that makes us what we are!"
> Sutherland looked around. "I still don't get it."
> "It's John Knox's house," Rebus said. "It's where he lived."
> "Bloody right, it is," Gray said, nodding. "Anybody else's mum bring them here?"
> "I came on a school trip," Jazz McCullough admitted.
> "Aye, me too,' Allan Ward said. "Fucking boring it was, too."
> Gray wagged his finger. "That's history you're insulting, young Allan. *Our* history."
> Rebus wanted to say something about how women and Catholics might not agree. He didn't know much about John Knox, but he seemed to recall the man hadn't been too keen on either group.
> "Knoxland," Gray said, stretching out his arms. "That's what Edinburgh is, wouldn't you agree, John?"
> Rebus felt he was being tested in some way. He offered a shrug. "Which Knox, though?" he asked, causing Gray to frown. "There was another: Doctor Robert Knox. He bought bodies from Burke and Hare. Maybe we're more like him...."[36]

Scotland, in a most reductive formulation, is cut off from its past by the hegemonic power of Knox's theology, "everything that makes us what we are," and then by the 1707 Act of Union. In the Rebus books, the repressed past both literally and metaphysically returns in a monstrous form: "The blood that had seeped into stone, the bones that lay twisting in their eternity, the stories and horrors of the cities past and present ... he knew they'd all come rising in the digger's steel jaws, bubbling to the surface as the city began its slow ascent towards being a nation's capital once again."[37] Here is a vision of profane resurrection one should be wary of.

In terms of myth, the underworld of Edinburgh, literally figured in the buried city we learn about in the opening pages of *Mortal Causes*, is the world of the dead both literally, again the murdered Billy Cunningham in *Mortal Causes* is found in Mary King's Close, and figuratively insofar as this is the world of those, like Rebus, who are in need of resurrection. The context here is wholly gnostic, for, as Hans Jonas tells us, the underworld in the gnostic myth expands to embrace all of human life, since all creation, separate from God, is in need of an awakening or resurrection: "[T]he world takes the place of the traditional underworld and is itself already the realm of the dead, that is, of those who have to be raised to life again."[38] Ian Rankin's repeated and often ironical references to Burke and Hare and to the "resurrection men" or "body snatchers," particularly in *The Falls* and in *Resurrection Men*, though found in almost every text from *Knots and Crosses* (e.g., 102) on, again invoke Stevenson, who wrote "The Body Snatchers," but they also remind us through the many uses of the word "resurrection" that Rebus's is a spiritually charged world: words such as "resurrection," "atone," "doomed," or "undertaker" (a word actually discussed in *Resurrection Men* 369) are just not neutral terms in the Rebus books. And this spiritual sense is built up through all of the novels: there are too many contributing elements to allow us to dismiss their presence as mere homage to the gothic. How, for instance, are we to reconcile the coincidental surnames of John Knox, sixteenth-century clergyman, Calvinistic reformer, and nation builder, with Robert Knox, scientist and anatomist whose shady involvement with Burke and Hare becomes a point of speculation in *The Falls* [39] and in *Resurrection Men*? There can be little doubt that Rankin plays on the coincidence with one Knox standing for the spiritual realm and the other grounded in the material and, for Rebus, criminal realm, to offer an image of a single, divided entity.[40] Indeed, in *Hide and Seek*, one of the murderers is described as "the most Calvinist-looking thing Rebus had ever seen" (249; similarly 5), an observation that suggests Knox's theology is not only inadequate but death-dealing, even criminal.

## Detective Fiction and Gnosticism

Work on detective fiction traditionally distinguishes two kinds of stories in terms of its formal qualities (see the essays by Auden, Grella, or Todorov for example) and in terms of its native British and American traditions (as elucidated in pieces by P.D. James or Glenn Most).[41] Each is usually seen to reflect its own epistemology with analytical or classical detective fiction, largely identified with the British tradition, offering a vision of an integrated universe that patient reason can understand, while hard-boiled detective fiction, often associated with the American tradition, offers a vision of a contingent and indeterminant universe. Detectives such as Lew Archer and Rebus may not believe in coincidence, implying they share the hermetic vision that Dupin, Holmes and other analytical detectives assume,[42] but the hard-boiled detective is not particularly sure that he or she can reduce the complexity of events to a cohesive narrative, for to do so inevitably involves distortion. As Stephen Marcus observes of Hammett's *Continental Op*, "the story, account, or chain of events that the Op winds up with as 'reality' is no more plausible and no less ambiguous than the stories he meets with at the outset and later"[43]; and the same is true for Rebus, who recognizes that his stories do not always make sense (*Let It Bleed* 282). From the point of view of the discourse, we also find that in hard-boiled fiction not everything in the narrative necessarily fits or is assimilated in the formulation of the solution, as is the case with the occultist elements in *Hide and Seek* or the details concerning Rosslyn Chapel in *Set in Darkness*, so the possibility of coincidence and contingency remains open.

While the classical detective story generally fits Auden's Judeo-Christian frame, we can profitably say the hard-boiled story reflects a darker spiritual vision. Again, the point should be clear to Rankin's readers and to those who have attended to the quasi-religious content of books such as Hammett's *Maltese Falcon* and Chandler's *Farewell, My Lovely* where religious practice, when it occurs, is usually regarded as some kind of "racket."[44] (Rebus's distrust of organized religion reflects an analogous position.) Jasmine Yong Hall comments that hard-boiled texts present "us with a secular world — a world in which religion does not provide a medium by which the material world can be translated into meaningful signs. If there is a transcendent power in *The Maltese Falcon*, it is the power of money."[45] But such an observation is only true in a limited sense. The hard-boiled detective often scorns religious belief, and is frequently correct in suspecting those who claim supernatural or divine awareness. Indeed, the manipulative cult, the faked seance, the bogus church (or, relatedly, the bogus clinic), and the like have become so cliched within the genre that we immediately suspect the tarot reader, crystal-gazer, or spiritualistic medium of criminal behaviour or worse.[46] However, the hard-boiled detective's obvious demystifying of the seemingly supernatural and the consequent materialist bias Hall sees in these texts work to mask hard-boiled fiction's gnostic content.

Even that most basic of narrative structures—the romance quest—conceals deep occult patterns. *The Maltese Falcon* and *Farewell, My Lovely* are more or less explicit about this matter insofar as both make pseudo-occultist religious practice part of their narratives, and the same is true of several of Rankin's books. In *The Maltese Falcon*, the story of the falcon and its connection to the Templars explicitly invokes a heretical and suppressed religious organization associated with dualistic belief.[47] Chandler often acknowledged his use of the grail myth,[48] and so rewrote a spiritually saturated myth in twentieth-century terms, and Rankin, too, explicitly evokes the same archetypal pattern: "Once upon a time, in a land far away, there was a king called Strathern. And one day, he called one of his errant knights to him with news of a perilous quest." (*Resurrection* 408). The Grail story, as Joseph Campbell observed, puts us firmly "in the realm of Gnostic traditions,"[49] for "[t]he Grail romance is of the God in your own heart, and the Christ becomes a metaphor, a symbol, for that transcendent power which is the support and being of your own life."[50] In hard-boiled fiction, this inner "transcendent power" is seen both in the detective's personal code of ethics and, more particularly, in his or her frequent "hunches," which are often registered as deep sensations: "What was his [Rebus's] interest? ... All he knew was that he felt something" (*Hide* 14; similarly, 21, 113, 156, or 231). Campbell's discussion of the Grail story emphasizes the pursuit of the transcendent, but his suggestion that the story is fundamentally gnostic is particularly intriguing if we consider that hard-boiled detective fiction and film noir share a sensibility that goes well beyond the sense of Campbell's remarks. The detective's hunch may be taken as the internalized conscience Sage and others argue is part of the Protestant tradition's legacy to fiction, but the intuitive quality of these hunches is something separate from conscience, and, though irrational, is often correct, as it is in *Hide and Seek* (156) or in *The Falls* (474–5) when Rebus senses early on (71) that Beverly Dodds is the source of the most recent coffin found at the falls. In this regard, Rebus is obviously similar to other hard-boiled detectives (Spade, Marlowe, or more recently Bernie Gunther in Philip Kerr's series) in that he follows his intuition, and so a hunch often and most suggestively stimulates and pushes an investigation towards justice.

Rankin's texts all reveal their author's deep learning and his developing awareness of the tradition in which he writes.[51] Although they draw on the police procedural, the Rebus novels are clearly tied to the traditions of American hard-boiled fiction and film noir (itself derived from numerous European strands including German Expressionism[52]). Rankin is not above using noir cliches to alert us to the link; for example, "But the night could be dark in other ways" (*Hide* 125), or Flight's remark in *Tooth and Nail*, "'Nowhere is safe these days,' he said. 'Nowhere'" (22)[53]; hence, we can understand James Ellroy's claim that Rankin has created "tartan noir."[54] In any case, Rebus, though a part of a huge organization, is, like other hard-boiled detectives, a self-constructed loner who feels separate from "the mass of the people just getting on with their lives.... The only thing you could be sure of was the inside of your head, and even that could deceive you" (*Hanging* 133–134). To the consternation of his colleagues, Rebus has resisted promotion (*Let It Bleed* 342), but their most frequent complaints about him are that he becomes obsessive, does not share information, and does not work well as part of a team (e.g., *Let It Bleed* 269). Their deeper suspicion, however, is that he is too close to and too much like Morris Gerald ("Big Ger") Cafferty, Edinburgh's notorious gangster and Rebus's nemesis (*Resurrection* 51). As an outsider, however, Rebus is able to succeed where others might fail because he has little to lose (*Set* 397); hence, he can challenge government corruption (*Let it Bleed*) though the consequence is professional exile to Craigmiller (*Black and Blue*). On the other hand, his marginal position can keep him in a tangential relation to the central case (as in *The Falls*), though he remains effective particularly through his mentoring of Siobhan Clark—ultimately another of Rebus's twins who, as the series goes on, finds herself having to choose between the two paths before her: One is Gill Templer's and the other is Rebus's. But beyond these concerns, we sense a brooding metaphysic in these novels that invests all action with spiritual importance.

To move from the Protestant tradition to the gnostic in a discussion of the Rebus books necessarily takes us through a consideration of genre (otherwise, Rebus's behaviour could be seen as almost entirely in keeping with his Presbyterian heritage), and in this regard we should remember that "the central narrative dynamic of every detective story is the movement from lack of knowledge to possession of knowledge — what we might call the gnostic imperative."[55] The detective story, as Michael Eaton points out in his short study of Roman Polanski's *Chinatown*, is "a species of gnostic initiation on the part of the investigator as acolyte; it can be seen that this journey—from the darkness of ignorance to the light of knowledge — must also necessarily involve a transformation on the part of the person who undertakes it."[56] Eaton doesn't pursue connections between gnosticism and detective fiction in *Chinatown*, though a photo caption identifies Noah Cross as "the patriarchal demiurge"[57] (his name ironically hints at his spiritual importance), but there can be little doubt that these connections exist. While "gnostic imperative," the pursuit of knowledge, grounds all detective fiction, the hard-boiled form particularly allegorizes the gnostic's vision of the universe and human endeavour.

For the Gnostics, "the knowing ones," knowledge of divine mysteries was obtained either by a personal experience of revelation or by initiation into a secret or esoteric tradition. In gnostic mythology, a "precosmic fall of part of the divine principle"[58] gives rise to a radical dualism between God and creation, between humanity and the world, because the fallen portion of divinity, a lesser or perhaps co-eternal god who is sometimes given characteristics associated with the God of the Old Testament,[59] creates the world so as to imprison the fallen elements of divine light in the darkness of matter and ignorance. The creating Demiurge is thus the inferior reflection of the essentially unknowable and alien God who remains identified with the realms of light, but is shrouded in "the cloud of unknowing." The individual person, then, is made up of the body, an astral soul, and the fallen sparks of divinity, or the pneuma, which consequently is doubly enclosed within both matter and an astral soul consisting of the accumulated psychic tendencies given by the seven Archons (lower powers separated from the divine and identified with planetary influences and pagan gods).[60] Lulled to sleep by the artifice of creation,[61] the pneuma forgets its origins and its purpose. Consequently, the Gnostics' world is a place of darkness, a prison for the pneuma which, if awakened from its torpor through revelation or initiation or the agency of "the alien man," longs to rejoin the godhead.

In this context, all creation is viewed as the product of god's adversary: It is fundamentally an error and our best evidence of separation from an alien god[62]; hence, "the world ... is itself already the realm of the dead, that is, of those who have to be raised to life again."[63] The gnostic's goal, then, is to seek the (forgotten) knowledge of the transcendent God to find "knowledge of the way" for the pneuma to return to the transcendent deity after death. Hans Jonas associates two extreme personality types with the gnostic vision: the ascetic and the libertine. The first avoids contact with a corrupting and wicked world. Sexual love and sensual pleasure in general are especially suspect since "the main weapon of the world in its great seduction is love,"[64] while procreation only furthers the dispersal of divinity. The libertine, on the other hand, regards the pneuma as "saved in its nature." All earthly laws, then, including the law of "thou shalt" and "thou shalt not," are further attempts by the Demiurge to prevent the pneuma from leaving the realm of matter. To flout these laws is to frustrate the demonical design of the Demiurge, an "evil god who must be opposed"[65] — a position Jonas sees as typically gnostic in its reversal of the hierarchy of good and evil.[66] Hence, gnostic accounts of humanity's fall emphasize the acquistion of knowledge as a desirable end linked to the light and to an awareness of the divinity beyond the Demiurge.

That some of gnosticism's structures have found their way into detective fiction is not surprising when we recall that gnostic tendencies can be seen in work by many writers such as Melville, Conrad, and Eliot.[67] After all, it isn't just the gnostic imperative in detective fiction that concerns us. In hard-boiled detective fiction and its cinematic counterpart film noir a shadowy world of pervasive evil is challenged by a detective who shares in the corruption, although he or she often struggles to find some individual moral code that, though perhaps only dimly understood, places the detective outside conventional systems of law and order, morality and ethics. Obviously, the detective's discerning of a personal code involves a kind of gnosis; it is the only source of meaning in a world abandoned by the alien god, but even so clarity of motive is often lacking. As Spade vaguely declares, "When a man's partner is killed he's supposed to do something about it. It doesn't make any difference what you thought of him. He was your partner and you're supposed to do something about it."[68] Only the gnostic, the knowing one, recognizes the importance of awakening to the godhead, yet the hard-boiled detective like Rebus is at best just dimly, though often uniquely, aware of this imperative.

In the hard-boiled tale, however, the detective is never more than partially successful, and the world continues to appear "devoid of spiritual and moral values, pervaded by viciousness and random savagery."[69] As the narrator in *Knots and Crosses* says, after the SAS, Rebus found himself in "an Old Testament land ... of barbarity and retribution" (25), presided over by "Our lady of perpetual Hell" (a graffitist's alteration of "Perpetual Help"on a church hoarding) (*Mortal* 13; *Hanging* 139). The vision of the world as a "hell" aligns creation with the work of the Demiurge. *Knots and Crosses* reinforces this association through the quoted passages from *Job* that Rebus reads (127), but more particularly through Rebus's vision late in the novel:

> If God swirled in his heaven, leaning down to touch his creatures, then it was a curious touch indeed that he gave them. Looking around, Rebus stared into the heart of desperation. Old men sat with their half-pint glasses, staring emptily towards the front door.... Rebus could not see behind their eyes.... Rebus, behind his eyes, was begging now, begging to that strange God of his to allow him to find Reeve, to explain himself to the madman. God did not answer. The TV blared out some banal quiz show [194].

While the television quiz show offers an ironic vision of "mysteries made to be solved,"[70] Rebus here sees an abandoned creation, touched by the demonic creator, but cut off from the alien, "strange" God who remains silent and apart. Only an inner knowing, separate from rational thought, can lead him to the truth: "Rationality could be a powerful enemy when you were faced with the irrational. Fight fire with fire.... And suddenly, for John Rebus as for Gill, it all seemed to fit.... My God, was nothing arbitrary in this life? No, nothing at all. Behind the seemingly irrational lay the clear golden path of design. Behind this world there was another" (*Knots* 206). The insight is crucial to the crime's resolution, but it is also a metaphysical prospect to which Rebus is awakened. Since early in the novel (17), he was aware that "clues are everywhere" (echoed in *Tooth and Nail* 155), but now he sees the truth of Reeve's taunt.

Within the hard-boiled darkness the detective may often be the only character to retain some memory of a deeper sense of purpose; nonetheless, he or she, like Oedipus, becomes "inextricably intertwined" with the investigation and its object[71] and so may even need his or her own savior.[72] Spade, for instance, becomes sexually involved with Brigid O'Shaughnessy, and Rebus, too, becomes sexually involved with a suspect (Lorna Grieve in *Set in Darkness*). It is often the case in hard-boiled fiction that only the finest of distinctions allows us to separate detective from criminal in any real moral or ethical sense: They are, as Tani observes, two sides of the same coin — "Each depends upon the other for his existence."[73] However, this same identification of detective and criminal can also take on more explicitly gnostic connotations. What, for instance, are we to do with Hammett's opening description of Sam Spade in *The Maltese Falcon*: "Samuel Spade's jaw was long and bony, his chin a jutting v under the more flexible v of his mouth. His nostrils curved back to make another, smaller, v. His yellow-grey eyes were horizontal. The *v motif* was picked up again by thickish brows rising outward from twin creases above a hooked nose, and his pale brown hair grew down—from high flat temples—in a point on his forehead. He looked rather pleasantly like a blond Satan."[74] Certainly such a description reinforces the connection between the genre and gnosticism that we can see in other ways as well.

Since, in the gnostic vision, the world conspires to encourage the detective's forgetfulness, we can read the frequent attempts to seduce the detective in hard-boiled fiction (by Brigid O'Shaughnessy in *The Maltese Falcon*, Carmen Sternwood in *The Big Sleep*, or Lorna Grieve in *Set in Darkness*, to give just three examples) in light of Jonas's comment that love is the world's main weapon against the awakening of gnosis. Equally, we can see the convention of the detective being "sapped" or drugged into unconsciousness in a similar way. Intoxication, a favorite metaphor in gnostic writing,[75] and unconsciousness keeps the detective "in the dark." And certainly, intoxication and forgetfulness (sometimes both) are never far from Rebus's ken (he periodically suffers from blackouts). We might, in this regard, look to the end of "Trip Trap," a rather insignificant Rebus short story reprinted in *Beggar's Banquet*:

> On his way out of the shop, he bought the final edition of the evening paper, and was reminded that this was 30 April. Tomorrow morning, before dawn, crowds of people would climb up Arthur's Seat and, at the hill's summit, would celebrate the rising of the sun and the coming of May. Some would dab their faces with dew, the old story being that it would make them more beautiful, more handsome. What exactly was it they were celebrating, all the hungover students, the druids, and the curious Rebus wasn't sure anymore. Perhaps he had never known in the first place.[76]

Rebus may never have known what was being celebrated but the emphasis here is on forgotten knowledge that, in this case, is tied to a forgotten religious belief.

Rebus, though, still feels the full burden of Knox's Calvinism and sees humanity as desperately in need of resurrection, though he considers himself beyond salvation (*Resurrection* 470). He is confirmed in this belief not only by his religious heritage but by the fact that the double he most often meets is Cafferty; however, dualism is everywhere in Rankin's fiction. His narratives repeatedly present Rebus in a world of "ghosts" and doubles who all seem to connect with him on psychological and metaphysical plains. Rebus may be Calvinistic in his thinking but his experience of the world leaves him uncertain about its spiritual underpinnings, so he is drawn to those, ranging from Vanderhyde to Fr. Leary, who offer opportunities for him to discuss spiritual matters, though Rebus finds neither particularly persuasive.

## Duality and the Spiritual World

As anyone who has read a couple of the Rebus novels quickly realizes, the relationship between Cafferty and Rebus is far more complicated than simple opposition: As Rebus confesses in *Set in Darkness*, "'Sometimes I feel closer to that bastard than I do....' He bit off the ending *to my own family*" (309, Rankin's italics). Cafferty claims they are like brothers— like Cain and Abel, adds Rebus (*Resurrection* 449)— and Rankin works hard to bring the two into a shared orbit. In fact, they can even, as happens in *The Hanging Garden*, serve each other's ends, for Rebus clearly prefers the devil he knows to its rivals. Sage reads this kind of pairing as the legacy of Calvinistic self-scrutiny with the monstrous double of gothic horror fiction being the textual manifestation of a hidden self discerned in the Calvinist's extreme self-examination. Sage's insights certainly apply to Rebus's "ghosts," generally figures who result from deep pangs of guilt, but it is debatable whether or not Cafferty should be read this way.

While carrying on Poe's legacy to the genre, the Cafferty-Rebus pairing exemplifies the basic dualism Cawelti says characterizes "the most powerful and influential forms of mystery." Cawelti points out that, for instance, contemporary adaptations of the Holmes stories, as in Jeremy Brett's portrayal or in Nicholas Meyer's accounts, tend to emphasize Holmes's struggle with Moriarty — a figure of limited importance in Conan Doyle's canon who was eliminated in the author's attempt to kill off Holmes — over, for example, Holmes the problem solver. This kind of doubling can be read in many ways, but Cawelti stresses the high "degree of tension in the self-other dialectic ... particularly ... [when] the other can appear as some sort of projection of the self." As Rankin implies in his comments both on Edinburgh in *Set in Darkness* (231) and on Muriel Spark, he considers duality characteristic of Scottish culture and of Scottish fiction.[77] At the heart of this split one might see, as Edwin Muir did, the impact of Knox whose new dispensation meant the repression of an older indigenous Scottish culture.[78] Equally, the Calvinistic emphasis on self-scrutiny Knox brought to Scotland exposes a sinful self that is normally repressed: "Reticence was an Edinburgh tradition. You kept your feelings hidden and your business your own. Some people put it down to the influence of the Church and figures like John Knox — she'd [Jean Burchill] heard the city called 'Fort Knox'" (*The Falls* 372; similarly *Set* 231). The duality, then, reflects, as in Stevenson, division within the psyche, but such a feature may be typical of hard-boiled detective fiction. As Ross Macdonald says of his characters, "The Platonic split between more worthy and less worthy substances, ideal and matter, spirit and flesh, ... suggests an image of man not only divided but at war."[79] Rankin's question, then, in *Tooth and Nail*, "Where was the religion for a man who believed that good and bad must co-exist, even within the individual?" (230), speaks to the same problem. For Macdonald conflicting forces within the psyche are at war, but this is more than a war between the rational and the irrational mind. Crudely, the repressed in Scottish culture and the national life of Scotland is its past, which is often, as Rankin notes, literally covered over (cf. *Set* 231). And in this regard, Rankin, like Ross Macdonald, often connects Rebus's investigations with episodes in the country's or his own past — *Black and Blue* is especially notable in this regard[80] — that are sometimes literally being unearthed. Again, the murder in Mary King's Close in *Mortal Causes*, the body found in Queensberry House in *Set in Darkness*, or the miniature coffins in *The Falls* all show the past returning in the present. Indeed, whenever we see this re-emergence of the past we see both the return of the repressed, an uncanny moment in the Freudian sense for characters and readers (think of the face screaming out of the carpet that Rebus sees in *Knots and Crosses*), and a kind of profane resurrection being enacted (Gordon Reeve is reborn as Ian Knott)[81]; as Cafferty says to Rebus in *Set in Darkness*, "[Y]ou're always try-ing to dig up the corpses. One foot in the past and one in the grave" (209). As often happens in Rankin's novels, we get a hint here, in the reference to digging up corpses, of themes that are subsequently developed in *The Falls* and *Resurrection Men*.[82] The duality of the criminal-detective pair-ing can also be read as mirroring in small gnosticism's larger separation within the godhead — Cafferty is said to laugh "with the confidence of the immortal" (*Set* 400), and he has seemingly escaped a sure death from can-cer. Of course, his "resurrection," his return to Edinburgh, is literally the result of false medical records, but the effect is that of undying evil. As in the gnostic myth, the criminal is the author or the creator of the plot.[83]

Rankin's books always emphasized dualism, and even with the weaker *A Question of Blood* they continue to do so. *Knots and Crosses* introduced Rebus and told us of his experiences with the British Special Forces. Part-nered in SAS training with Gordon Reeve, who is the text's villain, Rebus is presented as the successful half of a close pair. The same is true of his relationship with his brother Michael, whose criminality again metaphor-ically emphasizes duality. More explicit, though, is the drunken Rebus's attempt to strangle a woman he met at one of his brother's performances. The event isn't clearly motivated but it does bring Rebus's Mr. Hyde to the fore. Rankin's debt to Stevenson's text was especially, though hardly exclusively, developed in *Hide and Seek*— a title that puns on Stevenson's. As Rankin says, "I once heard Edinburgh's character described as 'public probity and private vice.' In this respect, the model of Edinburgh in human terms remains Deacon Brodie ... the inspiration for the dual personality of Jekyll and Hyde. Public probity and private vice — these are the two sides of the Scottish character that I investigate in all my mystery novels."[84] Although a religious questor, Rebus remains a damaged hero— as is evi-dent by his dependence on alcohol, his failed relationships, and his sense of being haunted by his past. He is a fallen angel who senses a higher realm and knows what should be done (he urges Jazz McCullough to confess while there is time [*Resurrection* 374]) but often settles for what can be done in the particular circumstances of the mundane realm, as the con-clusions of *Hide and Seek* or *Let it Bleed* demonstrate. After all, as we find at the end of *Resurrection Men*, "It was the deed that mattered, not the individual.... Allan Ward [a corrupt officer who saved Rebus's life] had changed his mind.... Sometimes that was all it took to effect a kind of resurrection" (480–481).

Intuitively and experientially Rebus knows he inhabits a spiritual world, but of what kind? In *Resurrection Men*, he uses the visit to Knox's house to underscore a theological message reminding his fellow officers of their own corruption and guilt. Ultimately, none recognize the moment for what it is, but Rebus's added comment that Knox was also the name of a surgeon who accepted corpses from the "resurrection men" (this Knox figures more prominently in *The Falls*) emphasizes the criminal complicity of the socially respectable (a hard-boiled theme prominent in *Hide and Seek, Let It Bleed, Set in Darkness*, and several other books) while undercutting the salvationary understanding of resurrection. That is, references to Burke and Hare, and to Robert Knox, the surgeon, speak to a kind of profane resurrection steeped in irony. The question is, which Knox are they like? Rebus speculates they may be like the latter, who rationalized criminal complicity, but there is no denying the presence of the former in Rebus's life. In *The Falls* Rankin points out the doctrinal position —"a dissected body cannot rise up again on the day of the Last Judgment" (97)— but in his texts the only tangible afterlife is a ghostly presence that haunts Rebus's conscience in the late hours. In *Resurrection Men*, the corrupt police, especially Francis Gray and Jazz McCullough, are beyond saving, yet Rebus's rhetoric nonetheless emphasizes the possibility and the need for spiritual atonement: "'You need to admit it while there's still time,' Rebus went on. 'Time for what?' Jazz asked genuinely curious. 'For resurrection,' Rebus answered quietly" (*Resurrection* 374) . The problem, though, is that he seems only to accept atonement or resurrection as an earthly event. As is the case at the end of "Trip Trap," the prose suggests a spiritual vision that Rebus only faintly discerns behind his clouded, often intoxicated vision. What we find is a divided character whose language suggests a spiritual awareness he is not fully conscious of, and so Rankin develops an indeterminant irony that leaves us uncertain where he stands.[85]

A good illustration can be found in *Set in Darkness* when Rebus and Clarke question Gerald Sithing, a member of the Knights of Rosslyn, about a suicide's interest in Rosslyn Chapel. Like the occultist apparatus we find in *Hide and Seek* or other Rebus novels, lore surrounding Rosslyn Chapel and the Templars suggests a number of gothic plots, reminds us of Nazism's ties to occultism (and so alludes to any number of texts that link the two) and, of course, points through the Templars reference to *The Maltese Falcon*.[86] At the same time, the discussion about Rosslyn Chapel

brings into the narrative an awareness of a complex spiritual environment — the chapel is "pantheistic" (225) — and is a reminder of what was
lost with Knox's Presbyterian ascendancy. (It can hardly be a coincidence
that three or four pages after the interview with Sithing a new chapter
begins with observations on Edinburgh that include, "The Presbyterian
ethos swept idolatry from the churches, but left them strangely empty and
echoing..." [231].) But as in *Hide and Seek*, overt occultism, such as that
which surrounds Rosslyn Chapel, plays little part in the outcome of the
case, though Rebus's and Clarke's interview with Sithing does yield important information. What is interesting from our point of view is that Rebus
is twice said to appear as a "magus" (226) to Sithing because Rebus has
guessed at aspects of Charles Mackie's or Freddy Hasting's interest in the
chapel. Sithing is stunned by Rebus's acuity. Desiring to preserve his belief
that Mackie/Hastings (the suicide, Freddie Hastings, had adopted the name
Charles Mackie) was genuinely interested in Rosslyn Chapel's mysteries,
Sithing refuses to think that Mackie/Hastings was only using him and the
Chapel as a pretext to find out about the owner's affairs. Rebus's response
is again telling: "'Look into your heart, Gerald', he intoned" (227). At this
point, Sithing realizes he may have been duped. Rebus's remark though,
coming on the heels of claims attributed in the narrative to Sithing's point
of view, suggests genuine religious import in Rebus: he is acting as a spiritual guide.[87] Immediately following the interview, however, we read,
"Siobhan smiled as she mimicked him. '"Look into your heart, Gerald."'
'Rum old bugger, wasn't he?' Rebus had the window down..." (227).
Rebus's dismissiveness, coupled with the fact that Sithing's claims have
already been treated skeptically in the text (161–163), and that Rebus failed
to acknowledge any affect the Chapel might have on him (225), leave us
thinking that Rebus was, in fact, exploiting Sithing's credulity to get the
answers he wanted. We are, in a sense, faced with the same kind of inde-
terminacy we saw in that early scene in *Knots and Crosses* when Rankin
has Rebus simultaneously dismiss the notion of past lives, question his
beliefs, and see the face in the carpet. In *Set in Darkness*, Rebus's position
as "magus" is ironical, yet the scene retains its power and its spiritual res-
onance because we know that Rebus is a spiritually conscious character,
though he is also unable to accept or articulate metaphysical certainty. It
may also be worth noting that, although Rosslyn Chapel and the details
around it are of limited importance to the narrative's outcome, Rankin
directs his readers to the chapel's website in his book's acknowledgments,
a fact which emphasizes its importance beyond what the narrative does on
its own. Again, one wonders if Rankin is not trying to have things both
ways.

## Conclusion

*Resurrection Men*, Rankin's next novel, continued developing his themes and preoccupations. The dual possibilities of its title suggest a similar dynamic to what we saw in *Set in Darkness*, but beyond the title, the book's opening line (and closing scene featuring Siobhan Clarke) again push us towards metaphysical readings, with "Why are you here?" being one of humanity's most basic questions—a fact Rebus picks up on before the narrative moves on to introduce Tulliallan, the Scottish Police College, "the last chance saloon" for cops who need "to atone, to be resurrected" (6). The language is, again, self-evidently religious, but its immediate application is to mundane and secular concerns. Still, the spiritual connotations can not be dismissed. In this novel, Rebus is a "mole" (307) investigating other officers, but he is also uncertain about whether he can trust his superiors. As we have come to expect, Rankin deftly works a dual investigation here as Rebus probes corruption among his colleagues while they work on an old a case relevant to his past, so he is again compelled to undertake a self-investigation. In *Resurrection Men* we see that Rankin has clearly absorbed the lessons of Greene, Le Carré, and other novelists of espionage (221; 333), but the book also echoes work by writers as diverse as Conan Doyle, Christie, and Ellroy. This novel, like so many of Rankin's later books, traces themes he explored in earlier texts, but what we find in the later books, especially after *Black and Blue*, is that Rankin's work has become increasingly complex both in terms of its plots and in terms of the intricacy with which he handles philosophical and religious questions. "Crime fiction," Rankin writes, "can do anything, explore any avenue, use myriad voices and locations" (Introduction), and in his Rebus novels, Rankin pushes his narratives towards investigations of the most fundamental questions facing the city, the country, the self, and the cosmos—a grand claim and wholly appropriate.

## Notes

1. Graham Greene, *The Pleasure Dome: Collected Film Criticism 1935–1940*, ed. John Russell Taylor [1972] (Oxford: Oxford University Press, 1980), 192.

2. Among the titles, the following are more or less explicit in foregrounding spiritual concerns: *Knots and Crosses, The Black Book, Mortal Causes, Dead Souls,* and *Resurrection Men*. Of course, three of his books also share titles with albums by the Rolling Stones (*Let It Bleed, Black and Blue,* and *Beggar's Banquet*), a fact that points to other underlying interests of Rebus and of Rankin.

3. Ian Rankin, *Knots and Crosses* [1987] (London: Orion, 2002), 8–9. All further references to *Knots and Crosses* are to this edition and identified (in parentheses) in the text.

4. "Gothic Scot. Ian Rankin Talks to Robert McCrum ...," *Guardian Unlimited* (*The Observer*), March 18, 2001, <http://books.guardian.co.uk/departments/crime/story/0,6000,458332,00.html> Date consulted September 10, 2003.

5. "Gothic Scot"; Nicholas Blincoe, "The other Edinburgh fringe," *Guardian Unlimited* (*The Observer*) July 26, 1998, <http://books.guardian.co.uk/reviews/crime/0,6121,98978,00.html>. Dated consulted August 20, 2002.

6. Paula Shields, "The *Fortnight* Interview: Ian Rankin Talks to Paula Shields," *Fortnight Magazine,* <http://www.fortnight.org/rankin.html>. Date consulted October 10, 2003.

7. René Girard, *Violence and the Sacred* [1972], translated Patrick Gregory (Baltimore and London: Johns Hopkins University Press, 1977), 19.

8. "These mysteries [detective stories, crossword puzzles, acrostics, etc.] made only to be solved, these horrors which he [the reader] knows to be mere figments of the creative brain, comfort him by subtly persuading that life is a mystery which death will solve, and whose horrors will pass away as a tale that is told" (Dorothy Sayers, introduction to *The Omnibus of Crime,* in *Detective Fiction: A Collection of Critical Essays,* ed. Robin Winks [1980] (Woodstock, Vermont: Countryman Press, 1988), 53.

9. David I. Grossvogel, *Mystery and Its Fictions: From Oedipus to Agatha Christie* (Baltimore and London: Johns Hopkins University Press, 1979), 15.

10. *Ibid.,* 13–14.

11. John G. Cawelti, "The Literature of Mystery: Some Suggestions." Part of this essay appeared in *Storytelling: A Critical Journal of Popular Narrative* 1.1 (Spring 2001). I quote from a typescript Professor Cawelti sent me.

12. Similarly in Ian Rankin, *Tooth and Nail* [1992], (London: Orion, 1999), 5. All further references to *Tooth and Nail* are to this edition and identified (in parentheses) in the text.

13. Ian Rankin, *Hide and Seek* [1990], (London: Orion, 1999), 82. All further reference to *Hide and Seek* are to this edition and identified (in parentheses) in the text.

14. The story of Theseus is, along with that of Oedipus, one of the two great antecedents for detective fiction. John T. Irwin is particularly good at elucidating the relationship between it and Poe's "The Murders in the Rue Morgue," which is usually considered the first modern detective story (John T. Irwin, *The Mystery to a Solution: Poe, Borges, and the Analytic Detective Story* [Baltimore and London: Johns Hopkins University Press, 1994] 176ff.).

15. Victor Sage, *Horror Fiction in the Protestant Tradition* (New York: St. Martin's, 1988), xvi.

16. "Gothic Scot."

17. Paula Shields.

18. Ian Rankin, "The Silence of the Lums," *Mystery Readers International,* <http://www.mysteryreaders.org/Issues/Brit1.html>. Date consulted September 10, 2003.

19. Paula Shields.

20. Ian Rankin, "The Deliberate Cunning of Muriel Spark," *The Scottish Novels Since the Seventies: New Visions, Old Dreams,* ed. Gavin Wallace and Randall Stevenson (Edinburgh: Edinburgh University Press, 1993, pp. 41–53), 43.

21. J. Kingston Pierce, "*January* Interviews— Ian Rankin: The Confidential Crime Writer," *January Magazine,* <http://www.januarymagazine.com/profiles/ianrankin.html>. Date consulted August 10, 2003.

22. "I came up with it [the name Rebus] when I was a smart-arse Ph.D. student who was doing lots of semiotics and deconstruction, and since I thought that since the crime novel was playing a game with the reader, I'd do more of the same–give him a

puzzle" (J. Kingston Pierce). "Rebus' very name is a joke.... A rebus is a picture puz-zle, and in *Knots and Crosses*, Rebus is solving tantalizing clues in the mail–knotted pieces of string and crosses made from matchsticks. If I tell you that in Britain we call Tic-Tac-Toe noughts and crosses, you'll see already the air around Rebus was thick with wordplay" (Ian Rankin, "Silence of the Lums"). In the novel, an acrostic is cru-cial to solving the case.

23. Eco discussed James Bond in an often reprinted essay, "Narrative Structure in Fleming" (*The Role of the Reader: Explorations in the Semiotics of Texts* [Bloomington: Indiana University Press, 1984], 144–172). He has also written on Holmes and edited, with Thomas A. Sebeok, *The Sign of Three: Dupin, Holmes, Peirce* (Bloomington: Indi-ana University Press, 1983). Eco's interest in semiotics and literary theory is also evi-dent in his novels, the first of which, *The Name of the Rose*, is a medieval detective story featuring an investigator, William of Baskerville. It hardly needs mention, but Rankin adopts the names Holmes (Brian) and Watson ("Farmer") for characters in his series.

24. Stefano Tani, *The Doomed Detective: The Contribution of the Detective Novel to Postmodern American and Italian Fiction* (Carbondale and Edwardsville: Southern Illi-nois University Press, 1984), 2.

25. Tani, 7, 25. Cawelti concurs: "[T]he best and most influential mystery stories usually retain an element of uncertainty no matter how clearly the mystery has been solved or the evil villain destroyed. The inherently serial character of the literature of mystery indicates this." Geoffrey Hartman also speaks of detective stories as "exor-cisms" ("Literature High and Low: The Case of the Mystery Story," in *The Poetics of Murder: Detective Fiction and Literary Theory*, eds. Glenn W. Most and William W. Stowe [San Diego, New York, London: Harcourt Brace Jovanovich, 1983, 210–219], 220).

26. Sage, xvi.

27. *Ibid.*, xv.

28. *Ibid.*, xvi.

29. *Ibid.*, xviii.

30. W. H. Auden, "The Guilty Vicarage" [1938], *The Dyer's Hand and Other Essays* (London: Faber, 1963, pp. 146–58), 154.

31. *Ibid.*, 147.

32. *Ibid.*, 151.

33. Similarly, see *Black and Blue* [1997] (London: Orion, 1999), 7. All further refer-ences to *Black and Blue* are to this edition and identified (in parentheses) in the text.

34. J. Kingston Pierce.

35. Similarly, see Ian Rankin, *Set in Darkness* (London: Orion, 2000), 231. All fur-ther references to *Set in Darkness* are to this edition and identified (in parentheses) in the text.

36. Ian Rankin, *Resurrection Men* [2001] (London: Orion, 2001), 135. All further ref-erences to *Resurrection Men* are to this edition and identified (in parentheses) in the text.

37. Ian Rankin, *Dead Souls* [1999], (New York: St. Martin's, 2000), 413. All further references to *Dead Souls* are to this edition and identified (in parentheses) in the text.

38. Hans Jonas, *The Gnostic Religions: The Message of the Alien God and the Begin-nings of Christianity* [1958] (Boston: Beacon, 1963), 68.

39. *The Falls* (London: Orion, 2001), 135–36. All further references to *The Falls* are to this edition and identified (in parentheses) in the text.

40. One can detect Rankin playing on Knox's name from the outset of the series. The title *Knots and Crosses* is already an elaborate pun on a character's name, on knot-ted sting and tied matchsticks, and the "Tic-Tac-Toe" game, but it also sounds an

awful lot like "Knox and Crosses," which further emphasizes the Christian connotation of "Crosses" while also inscribing the self-negating idea of "Knox" as the "zero" or the "nought"/ "not" of Scottish life.

41. Auden, "The Guilty Vicarage"; George Grella, "The Formal Detective Novel," in Robin Winks, ed., 84–102, and "The Hard-Boiled Detective Novel", in Robin Winks, ed., 103–120; Tzvetan Todorov, "The Typology of Detective Fiction," in *The Poetics of Prose* [1971], trans. Richard Howard (Ithaca: Cornell University Press, 1977, 42–52); P. D. James, "The Art of the Detective Novel," *Journal of the Royal Society of Arts* 133 (August 1985), 637–649; Glenn W. Most, "The Hippocratic Smile: John LeCarré and the Traditions of the Detective Novel," in eds. Most and Stowe, 341–365.

42. See, for example, Ross Macdonald, *The Barbarous Coast* [1956] (New York: Warner, [1990], 121; Ian Rankin, *Mortal Causes* [1994], (New York: St. Martin's, 1997), 107; Ian Rankin, *Let It Bleed* [1995] (London: Orion, 1996), 254. Again, further references to these Rankin novels are to these editions identified (in parentheses) in the text. The hermetic vision is well illustrated by Holmes's Book of Life, which tells us, "From a drop of water ... a logician could infer the possibility of an Atlantic or a Niagara without having seen or heard of one or the other.... By a man's finger-nails, by his coat sleeve, by his boots, by his trouser-knees, ... by each of these things a man's calling is plainly revealed" (Sir Arthur Conan Doyle, *The Complete Sherlock Holmes*, 2 vols. [Garden City, New York: Doubleday, 1930], 23).

43. "Dashiell Hammett," in eds. Most and Stowe (197–209), 202.

44. Raymond Chandler, *Farewell, My Lovely* [1940] (New York: Ballantine, 1975), 129.

45. "Jameson, Genre, and Gumshoes: *The Maltese Falcon* as Inverted Romance," in *The Cunning Craft: Original Essays on Detective Fiction Contemporary Literary Theory*, ed. Ronald G. Walker and June M. Frazer. (Macomb, Illinois: Western Illinois University, 1990, 109–119), 109–10.

46. In Graham Greene's *The Ministry of Fear* (1943) and, more elaborately, in Philip Kerr's *A Pale Criminal* (1990) fraudulent mediums work with Nazi officials to advance their darker goals. Nazism's links to occultism have been well explored in Nicholas Goodrick-Clarke's *The Occult Roots of Nazism: The Ariosophists of Austria and Germany, 1890–1935* (Willingborough, Northants: Aquarian Press, 1985). Greene is alluded to in *Black and Blue* (459), and Kerr, another Scottish writer, is the author of the brilliant *Berlin Noir* trilogy (*March Violets, A Pale Criminal*, and *A German Requiem*) and other books, one of which supplied Rankin with his epigraph for *The Falls*.

47. Stories about the Templars (The Knights Templars of the Temple of Solomon, founded as a military religious order in 1119) continue to fascinate (see *The Holy Blood and the Holy Grail* by Michael Baigent, Richard Leigh, and Henry Lincoln [1982] for example) and are often only remotely linked to historical fact. The Templars were prosecuted for heresy in the fourteenth century. Hammett and Rankin hardly need to draw on the latest historical research to support the use they make of the Templar story. Lewis Spence's account in his *Encyclopaedia of Occultism*, first published in 1920 (rpt. Secaucus, NJ: Citadel Press, 1974), is sufficient for Hammett's purposes.

48. I am thinking here of Marlowe's reflections on the painting he views in General Sternwood's house in *The Big Sleep*'s second paragraph, of his search for Velma (who, we find, has assumed the identity of Mrs. Grayle) in *Farewell My Lovely*, and of the title of his fourth novel, *The Lady in the Lake*. Any number of other items, including comments Chandler made in "The Simple Art of Murder" and elsewhere, might be cited to illustrate his self-conscious use of the romance paradigm.

49. *Transformations of Myth Through Time* (New York: Harper and Row, 1990), 247.

50. *Ibid.*, 211.

51. Literary allusions abound in Rankin's work. In *Hide and Seek*, for example, we find references to Keats (147), Whitman (186), the *Inferno* (203), *MacBeth* (204), and Raymond Chandler's Philip Marlowe (97), to list just a handful of allusions beyond the ubiquitous Stevenson references. *Hide and Seek*'s debt to Chandler is seen in other ways as well. In the course of the investigation, Rebus and Holmes question a photographer, Jimmy Hutton, who also produces pornography. Elsewhere, in discussing the occult with Poole, Rebus recalls a book of paintings by H. R. Giger that he once purchased (47). In Chandler's *The Big Sleep*, Marlowe also discovers a photographer, named A. G. Geiger, who is producing pornography and then using the images to blackmail rich women. Incidently, Chandler's gangster, Eddie Mars, may also be the source of the murdered Eddie Marbar's name in *Resurrection Men*.

52. For an interesting discussion of film noir and its relationship to hard-boiled detective fiction see James Naremore's *More Than Night: Film Noir in Its Contexts* (Berkeley: University of California Press, 1998).

53. Even John Milton is co-opted to this purpose: "Dark, dark, dark. Rebus recalled that line at least" (*Mortal* 72). Here, the allusion to *Samson Agonistes*, "O dark, dark, dark, amid the blaze of noon" (line 80), also ties acrostically to "SaS" (Sword and Shield), appearing immediately before the reference, and to the "SAS" (Special Air Service), both of which, in *Mortal Causes,* point to aspects of the mystery and of Rebus's past. The quotation from *Hide and Seek* echoes Chandler's description of the hard-boiled world in his introduction to *Trouble Is My Business* (1950): "The characters lived in a world gone wrong.... The streets were dark with something more than night" ([New York: Ballantine, 1972, vii–xi], viii).

54. Quoted on the back of the book jacket for Ian Rankin's *The Hanging Garden* (New York: St. Martin's, 1998). It is particularly remarkable that Rankin adapts the mostly American tradition to a context that is largely free of guns; that is, American hard-boiled novels and their police-focused descendants, such as Ellroy's books, contain extensive gunplay which is narrowly restrained in Rankin's texts. Nonetheless, we barely notice that Rebus is mostly unarmed; indeed, his possession of a gun in *The Black Book* (1993) becomes a plot point that reflects badly on his character and keeps him on the fringes of the policing community (London: Orion, 2001, 228–31).

55. Michael Eaton, *Chinatown*, BFI Film Classics (London: BFI Publishing, 1997), 40.

56. *Ibid.*, 41. Hans Jonas discusses patterns of light and darkness in Gnostic writings (57–58). This passage from darkness into light is nicely articulated by the epigraph Rankin chose for *Set in Darkness*: "Though my soul may set in darkness/ It will rise in perfect light, / I have loved the stars too fondly / To be fearful of the night" [Sarah Williams, "The Old Astronomer to his Pupil"] (*Set*, vii.)

57. Eaton, 66.

58. Jonas, 62.

59. *Ibid.*, 42–44.

60. *Ibid.*, 43.

61. *Ibid.*, 44.

62. For example, in *The Gospel of Philip* we read, "The world came about through a mistake. For he who created it wanted to create it imperishable and immortal. He fell short of attaining his desire. For the world never was imperishable, nor, for that matter, was he who made the world" (*The Nag Hammadi Library*, general editor James M. Robinson, third revised ed. [San Francisco: Harper, 1990], 154).

63. Jonas, 68.

64. *Ibid.*, 72.

65. Ioan Petra Culiani, "Gnosticism from the Middle Ages to the Present," in *Encyclopedia of Religion*, Mircea Eliade, editor-in-chief (New York and London: Macmillan, 1987, 574–578), 577. Jonas, 46.

66. Jonas, 92.

67. On Eliot, "'Others but Stewards': T. S. Eliot's Gnostic Impulse" in William Monroe, *Power to Hurt: The Virtues of Alienation* (Urbana and Chicago: University of Illinois Press, 1998), pp. 134–154. On Conrad, "*Heart of Darkness* and the Gnostic Myth" by Bruce Henricksen (*Mosaic*, 11.4 [1978], 35–44). Richard Smith's "Afterword: The Modern Relevance of Gnosticism" (*Nag Hammadi* 532–549) notes gnostic belief structures in the work of many writers. The links between gnosticism and theosophy as well as other occult systems remind us that the structures of gnostic belief survived the various sects that profess those beliefs. Hans Jonas has found significant parallels between gnosticism and existentialism, and Cairns Craig finds parallels between existentialism and Calvinism (*The Modern Scottish Novel: Narrative and the National Imagination* [Edinburgh: Edinburgh University Press, 1999], 107), but from a literary point of view, again, gnostic belief structures have often merged with hermeticism. Early in the twentieth century, G. R. S. Mead translated and published many of the then available gnostic texts in books such as *Fragments of a Faith Forgotten*. Since Mead also inhabited literary communities, his books were read by more than theosophists, occultists, and members of the Society for the Psychical Research (see Leon Surette, "*The Birth of Modernism*": *Ezra Pound, T. S. Eliot, W. B. Yeats and the Occult* [Montreal and Kingston: McGill-Queen's University Press, 1993], 132 ff.). As Surette and Demetres Tryphonopoulos (*Literary Modernism and the Occult Tradition*, ed. Surrette and Tryphonopoulos [Orono, Maine: National Poetry Foundation, 1996]) show, Mead played a significant role in early modernism, and he is one of many sources we can point to for the dissemination of gnostic belief.

68. Dashiell Hammett, *The Maltese Falcon* [1930] (New York: Vintage, 1972), 226.

69. George Grella, "The Hard-Boiled Detective Novel," 110.

70. Sayers, 53.

71. Most, 347.

72. See Jonas, 79, on this point.

73. Stefano Tani, 6. He continues: "[T]he murderer, in effect, 'invents' the detective who must necessarily follow (and chase) the murderer; in other words the detective exists–is made possible–because the murderer exists. The criminal is simply 'creative'; the detective both stifles and, ironically, *realizes* the criminal's creativity by bringing to light the full nature of the criminal act and then imposing on the criminal the detective's 'resolvent' power, defusing creative anarchy with common-sense morality" (6).

74. Hammett, 3. This isn't the place to develop the discussion, but John T. Irwin devotes considerable space to elucidating the emblematic importance of the "V" shape for Thomas Browne, Poe, and Borges: "the V shape —considered as a geometric representation of the fold of the hand — is an appropriate figure of intelligibility precisely because the basic metaphor of human knowledge (basic because derived from the givenness of the body's structure, the physical basis of the functioning intelligence) is one that figures thought as the mental grasping of an object" (147). That such a figure of intelligibility is associated with Spade and then Satan evokes the gnostic revaluation of Satan's role in the human story.

75. Jonas, 71.

76. "Trip Trap" [1992], *Beggars Banquet* (London: Orion, 2002, 5–22), 21.

77. "The Deliberate Cunning of Muriel Spark," 51.

78. Cairns Craig, 15, 18–19.

79. "A Preface to *The Galton Case*," in *Afterwords: Novelists on Their Novels* [1969], ed. Thomas McCormack (New York: St. Martin's, 1988, 146–59), 152.

80. "As a detective, he lived in people's pasts: crimes committed before he arrived on the scene; witnesses' memories ransacked. He had become a historian, the role had bled into his personal life. Ghosts, bad dreams, echoes" (*Black and Blue* 461).

81. For Freud, "The uncanny is that class of the terrifying which leads back to something long known to us, once very familiar" ("The Uncanny," in *On Creativity and the Unconscious: Papers on the Psychology of Art, Literature, Love, Religion*, selected with introduction and annotations by Benjamin Nelson [New York: Harper and Row, 1958, 122–61], 123–24). "[T]he uncanny is in reality nothing new or foreign but something familiar and old-established in the mind that has been estranged only by the process of repression" (148). Sage notes that Freud's word, *unheimlich*, literally means the unhomely; that is, that which is strange or not like home in the sense of the familiar and the comfortable (xviii–xix). Curiously, the appearance of the body in Queensberry House in *Set in Darkness* renders the future home of the Scottish Parliament an unhomely space. It speaks to the buried past of the Scottish people and their nation.

82. Similarly, the passage I quoted from late in *Dead Souls* about bodies being unearthed in the construction for the new parliament leads into *Set in Darkness*'s opening pages. In *Black and Blue* material related to the murderer's (Slocum's) interest in the Nazi's and the Second World War cue *The Hanging Garden*.

83. Peter Brooks develops this idea particularly well and influentially in his *Reading for the Plot*. Taking Conan Doyle's "The Musgrave Ritual" as paradigmatic, Brooks used Todorov's well-known description of the two-story structure of detective fiction (of the investigation and of the crime) to show how the detective's retracing of the criminal's path involves a retracing of an already present plot, and so reflects the dynamics of narrative itself.

84. Ian Rankin, "The Silence of the Lums."

85. Rankin has often remarked on several uncanny experiences in his life since he published the first of the Rebus novels (see Pierce for instance), though he refrains from commenting on what these experiences might suggest.

86. Earlier, I noted that the discussion of the Templars in Lewis Spence's *Encyclopaedia of Occultism* (1920) may have served Hammett's purposes. Rankin's readers will be surprised to see that Spence signed his preface and his introduction to the volume with his address "66 Arden St., Edinburgh." Arden Street is a long street, but Rebus lives on it.

87. In *Resurrection Men*, Rebus performs a similar function leading Siobhan Clarke to discover something she already knows: "She could see all of a sudden where Rebus had been leading her" (458).

# 9

# Gender and Ethnic Otherness in Selected Novels by Ann Granger, Cath Staincliffe and Alma Fritchley

MARTA VIZCAYA ECHANO

This essay will study the connections between the detective and the ethnic other in Ann Granger's *Running Scared* (1998),[1] Cath Staincliffe's *Stone Cold, Red Hot* (2001),[2] and Alma Fritchley's *Chicken Feed* (1998),[3] detective novels with female protagonists who are manifestly aware of their white British identity but who also occupy liminal positions in society due to their gender, class or sexuality. While the three novels show marked feminist concerns, their protagonists occupy different cultural spaces that affect the stories' depiction of the racial other. Encountering this other alters the protagonists' sense of identity together with their conceptualization of the communities within which such identities are constructed.

If formula fiction is a cultural product shaped by popular demand, *Running Scared, Stone Cold* and *Chicken Feed* indicate the variety of social groups writing and reading detective fiction who want to see their concerns treated in it. Their different portrayals of British ethnic communities reflect an increasingly widespread awareness of how these groups' presence is making mainstream society reimagine itself in ways that, as *Stone Cold* exposes, sometimes result in prejudiced and brutal acts. In undertaking this study of gender and ethnic otherness, I will first consider how these novels' social concerns and their portrayal of the dominant ethnic group's relations with the racial, cultural, and social other place them in the tradition of women's detective fiction, ethnic detective fiction and, in the case of Fritchley's work, lesbian detective fiction. I will also explore how the authors use intertextual strategies to engage readers in the exploration of social injustices represented in the stories. Finally, I will analyze the various tensions arising from and problems inherent in the detectives' and readers' attempts to understand or portray the predicament of the ethnic other.

Staincliffe's Sal Kilkenny series features a single mother who sets up a private investigation agency thanks to an Enterprise Allowance governmental scheme. In *Stone Cold*, Sal investigates the brutal racial harassment experienced by a family of Somalian refugees living in an impoverished Manchester council state. Ann Granger's Fran Varady series follows the trajectory of its protagonist, an unemployed young woman with no family who lives in London's squats until an acquaintance gives her shelter and her best friend, Ganesh, offers her a part-time job at his uncle's newsagents'. An amateur sleuth (who is also attempting to help a homeless, drug-addicted girl), Fran becomes involved in various cases including a murder near her house. Finally, Fritchley's *Chicken Feed* is the second book in a series starring Letty Campbell, a middle-aged lesbian farmer living in Calderton, West Yorkshire. In the novel, Letty finds herself at the center of a series of violent events following the sudden disappearance of Sita Joshi, a controversial lesbian politician of Indian background with whom an ex-partner of the protagonist had become involved.

I will approach these novels as pieces of multicultural and ethnic writing, terms that need to be defined more specifically before proceeding further. Since the works are written by women — and, in the case of Fritchley, by a lesbian — they can be considered multicultural detective fiction according to Adrienne Johnson Gosselin's understanding of the term as stories "in the hands of authors whose cultural communities are not those of the traditional Euro-American male hero, whose cultural experiences have been excluded from the traditional detective formula, and whose cultural aesthetic alters the formula itself."[4] They could also be called multicultural in that they deal with the relations and tensions between various social groups differing in their gender, sexual preference, class, and ethnicity. This last factor also makes them ethnic crime fiction, following Ray Browne's definition of the genre as "literature about crime ... involving people of at least two ethnic groups."[5]

Like much contemporary writing within the genre, the works of Staincliffe, Fritchley and Granger also show a marked social consciousness. It manifests itself most clearly in how the works seek "to subvert the social order rather than preserve it" and portray its characters' selves as "fluid and multivalent," varying according to personal and socio-cultural circumstances.[6] The authors' depiction of identity as relational seeks to avoid gender, sexual, class, and ethnic essentialisms while exploring the differences and convergences between mainstream groups and those perceived or perceiving themselves as "other." However, as I argue later on, when it comes to the representation of ethnic characters, these writers do not fully succeed at avoiding stereotypes and tokenism.

With their strong female protagonists, feminist consciousness and social concerns, *Stone Cold, Chicken Feed* and *Running Scared* have as direct influences the hard-boiled female detective fiction of the 1980s. Popular novels by women writers with a female sleuth as a protagonist became a phenomenon in the late 1970s and particularly in the early 1980s with the debut of writers like Marcia Muller (1977), Sue Grafton (1982) and Sara Paretsky (1982). As Walton and Jones point out, by the 1980s women were no longer mere consumers of household products but "buyers with significant disposable incomes whose needs were independent of the domestic context"[7] and who were influenced by the social debates caused by the feminist movement of the 1960s and 1970s. This readership demanded strong female characters reflecting "the growing numbers of women in the workforce, women who chose to be single, were extremely efficient at their jobs, could defend themselves physically and constantly questioned the patriarchal society in which they functioned."[8] Women detectives in 1980s novels thus face new personal and social problems related to women's changing circumstances as well as to their political awareness.

Written from the 1990s onwards, the works I am examining portray situations that have become increasingly common for women in the last decades. Granger's Fran, a twenty-one-year-old orphan living in the streets and squatting for much of her teenage years, underlines the downward social mobility, poverty and homelessness afflicting sectors of the population frequently ignored by mainstream society. Staincliffe's Sal brings to the fore the struggle of single mothers to combine work and home responsibilities. Her living arrangements sharing a house with her friend Ray and his son Tom also call the reader's attention to the increasing number of non-traditional, non-nuclear family and family-like units. So too does the lifestyle of Fritchley's Letty, who shares her farm with her long-term partner, Anna, her niece AnnaMaria and, once she gives birth, the baby who AnnaMaria is having from a man who is not her boyfriend.

The first writers of female hard-boiled fiction faced the problem of how to combine the influence of traditional generic conventions, which were considerably misogynist, with the kind of female figures and worldview that they wanted to portray. They did so by giving a central place in their writing to three interconnected thematic strands: the protagonist's daily and emotional life; wider social problems regarding women's social roles and status; and other instances of inequality and injustice examined from a feminist perspective.[9] This stress on the sleuths' networks of social and personal relationships has become a distinctive feature of detective novels in the 1990s.[10] Traditional Golden Age male detectives like Poirot showed a "legendary clear-sightedness ... achieved at a distance from people," an individualism inherited by the American hard-boiled detectives. In contrast, in the 1980s and yet more so in the 1990s, sleuths manage to "see things clearly because they are close enough to others to understand what motivates people."[11]

In both U.S. and British women's detective fiction since the 1980s, female friendship appears as a prominent structuring and thematic element. It allows authors to examine the bonds linking people of different age and backgrounds, to study the differences between them, and to explore "the possibility of individual and collective female agency and the effects of such agency on patriarchal systems."[12] In *Chicken Feed*, Letty is surrounded by Anne, AnnaMaria, her friend Julia, local journalist Janice, and several other female secondary characters. And both *Running Scared* and *Stone Cold* illustrate the growing tendency in the 1990s for the development of the friendship theme to include female detectives' bonds with men. For instance, while she has an affectionate rapport with her elderly landlady Daphne and she cares for Tig — a teenage prostitute that she met in a squat — Fran's closest friend is Ganesh, a young shopkeeper of Indian origin. Similarly, Sal has artist Diane as her main confidante and also turns to her lesbian friend Chris, but she also often seeks the company and the help of housemate Ray.

Critics like Susan Elizabeth Sweeney argue that, through their themes and their characterization of female protagonists, novels like *Chicken Feed*, *Running Scared* and *Stone Cold* succeed in subverting the genre's conventions and patriarchal ideological framework instead of merely substituting a female sleuth for a male one.[13] Patricia Walton and Manina Jones also contend that these novels endow the presence of the woman sleuth with political significance, contesting and altering the traditional parameters of a genre that has often demeaned and stereotyped women. The detective novel thus provides a site for the negotiation of literary and social concerns by both authors and readers, part of whom would not necessarily face some of these issues in any other areas of their lives.[14] It constitutes a potential space for collaborative agency between people of different backgrounds as they examine the motives, circumstances and consequences not just of specific crimes but of wider collective problems closely connected with them.

In contemporary women's detective fiction, most instances of injustice and crime are not depicted as isolated events but as the result of social organizations based on patriarchy and on racial, cultural, class and sexual hierarchies and discrimination. As Sweeney observes, although the blame might be directly ascribed to a single person, feminist detective fiction explores how "this individual's actions reflect a broader social practice" and makes it clear that "truly solving the crime would entail changing that practice"[15] together with changing widespread societal perceptions. Sal, for instance, realizes that the racist attacks against the Ibrahims are only the most extreme manifestations of more extended prejudices towards asylum seekers and people of color. Similarly, when Fran realizes that Tig had been raped by an educated, well-off police officer, she is also aware that the root of the problem lies in mainstream society's tendency to see homeless people and prostitutes as not "human, ... just a thing.... Something to be used and chucked back in the gutter" (*Running Scared*, p. 290).

The adequacy of the detective fiction genre to act as a common space for the examination of social topics has been questioned on the basis of its alleged conservative conventions and ideology. While the mystery and crime novel deals, by definition, with transgression and violence, the detective's resolution traditionally facilitates a restoration of social and ethical order and supports the primacy of rational discourses.[16] However, like many other contemporary sleuths, Letty, Fran and Sal sometimes solve the mystery by chance rather than by wit. They also make mistakes or endanger their lives. The detective's flawed character and limited powers in these novels follow the increasing trend to present her "not as Great Detective, but as fallible and suffering human being,"[17] something which Sal, Fran and Letty acknowledge themselves.

Justice is often achieved only partially and in unsatisfactory terms, and sometimes it is not achieved at all. For instance, Fran discovers that she has started dating the policeman who raped Tig and confronts him, but he is never punished for his crime: Fran has no evidence apart from Tig's word, the girl refuses to report him to the police, and, even if she were to do so, she is unlikely to be believed because of her past as a prostitute. Sal, in turn, finally gets the sound evidence of racial harassment required by the council before acting against the Ibrahims' attackers when she witnesses the arson of their house. Although the Ibrahims will now probably get new housing and see their victimizers taken to court, this comes as a meager consolation after the death of their son in the fire.

Formula literature's conditions of production and reception have also contributed to the consideration of the detective novel as a conservative means of expression. Since it is aimed at a mass readership, formula fiction is often seen as "(commercially) reproducing, rather than changing, the hegemonic literary and social values of the past."[18] However, if mystery and crime novels—like other formula fiction — must be immediately identifiable as belonging to a specific genre, they also have to be unique, departing in some way from its conventions and thus modifying readers' expectations of that type of literature. As their societies change, readers demand to see these new circumstances and values reflected in formula fiction and reward the type of novel that answers their requirements through their buying power. Consequently, like other manifestations of popular culture, detective fiction cannot be considered either conservative or progressive. Genre, quoting Walton and Jones, "serves as a relational, conventional, and contradictory location that tends to complicate in practice any simple either/or categorization."[19] Detective novels simultaneously convey the ideological generic restrictions inherited from the past as well as the potential for literary and social change.

This dynamism is evident for instance in the transformation of the British cozy into the American hard-boiled novel,[20] as well as in the responses that writers like Muller, Cody, Paretsky or Grafton made to the patriarchal values and the often misogynistic male protagonists in this subgenre. Mid–1990s female sleuths like Granger's Fran, Fritchley's Letty and Staincliffe's Sal are in turn "softer" and more focused on affective relationships and family life than their predecessors. These shifts show the evolution in the views and expectations of both women and detective fiction held by feminist writers as well as by the genre's readership and society at large. Writers like Staincliffe, Granger and Fritchley both reflect and promote certain social changes from within the genre, acknowledging its history of ideological conservatism while pushing its thematic and formal limits each in her own way. The alternative of rejecting detective fiction is not a viable option since the writers presumably enjoy writing and reading it — Staincliffe's biographic information in Looking for Trouble, for instance, presents her as "an avid reader of crime fiction."[21]

Added to this, the novels suggest that the most effective way of instigating social change is from within society. Although single motherhood, homelessness and sexual preference have respectively placed Sal, Fran and Letty in social positions considered marginal, the characters engage with collective concerns which do not always affect them directly and give the impression of considering themselves very much a part of society. However, even if they constitute a force facilitating change and advocating equality, they are presented as people in evolution who show personality flaws, biases, and sometimes ignorance. In this last point they resemble the societies of which they are simultaneously products, observers and critics.

The emergence of novels with lesbian or ethnic minority sleuths in the 1990s constitutes another important stage in the genre's evolution, and so does the increasing awareness in works by and about straight white women of the problems faced by ethnic minorities and other marginalized collectives—problems that are depicted as concerning society as a whole. In this sense, works like those of Staincliffe, Granger and Fritchley present themselves as ethnic narratives in that their white female first-person narrators are conscious of their ethnicity — no longer experienced as a non-marked racial category — as well as of its historical construction, implications, and privileges. On several occasions the characters resort to their own experiences of prejudice and marginalization because of their gender and social status in order to empathize with those who are subjected to other kinds of oppression. The novels also make it clear that the protagonists' efforts to empathize are done with an awareness of the specificity of each case of inequality and abuse, and hence of their limitations when it comes to understanding what others are going through. However, while it is acknowledged that there exist personal and cultural differences between characters which might prove irreducible, the authors refuse to present each instance of oppression as so unique and impossible for others to grasp that solidarity and collaboration between different people towards constructing a fairer society becomes impossible.

The intertextual references in the works acknowledge their place within crime and mystery writing as well as the readers' likely familiarity with their literary contexts, while also playing with the boundaries between fiction and reality. The one overt allusion of this kind in Staincliffe's *Stone Cold* is Sal's joke about her investigative work being "[j]ust like they do in the movies" (p. 51). To the readers, Sal's universe is as fictional as the films she mentions are to her, although many of her personal and social concerns might nevertheless "ring true." As they follow the protagonist's dilemmas throughout the series when facing complex instances of racism, sexism, domestic violence, poverty and child abuse, they have to consider what Sal's fictional world tells them about their own. The humorous allusion to "the movies" also underscores the connections among different forms of popular culture, specifically mystery and crime plots in literature and cinema.

The distance between Staincliffe's work and the early mystery and crime novel is explicitly established in *Looking for Trouble*, the first book in the Sal Kilkenny series, when Sal confesses not being able to concentrate on "[a] crime set on a cruise ship in the 'thirties'" since its "mannered dialogue was too much effort" and she "didn't really care whodunit or why" (p. 82). The characteristics of the book that Sal is reading strongly contrast with the realistic dialogue, contemporary settings and psycholog-ical depth in Staincliffe's writing. *Looking for Trouble* also depicts the pro-tagonist as an avid reader of crime thrillers by Loren D. Estleman — a pivotal figure in the revival of the P.I. novel in the 1970s and early 1980s who also writes historical westerns — as well as of the Sue Grafton Alpha-bet series (p. 163), which offers an independent, complex female protag-onist with whom Sal shows strong links. The fact that Sal enjoys writers like Estleman and Grafton also points to the cross-pollination processes between U.S. and British crime and detective fiction.

Similarly, Fritchley's *Chicken Feed* mentions influential points of ref-erence within the crime and mystery genre in a way that pays homage to them while humorously highlighting its differences from them. After being involved in several dangerous incidents, Letty — who acknowledges liking *The Bill*—feels like she has "fallen into a Dashiel Hammett thriller" (p. 183). When she is trapped by the criminal, she compares the latter's threats to "a menacing retort ... from a gangster movie" (p. 202), and finds herself "playing for time" like she has seen "in countless movies" (pp. 204–205). Considering her predicament, Letty states: "This wasn't like *Cracker* or *Prime Suspect*. On telly a negotiator turns up and everyone gets cosy and clever. This was proving to be more of a 'Cagney' than a 'Lacey' situation" (p. 209). As in Staincliffe's writing, the character's feelings of unreality when certain circumstances remind her of parts of a book or film make the reader examine the boundaries between reality and fiction. These ref-erences also stress the crossover between the consumers of different forms of popular culture — in this case, mystery and crime books, films and tel-evision programs— suggesting that a similarly wide range of influences has inspired Fritchley's writing.

Granger's Fran Varady stresses both her links and her contrasts with previous detective fiction figures when she states that she is "quite a good detective ... *You know my thesis, Watson*" (*Running Scared*, p. 10). We are told that she sometimes reads "an Agatha Christie or an Ngaio Marsh" (*Running Scared*, p.10), and she is warned by a police officer not to start pretending that she is Miss Marple (*Running Scared*, p. 84). After finding a corpse by her flat's door she states that for her landlady, a fan of crime and mystery novels, "[t]his must beat reading about murder in one of the whodunits lining her shelves. This was the real thing" (*Running Scared*, p. 80). Fran also describes a later event as "a turn up for the books" (*Run-ning Scared*, p. 281). When reporting to the police that she has not had any further contact with the criminal related to the murder by her flat, Fran feels "perfectly ridiculous..., as if [she]'d escaped from a spy thriller" (*Run-ning Scared*, p. 254). Finally, the circumstances in which Fran becomes first an amateur sleuth and then is invited to join a professional detective agency after the death of its owner recall those of P. D. James' Cordelia Gray.

By making references to other crime or detective stories to which they owe a literary debt, show parallels or contrast strongly, these novels set the parameters for their critical evaluation. In this sense, the allusions to other narratives within the genre can be read as metafictional gestures that give clues about the works' literary aesthetics to those readers familiar with mystery and detection writing. At the same time, the intertextual allusions emphasize the novels' status as literary artifacts, disrupting the sense of reality that the worlds they portray might convey to the engrossed reader. This strategy allows the authors to play with the boundaries between fiction and reality. Cases in classic whodunnits might seem unreal to Fran, Sal, and Letty (although they often mirror loosely their investigations), yet even as contemporary readers are encouraged to recognize the fictionality of these novels they are cautioned not to dismiss the more real and relevant social tensions in *Running Scared, Stone Cold* and *Chicken Feed*. The fact that the narrators of *Running Scared* and *Chicken Feed* address the readers directly highlights further the latter's participation in (re)creating the narrative events and atmospheres, stressing the connections between the fictive and "real" world.

The device of acknowledging the readers' involvement in the problems exposed in the story emphasizes further the status of the detective novel as a potential site of collective agency for writers and readers. This communal aspect of the genre is also present at plot level particularly in the case of works showing a feminist consciousness, which "tend to privilege collaboration, relational thinking, [and involvement] over the lonely individualism of classic, Golden Age, and hard-boiled tales."[22] In women's detective fiction, the sleuth often becomes personally affected by the process of solving the mystery or bringing the criminal to justice, and her experiences during these undertakings affect her worldview significantly. Not only does she define herself relationally according to her circumstances and social interactions, but she is aware of doing so as well as of the relativity of her knowledge, sense of truth and justice. Readers, traditionally invited to identify with the detective and involved in a parallel process of solving the mystery, also face a similar self-examination, gaining awareness of their implication in other people's predicament.

As has been previously mentioned, ethnic detective fiction gained momentum in the 1980s and 1990s. Among the reasons for the increasing popularity of this type of novels—and, one would argue, of those by women, gays or lesbians, and other historically marginalized collectives—

Browne includes the authorial search for distinctive settings, stories, and characters that might attract readers seeking new possibilities of geo-social "armchair tourism." A second factor would be the wish of politically aware writers to challenge prejudices against certain ethnic groups, which may not necessarily be those of the authors themselves.[23] Finally, well-written ethnic crime novels can become "a kind of affirmative fiction," examining the tensions between different social sectors, pointing out the worries and misconceptions of dominant groups, and "demonstrating remorse and atonement for former and present social injustices."[24] *Chicken Feed, Running Scared* and — most prominently — *Stone Cold* show that, while the first factor will inevitably affect the writing of commercially successful formula fiction, the second and third are equally important if not more so for socially committed women writers.

One aspect differentiating British detective fiction from its U.S. counterpart is the scarcity of detective figures from ethnic minority backgrounds despite the waves of immigration mainly from Caribbean, African and Asian countries, which Mary Hadley reads as a reflection of a "generally more conservative society."[25] Added to this, Hadley observes that there are few secondary characters of nondominant ethnic backgrounds.[26] The works I am studying challenge this second point in that they portray their white protagonists' regular contact with a range of secondary characters from other ethnic, racial or national backgrounds. The depictions of the relations between these characters and the detective or other figures representing attitudes common in mainstream society, however, make it clear that interactions between dominant and non-dominant groups are still not normalized and might result in frictions and violence. At the same time, the novels explore how certain ethnic and national groups are racialized while others' difference is not perceived as equally significant and problematic.

Granger's *Running Scared* starts with a depiction of the strong friendship between Fran and Ganesh, whose background is Indian. Ganesh plays a central role throughout the whole Fran Varady series, which explores the characters' bonds as well as the differences between them — which both accept that they cannot always understand. Some of the main points on which they agree to disagree, for instance, are Ganesh's relationship with his family, whose wishes he often follows to the detriment of his own preferences, and Fran's individualism and fear that romantic commitment might spoil their friendship. Anita Naoko Pilgrim suggests that when readers evaluate the representation of non-white characters in prose fiction by white authors, we should consider whether these figures are well integrated in the story or are included mainly as token figures in order to provide positive representations of ethnic minorities or give more a balanced portrayal of a community.[27] Arguably, Ganesh can be seen as stereotypical to a certain extent in that he works in his relatives' corner shop, generally follows his family's wishes, and occasionally provides a humorous dimension to the novel. However, his presence is central to the narrative, which would be substantially different and flatter without him. His advice and support are invaluable to Fran, he is the only person whom she trusts with her feelings and thoughts, and his concerns and aspirations are explored side by side with the protagonist's.

In Fritchley's *Chicken Feed*, Sita Joshi and Tracey Pekec occupy important roles in the narrative as the former is the story's victim and Julia's new lover and the latter is the criminal. Born and educated in England, Sita returned to her parents' birthplace, Bombay, to become a film director. Although she is depicted as "a feminist whose work behind the camera was a radical departure from mainstream Asian cinema" (p. 81), her career comes to an end when the press gets hold of her lesbianism. Sita's predicament is described by Letty as the result of being "a dyke in a conservative part of the world and a woman in a male-dominated industry" (p. 81). Sita then heads for Australia to create there a center for women adventurers, after which she travels to Holland and gets involved with the Green movement. Once back in Britain, she becomes first a councilor for Manchester and then an MP for CalderVale, antagonizing "the usual motley crew of the religious right, who hated her because she was neither white, Christian nor straight" (p. 82), and receiving several death threats.

Sita's portrayal goes against stereotyped images of the ethnic other as a poor immigrant, and her circumstances and career choices arguably make her a much more innovative creation than Granger's Ganesh. The charismatic politician and women's rights activist is not presented as a powerless victim or a flawless idealist, but as a driven woman of sometimes ambiguous motives. The threats she suffers in the novel are triggered not by racial, gender, or sexual prejudice but by the wish for revenge of a former employee — Tracey — obsessed with her. However, one does get the impression that the character is a bit of a token figure in that, paraphrasing Anita Naoko Pilgrim's phrase, she is not in the story purely in her own terms.[28] While Sita continues to appear in the series as she becomes Julia's partner, she is not developed much further than in *Chicken Feed*. She remains a vague character whose interventions in the novels are brief, and we do not become familiar with her personality and concerns— apart from her political activities— in the same way as we do with Ganesh's.

In *Chicken Feed* Sita is threatened by Tracey Pekec, who was Anna-Maria's first lover but who falls in love with Sita when working at her adventure center in Australia. Tracey resents her indifference, feels wrongly blamed for the death of a climber — a death which she instead ascribes to Sita's acquisition of cheap sport materials— and resorts to blackmailing the ambitious politician. We are told that Tracey's parents were Romanies staying temporarily round Calderton, but the character's ethnic background does not add much to the narrative apart from stereotypically stressing her wild, passionate and extreme nature. The mixed background of Kim Stove, a singer and activist who is also Sita's ex-partner and friend, is similarly assigned a metaphoric value which is the character's main contribution to the story apart from helping carry the plot forward at certain points. Kim was born in Holland to a Persian mother and a Dutch father; she has "a dark and dangerous beauty" (p. 100); and her art, combining Persian and European influences, "would appeal to any sexuality, any age, anyone who could suspend their own preconceived ideas" (p. 103). Kim thus represents the possibility not only of crossover audiences but of the harmonious coexistence of different national, racial and socio-cultural groups.

Staincliffe's use of the ethnic characters in *Stone Cold* is substantially different from Fritchley's and Granger's. While Frichley's Sita becomes a victim of criminal activities because of particular reasons related to her personal life, Mr. Ibrahim and his wife Mrs. Ahmed suffer racial and socio-economic prejudices due to their refugee status. Sal is hired by the Neighbor Nuisance Unit at Manchester City Council to witness and film the racist abuse endured by the couple and their children, who had come to Britain from Somalia in 1998. After living in accommodation for homeless families, they are housed in a deprived, run-down area of Manchester, where they become the object of verbal insults and have graffiti written on their house as well as stones thrown at it. The escalating violence experienced by Mr. Ibrahim's family ends with an arson attack causing the death of one of their children and of a police officer who tries to save him.

The abuse against the family is orchestrated by two local adults and their teenage sons, who believe that the country is being "swamped by immigrants, taking houses and jobs" (*Stone Cold*, p. 85). While their behavior is repudiated without reserve by Sal and by most of the local community, the novel also suggests that this kind of virulent hatred is most likely to arise among the socially alienated urban poor, who feel that they are competing with people like the Ibrahims for jobs, housing and welfare resources. Those better-off will most probably express their antagonism against individuals perceived as foreign or inferior in less extreme ways, but Sal blames them equally for the climate of vilification of asylum seekers and economic immigrants in the late 1990s and 2000s. For instance,

Caroline Cunningham, one of the witnesses that Sal has to visit in order to solve a parallel case, tells the protagonist: "[I]t's all gone too far really ... I go to the shops round here and I'm the only person speaking English. Little Pakistan. And no-one dares to say anything about it" (p. 104). Sal, in turn, wonders how this character would judge the racist attacks against the Ibrahims, thinking that "she'd probably be appalled — not recognising that her own attitudes helped create a climate in which their violent racism could flourish" (p. 109). Caroline, who is also homophobic, is portrayed in an unsympathetic light although Staincliffe avoids demonizing her and makes her remarks evoke wider social problems.

Caroline's words illustrate the uncertainty, fear and resentment experienced by some white British sectors as they face a society in transformation in which their own place and role are changing too. Their unrest is augmented by a lack of awareness or acknowledgment of the socio-historical relations that have triggered migratory movements from parts of Africa, Asia and the Caribbean to the country, as well as of the contribution of immigrant populations to the construction of contemporary Great Britain. While the country can be defined as multicultural, multiethnic and multilingual, actions like those of the Ibrahims' attackers and views like Caroline's indicate a still insufficient understanding, interaction and social cohesion between different communities. In this context, people like Caroline experienced the political correctness of the 1980s and 1990s— unaccompanied by a wide enough social education and dialogue about Great Britain's past, present and potential future— not as a collective advancement but as an inability to voice their opinions and concerns.

Staincliffe makes it clear that the Ibrahims' predicament is the result not just of the isolated actions of a few individuals but of widespread social and institutional deficiencies. More specifically, the harassment against the characters reaches such limits due to a combination of factors like their neighborhood's failure to confront the attackers, the Council's lack of personnel and resources to stop the incidents or relocate the family, and the racist views of the police officer in charge of the case. This same officer arrests without justification a taxi driver of Asian origins who takes Sal to the Ibrahims' during a particularly vicious attack. The officer's behavior leads Sal to state that "[i]t wasn't all that long since the Chief Constable had admitted to institutional racism in his own force in the wake of the Stephen Lawrence enquiry" (*Stone Cold*, p.229). In a case well known to British readers but not to Americans, eighteen-year-old Stephen Lawrence was stabbed to death by a group of white youths in London in 1993. The biased views of the police who investigated the case severely diminished the chances of finding the murderers of the black teenager and bringing them to justice. Although there were clear suspects, nobody was convicted, and the police body was subsequently subjected to an inquiry and found institutionally racist. Staincliffe thus points to the connection between cases of racism in the novel and their real-life counterparts, making the reader link specific incidents to the social atmospheres which favor their occurrence and condone them.

In their portrayal of the prejudice often experienced by those of different ethnicity, Staincliffe, Granger and Fritchley are aware of the danger that speaking for the oppressed might result in depriving them again of their voice and agency. The ways in which their works depict ethnic minority characters indicate that the reader is invited to question not just the efficiency and fairness of a society's legal and judicial systems but also the protagonists' legitimacy to present and interpret these characters' case. One means used in the three novels to acknowledge the limitations in the detective's knowledge and the biases in her worldview is the use of a located, non-omniscient first-person narration. This narrative choice is accompanied by the detective's or other people's explicit statement of her limited perspective as well as by her gradual recognition of the personal and socio-cultural factors shaping her impressions.

The narratives of Granger, Staincliffe and Fritchley challenge Maureen Reddy's statement that while "white female detectives' plots often include discussions or illustrations of ways in which gender bias works against them, they never reflect upon the ways in which their race offers them privileges and thereby complicates gender discrimination."[29] As we have seen, the cases in which Sal, Fran and Letty become involved make them aware of the complexities of racial and ethnic identifications as well as of their intersections with gender, class, sexuality and other factors. In the Sal Kilkenny and Fran Varady novels, the exploration of instances of racial discrimination and the harsh realities of poverty-led immigration extend to other books in the series.

In the case of Fritchley's Letty Campbell stories, the unraveling of the mystery, the discovery of the criminal and the exposition of social injustices are often connected to her own experiences as a lesbian. Chicken Feed and other works in the series belong to the subgenre of lesbian detective fiction, which gained momentum in the 1980s with the appearance of such series as Katherine V. Forrester's Kate Delafield mysteries and Barbara Wilson's Pam Nilson novels. As Maureen Reddy observes, many of the first books in these early series constituted a mixture of mysteries and coming-out stories, which had been an important subgenre of the lesbian novel in the 1970s and 1980s.[30]

Chicken Feed describes how Sita Joshi's lesbianism and ethnicity had intersected to hinder her film career as well as the significance of her position as the "first 'out' lesbian MP"(p. 83), using Letty's words. However, the novel also portrays everyday instances in which lesbians are subtly discriminated against and rendered invisible. When saying goodbye to her partner Anne, who is about to leave for the States for several months, Letty describes how "Manchester Airport was witness to a lesbian ritual as old as time itself. Tears, fears and promises were exchanged as other travellers pretended we didn't exist" (p. 2). Similarly, Kim Stove's relationship with Sita is described by a local journalist and friend of Letty's as "her connection to Sita Joshi," which makes Letty observe sarcastically: "'Connection' was an odd way of describing a lengthy and intimate relationship. Newspeak, I guessed, known only to the initiated" (p. 181).

The novel, however, also offers a critique of political positions characterizing previous stages of feminist and lesbian political activism in the 1970s and 1980s such as separatism. Marilyn Frye defined this political stance as a "separation of various sorts or modes from men and from institutions, relationships, roles, and activities which are male-defined, male-dominated, and operating for the benefit of males" which is "initiated or maintained, at will, by women."[31] At the basis of separatism is the idea that males generally go through life as parasites of females since it is "the strength, energy, inspiration, and nurturance of women that keeps men going, and not the strength, aggression, spirituality, and hunting of men that keeps women going."[32] Separatism thus constitutes a refusal and reallocation of resources or services, a seizure of power by women as they redefine social relations between the genders.

However, political strategies like separatism underwent severe reexaminations as new understandings of what being a woman or a lesbian means gained popularity and ideological disagreements splintered the lesbian community from the mid–1980s onwards. A gradual rejection of women as essentially better and more caring than men has developed side by side with an awareness of divisions among women along the lines of class, ethnicity, sexuality and other factors. These differences also imply power differentials that have often led to some women's oppression of others. Feminists and lesbians of color as well as working-class activists have vigorously denounced middle-class western feminist constructions of "woman" as a monolithic category constituting the primary element in self-definition. Such an ideological positioning — and political strategies like separatism deriving from it — would deny them equally important connections with their ethnic and socio-cultural communities, and would place their duties as feminists in conflict with their allegiance to these groups. Finally, there has also been a shift towards seeking to change society from within, as part of it, as opposed to separatist forms of activism. Although these points are not explicitly mentioned in *Chicken Feed*, presumably they are part of what triggers the sarcastic comments that Letty's friend Julia makes about the sister of Letty's lover: "Men? ... She can't abide them. I thought separatists had died off long ago, but they're still breeding them somewhere and Laura's the leader of the pack" (*Chicken Feed*, p. 37).

Anna Wilson sees the rejection of separatism as characteristic of the lesbian detective novel, which "[i]n repudiating female essence as embodied in the separatist structures of lesbian nation ... repudiates not merely the capacity of lesbian nation to fulfil the function of home but also the idea of home itself."[33] Although Letty leads a woman-focused life in that practically all the characters around her — whether friends or family — are female, she does not seem to believe in any essentialist idealizations of womanhood or of lesbian communities. Her social circle is not any less free of power-conflicts, violence and crime than society at large, and she also chooses to interact with neighbors and other Calderton villagers. In Wilson's words, lesbian detective fiction promotes "a return to the streets and thus to the mainstream" in the sense that it presents self-definition and political activism as taking place within society.[34] From this perspective, changes would be effected most productively in interaction — meaning here both connection and confrontation — with social structures which earlier forms of lesbian feminism had wanted to challenge through rejection and detachment.

This "mainstreaming" tendency within certain feminist and lesbian sectors has in turn been criticized by more radical activists as a conservative, compromised political stance which is caricatured in the figure of the New Lesbian, "dedicated to lifestyle, integration with gay men and conservation of heterosexual values, and losing the connection with feminism with its analysis of male power and heterosexuality."[35] Thus, if Fritchley's character Julia considers Laura's views extreme and out of touch with the times, Julia could be criticized as representing this more conservative, less militant strand of lesbian politics by those not agreeing with the return to the mainstream advocated by theorists like Wilson. Fritchley's book thus acknowledges in an indirect way the different ideological positionings and debates shaping contemporary understandings of lesbianism.

Together with her choice and treatment of criminals, Fritchley's portrayal of Letty's relationships differentiates her writing from the type of lesbian detective fiction prominent during the previous decades. In the 1970s and 1980s, there was a certain pressure to write "politically correct" works in which the lesbian characters were portrayed positively and were often the victims of discrimination and crime while the culprit was generally male.[36] In *Chicken Feed*, characters like Tracey and Sita are depicted as being as capable of jealousy, ruthless ambition, revenge, violence or criminal acts just like heterosexuals.

Critics like Jill Radford have asked writers to examine carefully the construction of the lesbian as a criminal or killer, considering whether the novel is directed to a mainstream audience or to a lesbian one — as would be the case of books with marked lesbian thematics published by smaller, specialized presses— in which case the influence of negative depictions of lesbians on the general public would be minimal. In "mainstreamed" lesbian narratives, Radford argues, the use of lesbian villains could reinforce existing prejudices in certain sectors of the readership: "What makes for attractions for lesbian feminist readers could be read and used differently by others."[37] Fritchley's Letty Campbell books, dealing mainly with lesbian characters and published by the Women's Press, are not likely to reach a mainstream audience. However, what proves a more effective political strategy when presenting negative portrayals of lesbian characters is that these are balanced out by the fact that the "good ones" also share the same sexual preferences, which allows no readership to draw generalizations.

Fritchley's portrayal of the emotional lives of Letty and her circle also engages with various points of contention regarding feminist and lesbian writing. *Chicken Feed* shows Letty in a long-term relationship with live-in partner Anne — although in later novels Anne abandons our protagonist for another woman, leaving Letty in distress until she meets a new romantic interest. Similarly, Letty's ex-lover Julia finds a stable partner in Sita Joshi after a long string of relationships. The depiction of these bonds has to be read against the fact that certain representations of lesbian relationships in the 1990s have been found problematic by critics like Lynne Harne since they are seen as reproducing the models promulgated by heterosexual literature, implying that "to be a lesbian you have to be in a romantic and sexual relationship and that the fundamental goal of all lesbians is long-term domestic coupledom."[38] This type of representations of lesbian sexual and romantic life has been considered the result of a shift towards conservatism after the debates surrounding libertarianism and S&M in the 1980s.[39] A related objection is that non-sexual bonds such as friendships or political and work relationships are seldom foregrounded in 1990s narratives.[40] In the case of Fritchley's novels, while Letty and Julia become involved in monogamous long-term relationships, their choices are not portrayed as prescriptive but merely as reflecting the fact that some women — whether lesbian or heterosexual — find this kind of relationship most suitable or fulfilling. Added to this, whether searching for a partner or living with one, the characters also cultivate other friendships, family and social bonds that are depicted as being equally important to them.

While politically aware, Letty does not appear as particularly interested in a more direct activism whether lesbian or of any other ideological leaning. In a long-term relationship with Anne, and living comfortably as a farmer thanks to an aunt's inheritance, Letty has a pretty mainstream lifestyle in many senses. However, as Walton and Jones argue, the act of featuring a "mainstreamed" lesbian character matter-of-factly, with sexuality as only one of the many factors defining her, still "necessarily involves a politics of identity, for lesbian writers as for women writers in general."[41]

The detective has generally been male and heterosexual throughout the genre's history until the late 1970s and 1980s, with women and homosexuals occupying secondary roles either helping to carry the plot forward or acting as counterpoints to the male main character and contributing to his characterization. The increasing presence of female heterosexual and lesbian protagonists thus constitutes a drastic shift in that it makes "the traditional 'other' of crime fiction"—in this case, the characters marked as "other" because of their gender and sexuality—"the focus of the private eye narrative."[42] It places in the mainstream a social group—women, and particularly lesbians—which has been historically marginalized and whose sense of self has partly been built as a reaction to this background of discrimination. Characters like Letty represent not just the mere substitution of a female detective for a male one, but a change in the tone, crimes, and social concerns of the narrative as well as in the expectations that both writers and readers have from the genre.

I have argued before that while the works of Staincliffe, Granger and Fritchley show an awareness of being written by and about white British women, they portray their main characters' interactions with those of other ethnic or national backgrounds as a prominent element in the narrative. Staincliffe also dwells on Sal's awareness of gays' and lesbians' problems mainly through her friendship with Chris, who, as the protagonist acknowledges in *Looking for Trouble*, "is quick to spot oppressive behaviour" and does not tolerate it from Sal (p. 173). However, as with ethnic characters, there is no assumption that having endured discrimination and prejudice automatically makes lesbians less likely to oppress others. In fact, one of the cases Sal deals with in *Bitter Blue* is the physical violence inflicted on a woman by her lesbian partner, "a story [Sal had] heard many times but it had always been a he before."[43]

Throughout the genre's evolution, detectives have frequently been "ambiguously positioned as an insider/outsider figure"[44] through whom both authors and readers "can explore in fantasy the border between the law and unlawfulness, between social norms and deviancy, between social security and individual risk."[45] As we have seen in *Running Scared, Stone Cold* and *Chicken Feed*, the contemporary sleuth's partially marginal position often derives from socio-cultural factors such as gender, sexual preferences, class, or ethnicity. These novels also illustrate the tensions experienced by the detective when facing a victim or a criminal who undergoes a different kind of discrimination becoming her racial or social other. To solve the case, the detective has to understand these others' circumstances while confronting the often deep differences between her and them.

As Sal witnesses the racist abuse against Mr. Ibrahim and Mrs. Ahmed, *Stone Cold* also focuses on her inability to understand the attackers' thoughts and behavior as well as on her inability to imagine the extent of the victims' pain. Having a daughter herself, she frequently wonders how the mother feels and copes when facing each violent incident. However, as Mrs. Ahmed does not speak English, Sal cannot communicate with her, empathize, or offer comfort. Even when she meets Mr. Ibrahim, who does know the language, what she gets is not the conversation that she would like to have but his statement that the council for whom Sal worked "should never have left [them living] there" (p. 231). *Stone Cold* suggests that there are limits to what the detective and the reader — who is often invited to identify with her — can know about o/Others unless the latter willingly share it. In Linton's words, there are times in which, whether supporting the victim or condemning the wrongdoer, "a forthright recognition of difference is a stronger response than trying to resolve it."[46]

However, in the case of characters like *Running Scared*'s Ganesh, it could be argued that not providing a more detailed explanation of the other's worldview risks confirming clichéd racial and cultural preconceptions. Fran's depictions of Ganesh's respect towards his family together with his occasional naivete could be read as placing him in a childlike role which sometimes becomes a source of humor. Ganesh would thus be presented more as a means to illustrate particular dimensions of Fran's personality and cultural identity rather than as a complex subject who deserves proper exploration on his own terms. This could be seen as a reification of the racial other precisely by a protagonist, Fran, who continually strives to challenge other people's preconceptions of her on the basis of her gender, poverty and homelessness. However, these potential interpretations of Ganesh's characterization and narrative roles are prevented by the fact that Fran acknowledges the traits in her character — lack of relatives, a fear of emotional or financial dependence and an individualistic, suspicious attitude resulting from living in the streets — which taint her impressions of her friend.

Each in its own way, Granger's *Running Scared*, Staincliffe's *Stone Cold* and Fritchley's *Chicken Feed* illustrate the importance of the figure of the ethnic other in the evolution of British detective fiction. In an article published in 2000, Birgitta Berglund envisions the genre's future as involving an increasing blurring of the frontier between the soft- and the hard-boiled, the growing vulnerability of the detective, and a greater number of "'ordinary' women who juggle families and careers while staying in charge of the case."[47] These three novels and others in their series show that these shifts were already taking place in the mid- and late 1990s, and are likely to continue. We are also likely to see characters from ethnic minorities play more frequent and important roles in narratives by and about white British authors, while their characterization and their interactions with the detective will be undertaken in more sophisticated ways. At the same time, as Mary Hadley suggests, there is likely to be a growing number of detective fiction writers from Asian, African and Caribbean backgrounds answering with their work the tenets of both traditional and contemporary works within the genre.[48] Finally, the expansion of Europe and other geopolitical changes will bring new immigrants to Britain with the potential to become the new ethnic other, triggering new social and literary questions to be explored as Britain reconfigures its self-image.

## Notes

The research leading to the writing of this paper was undertaken thanks to a Basque Government doctoral research grant.

1. Ann Granger, *Running Scared* (London: Headline, 1998). Subsequent citations will be in parentheses within the text.
2. Cath Staincliffe, *Stone Cold, Red Hot* (London: Allison & Busby, 2001). Subsequent citations will be in parentheses within the text.
3. Alma Fritchley, *Chicken Feed* (London: The Women's Press, 1998). Subsequent citations will be in parentheses within the text.
4. Adrienne Johnson Gosselin, preface to *Multicultural Detective Fiction: Murder from the "Other" Side*, ed. Adrienne Johnson Gosselin (New York and London: Garland, 1999), p. xii.
5. Ray B. Browne, "The Ethnic Detective: Arthur W. Upfield, Tony Hillerman, and Beyond," in *Mystery and Suspense Writers: The Literature of Crime Detection and Espionage*, eds. R.W. Winks and M. Corkigaw (New York: Scribners, 1998, vol. 2, pp.1029–1046), p. 1029.
6. Susan Elizabeth Sweeney, "Gender-Blending, Genre-Bending and the Rendering of Identity in Barbara Wilson's Gaudí Afternoon," in *Multicultural Detective Fiction*, ed. Adrienne Johnson Gosselin (pp. 123–142), p. 123.
7. Patricia L. Walton and Manina Jones, *Detective Agency: Women Rewriting the Hard-Boiled Tradition* (Berkeley: University of California Press, 1999), p. 51.
8. Mary Hadley, "New Directions in Crime: Innovative British Female Detective Writers," Ph.D. diss., University of Reading, 2000, p. 8.

9. Hadley, pp. 5 and 6.

10. Margaret Kinsman, "A Band of Sisters," in *The Art of Detective Fiction*, eds. Warren Chernaik, Martin Swales, and Robert Vilain (London: Macmillan, 2000, pp. 153–169), p.161.

11. Kinsman, p. 161.

12. Kinsman, p. 154.

13. Sweeney, p.124.

14. Walton and Jones, p. 63.

15. Sweeney, p. 125.

16. I will use the terms detective, crime and mystery fiction somewhat interchangeably when referring to *Chicken Feed, Running Scared* and *Stone Cold* since these works illustrate an increasing tendency to blur the boundaries between the three subgenres.

17. Marilyn J. Kurata, "The Serialization of the Detective," *Clues: A Journal of Detection* 22 (Spring–Summer 2001, pp 119–126), p. 119.

18. Walton and Jones, p. 46.

19. Walton and Jones, pp. 88–89.

20. Walton and Jones, p. 48.

21. Cath Staincliffe, *Looking for Trouble: A Sal Kilkenny Mystery* (Manchester: Crocus, 1994), unpaged. Subsequent citations will be in parentheses within the text.

22. Sweeney, p. 125.

23. Browne, p. 1029.

24. Browne, p. 1029.

25. Hadley, p. 16.

26. Hadley, p. 16.

27. Anita Naoko Pilgrim, "Blackening my Characters: Race and Characterisation in Lesbian Fiction," in *Beyond Sex and Romance? The Politics of Contemporary Lesbian Fiction*, ed. Elaine Hutton (London: The Women's Press, 1998, pp. 106–123), p. 111.

28. Pilgrim, p. 111.

29. Maureen Reddy, "The Female Detective: From Nancy Drew to Sue Grafton," in *Mystery and Suspense Writers*, eds. R.W. Winks and M. Corkigaw (pp. 1047–1067), p. 1063.

30. Reddy, p. 1062.

31. Marilyn Frye, "Some Reflections on Separatism and Power," in *The Lesbian and Gay Studies Reader*, eds. Henry Abelove, Michele Aina Barale and David M. Halperin (New York and London: Routledge, 1993, pp. 91–98), p. 92. First printed in *Sinister Wisdom* 6, Summer 1978.

32. Frye, p. 93.

33. Anna Wilson, "Death and the Mainstream: Lesbian Detective Fiction and the Killing of the Coming-Out Story," *Feminist Studies* 22. 2 (Summer 1996, pp. 251–278), p. 265.

34. Wilson, p. 266.

35. Elaine Hutton, "Good Lesbians, Bad Men and Happy Endings," in *Beyond Sex and Romance? The Politics of Contemporary Lesbian Fiction*, ed. Elaine Hutton (London: The Women's Press, 1998, pp. 175–201), p. 176.

36. Hutton, pp. 176–177.

37. Jill Radford, "Lindsay Gordon Meets Kate Brannigan — Mainstreaming or Malestreaming: Representations of Women Crime Fighters," in *Beyond Sex and Romance? The Politics of Contemporary Lesbian Fiction*, ed. Elaine Hutton (London: The Women's Press, 1998, pp. 80–105), p. 103.

38. Lynne Harne, "Beyond Sex and Romance? Lesbian Relationships in Contemporary Fiction," in *Beyond Sex and Romance? The Politics of Contemporary Lesbian Fiction*, ed. Elaine Hutton (London: The Women's Press, 1998, pp. 124–151), p. 124.

39. Harne, p. 125.
40. Harne, p. 124.
41. Walton and Jones, p. 21.
42. Walton and Jones, p. 21.
43. Cath Staincliffe, *Bitter Blue* (London: Allison & Busby, 2003), p. 192
44. Patricia Linton, "The Detective Novel as a Resistant Text: Alter-Ideology in Linda Hogan's Mean Spirit," in *Multicultural Detective Fiction*, ed. Adrienne Johnson Gosselin (pp. 17–36), p. 18.
45. Walton and Jones, p. 191
46. Linton, p. 23.
47. Birgitta Berglund, "Desires and Devices: On Women Detectives in Fiction," in *The Art of Detective Fiction*, eds. Warren Chernaik, Martin Swales, and Robert Vilain (pp. 138–152), p. 150.
48. Hadley, p. 18.

# 10

# Putting the "Black" into "Tartan Noir"

## PETER CLANDFIELD

Distinctive crime and detective novels are part of the international success of recent Scottish writing. Vivid urban settings and other cannily deployed genre conventions in these works have attracted the tag "Tartan Noir."[1] The novels most often grouped into this category, such as those of Ian Rankin, Christopher Brookmyre, and Denise Mina, are quite different from one another, and are most significantly and similarly "noir" not in their use of specific settings, plots, or tropes, but in their mutual interest — which they share not just with American writers but also with longer-established Scottish ones, such as William McIlvanney — in using genre-based fiction toward social commentary and critique.[2] Rankin's Inspector Rebus series has noted the enduring legacies of imperialism, sectarianism, and class inequity, and its recent installments also address prospects for Scotland in the current era of increasing political autonomy. More recently still, however, Brookmyre and Mina have looked even farther beyond historical Scottish-English or Catholic-Protestant tensions to register the enriching effects upon Scotland of postwar patterns of immigration and demographic evolution. They not only acknowledge the increasing racial and ethnic diversity of Scottish society, but suggest cautiously that the embrace of this diversity offers ways around traditional religious, social, and political tensions and toward a cosmopolitan future for Scotland, within and beyond the Britain of New Labor. Brookmyre, in his novels *A Big Boy Did It and Ran Away* (2001) and *The Sacred Art of Stealing* (2002), and Mina, in her *Garnethill* trilogy (1998–2001), use generic hybridity as a fitting vehicle for the investigation of cultural hybridity.

Scotland is less obviously multiracial than are parts of England, but it has a substantial population of people who identify as other than "white."[3] In Britain, the term "black" is often used politically to refer not only to people of Afro-Caribbean descent, but also to those of South Asian and even East Asian descent. The geographical reach of the British Empire, combined with the ideological ambition that regarded imperialized peoples as subjects of Britain, meant that the British isles received settlers from all over the world, particularly between the late 1940s and the early 1960s when labor was in demand. As journalist and cultural critic Yasmin Alibhai-Brown explains in her book *Imagining the New Britain,* "the experience of racism here on this island began a movement which brought together the activated ex-colonial subjects under the common term 'black.'"[4] Alibhai-Brown also points out that reliance on this broadly political definition of "black" can obscure the important differences among the experiences of particular groups of settlers.[5] Yet, in itself, the debate over the category "black" highlights the constructedness and context-specific nature of all concepts of race and points to the ways in which race itself is a fiction; political "blackness" is not necessarily more metaphorical than physical "blackness." Most of the fictional characters discussed in this essay are actually of South Asian heritage, but they identify themselves most often by skin color — or are constructed by their authors as so doing — thus foregrounding the political dimensions of "blackness." Therefore I will use "black," hereafter without quotation marks, to designate these characters collectively, while occasionally employing more specific terms to refer to individual characters.

Both Brookmyre and Mina are white, which may circumscribe some of their achievements in the depiction of multicultural Scotland, yet heighten others. Maureen T. Reddy, in her 2003 book *Traces, Codes and Clues: Reading Race in Crime Fiction,* points to pitfalls of bias and blindness for white writers who adopt non-white protagonists out of a "desire to offer a corrective to the more usual positioning of people of color as Others, villains and/or victims"; Reddy argues that the resulting "well-intentioned texts end up reinforcing racist attitudes by reinscribing binary thinking."[6] If neither Brookmyre nor Mina avoids all idealization of their black characters, both move well beyond binarism. Questions of racial otherness are largely peripheral to the actual crimes around which Brookmyre's and Mina's books turn. The tangential and sometimes implicit relationships between such questions and major plot events, however, may actually add to the books' value as social documents. They register multiethnicity in context as a contemporary Scottish fact. Black characters are among the *least* mysterious elements in these long and complicated narratives, but they emerge as strong anti-"noir"forces, who represent remedies for or alternatives to corruption, neurosis, and violence.

Alibhai-Brown notes that the contemporary British face "challenges which are likely to encourage clannish tendencies and magnify the fear that, as the centre cannot hold, things will fall even further apart." She cites the stresses of globalization and notes the reconfiguration of Britain as it devolves political power to Scotland (and other distinct societies within the United Kingdom) even as it becomes increasingly integrated into the European Union. "Yet many of the feelings being experienced by the English today — the loss of their cultural roots— have been our [immigrants'] fears for decades," she writes, suggesting that white Britons have much to learn from black ones.[7] Brookmyre and Mina promote the same view. In their depictions of black Scots— and through their popular and critical success— they do not so much move "others" from margin to centre, as suggest that the centre itself, both of Scotland as a nation and detective fiction as a genre, can hold more than traditional models might suggest.

## Hybridities and British Culture

Black British theorists, preeminently Stuart Hall, are insightful guides to ways in which cultural products both reflect and help to create collective identities, whether national, diasporic, or something in between. "Everybody now inhabits the popular," Hall has remarked,[8] and his work offers useful ideas about interactions between popular culture and the multiracial, multicultural society of postwar Britain. As Hall notes, high culture has not always been quick to address this evolving society.[9] Thus, it has lost some ground to emerging forms of popular culture, so that popular music and fashion, for instance, have become important arenas of social identity-formation and intellectual innovation. Reddy mentions the experience of black English detective novelist Mike Phillips, who "turned to crime fiction after setting out to write nongenre fiction but being stymied by the marketplace" (113). In using a popular genre to address contemporary questions of ethnicity and culture, "tartan noir" writers are, in a general way, drawing on the work done by black cultural producers— and others excluded from the mainstream — to establish popular forms as vehicles for serious inquiry. The work of Peter Stallybrass and Allon White, in *The Politics and Poetics of Transgression* (1986), helps to show how, in a sense, popular fiction is literature's "other." Stallybrass and White define one form of hybridity as resulting from "the inmixing of binary opposities, particularly of high and low, such that there is a heterodox merging of elements usually perceived as incompatible, ... [which unsettles] any fixed binaryism."[10] There is a structural parallel between generic and cultural hybridity: both find the "low-other"—the subordinated, disdained, and marginalized—inmixing with, and working to change the meanings and possibilities of, elements of the dominant social and cultural force.

Along with its theoretical implications, cultural hybridization brings practical concerns. New settlers may be changing Britain and Scotland, but their experience affects them too, and not always comfortably. Some indication of the current complexity of Scottishness is available from the 2002 collection *Being Scottish: Personal Reflections on Scottish Identity Today*, which presents one hundred short essays by what the editors describe as "one cross-section of Scottish people."[11] The Sudanese-born, Aberdeen-based novelist Leila Aboulela provides one snapshot of hybridity in her account of a blonde, blue-eyed Scottish friend who has converted to Islam: "I sat on a bench and watched Aisha and the children play ball. Aisha running, black headscarf, long coat, and me mesmerised by the children: Sudanese, Lebanese and half–Bengali, speaking in the Scottish accent of Froghall and Tillydrone."[12] Other contributors vary greatly in their emphases. Bashir Maan, a Glasgow city councilor born in what was to become Pakistan and resident in Scotland since 1953, notes that "[t]he Celts, who make up the majority of the present population of Scotland, are descended in part from the Aryans and so are the people of northern India, from where I come." Maan adds, "I now feel privileged in being Scottish."[13] In sharp contrast is the frustration of Robina Qureshi, a younger Glaswegian of Pakistani ancestry. Qureshi reports that her "childhood in Pollokshields, [a middle-class neighborhood] where there was— still is—a large Pakistani and Indian community," gave her a sense of belonging, but that her experiences of racism in the city at large have made it "difficult to feel Scottish." Qureshi's closing words capture the ambiguity of her situation: "I remember the first day of my wee boy's school, and the headmistress asking Ibrahim rather sternly 'And what is your name?' He replied, for the first time ever pronouncing his name 'Abraham' instead of 'Ibrahim'. Still pisses me off, that."[14] Unhappy at her son's Anglicization (or Christianization) of his name, Qureshi nevertheless describes both the "wee" boy and her "pisse[d] off" condition in a recognizably Scottish idiom, implicitly asserting a hybrid Scottish Muslim identity.

Certain white contributors to *Being Scottish* also shed light, albeit perhaps inadvertently, on Scotland's current demographics. Irvine Welsh, one of contemporary Scotland's best-known cultural figures, is sympathetic to the prospect of racial and cultural diversification, yet apt to discount its actual presence: he claims of Edinburgh that "[t]he lack of a substantial visible multi-ethnic presence, at least compared to cities in England, is quite visually overwhelming."[15] Welsh has ventured into detective territory with his novel *Filth* (1998), whose scheming, substance-abusing central character, Edinburgh detective sergeant Bruce Robertson, reads like a savage caricature of Rankin's Rebus. Robertson reluctantly investigates the racially motivated murder of a visiting Ghanaian journalist. His crass bigotry, like virtually everything else about him, is treated hyperbolically: He appears to hate not only black people but also virtually any group that can be labeled. His attitude toward others is presented as both pathological in itself and as arising from larger social dysfunctions (one clue that he stands for things beyond himself is the fact that his name remixes that of one of Scotland's heroes, Robert the Bruce). Still, the book itself is based substantially upon the assumption that black people are still others and outsiders in Scotland.

## *Ian Rankin and William McIlvanney: Clues to a Multicultural Scotland*

Ian Rankin also seems to see Scotland as largely uniracial. Despite the panoramic scope for which the Rebus books have (understandably) been praised, they limit non-white Scots largely to roles as nameless minor characters. A case in point is *Black & Blue* (1997), which reads as if designed in part to map contemporary Scotland for Rankin's international audience. The narrative does touch on the demographic evolution of Edinburgh, notably in a scene where Rebus takes his investigations to Niddrie, one of the bleakly dysfunctional residential areas on the city's periphery:

> He walked over to the corner shop, asked the kids a few questions, handed out mints to anyone who wanted one. He didn't learn anything, but ended up with an excuse to go inside. He bought a packet of extra-strong, put it in his pocket for later, asked the Asian behind the counter a couple of questions. She was fifteen, maybe sixteen, extraordinarily pretty. A video was playing on the TV, high up on one wall. Hong Kong gangsters shooting chunks out of each other. She didn't have anything to tell him.
> 'Do you like Niddrie?' he asked.
> 'It's all right.' Her voice was pure Edinburgh, eyes on the TV.[16]

Rebus's question suggests that he assumes, like Welsh, that Asians are still new to Scotland. However, the reference to the girl's local accent implies that he is out of date in his awareness. Then again, the text barely gives her a voice, and it fails to specify what part of Asia she comes from. Alibhai-Brown reports that "South Asian Britons own 70 percent of independent.... neighborhood shops,"[17] so perhaps the girl's environment indicates her heritage. Yet the Hong Kong movie implies that she could be of East Asian descent. The ambiguity is not so much provocative as frustrating: the passage hints that the girl has things worth telling, but offers few clues to allow the reader to imagine them.

Later in *Black & Blue* Rebus has an Indian restaurant meal which includes "a nan bread big enough to be plotting world domination."[18] This may be a witty piece of personification, but it also illustrates the way in which South Asian food gets more of Rankin's attention than do people who produce it. As in the corner shop episode, the services provided by Asians, or Asian Scots, seem to stand in for the people themselves. Alibhai-Brown points out the centrality to contemporary British culture of Indian food, which, she reports, is recognized as "'the national food of this country'" even by the right-wing *Telegraph* newspaper.[19] The Rebus series may show that Scotland partakes in British culinary multiculturalism (or multiculinarism?), but it also seems to bear out Alibhai-Brown's assertion that the "enthusiasm to receive and learn from the 'other'" has been slow to migrate beyond dietary matters.[20]

More observant and imaginative than the Rebus books where presences other than white are concerned are the slightly earlier detective novels of William McIlvanney, whose protagonist, Chief Inspector Jack Laidlaw, takes an intense interest in the evolution of Glasgow. In *The Papers of Tony Veitch* (1983), Laidlaw's investigation of the disappearance of the title character, a student, brings him into contact with several forms of ethnic and cultural otherness in the city. An Indian doctor has a voice that is "a startlingly pleasant contrast to the gutturals of Glasgow, soft with the consonants and original with the intonations."[21] While the doctor is treated as an honored guest in the city, Laidlaw goes on to note the established South Asian presence in Pollokshields. In itself, his impression that "[a] few" of the district's houses "had become self-contained Pakistani villages" (71) could suggest anxiety about demographic developments, but in the context of the book as a whole, the observation may also be linked with the suggestion that Glasgow, and Scotland, will benefit from cultural diversification.

The book's most complex encounter with enriching cultural otherness involves not Laidlaw directly, but Tony Veitch's friend and fellow student, Gus Hawkins. The thirteenth chapter opens with a quotation that is at first unidentified: "'... in this crowd deaf to its own cry of hunger and misery, revolt and hatred, in this crowd so strangely garrulous and dumb'" (80). The passage comes (in translation) from *Return to My Native*

Land (*Cahier d'un retour au pays natal*), the classic long poem (1939/56) by the Martinique writer Aimé Césaire, whose theme, according to editor and annotator Abiola Irele, is "what Césaire himself has formulated as 'la postulation agressive de la fraternité'— in other words, the passionate insistence upon a humane order of life as a principle of coexistence in an interdependent world."[22] Gus, reading Césaire in his parents' flat, is interrupted when his elder brother Jim, a scarred gangster, arrives with a fellow "hard man" and questions him about Tony, whom they claim owes them money: "Gus said nothing. Half of his head was still dealing with Aimé Césaire's *Return to My Native Land*. He hadn't worked out how he came to be standing ... with his brother and another heavy" (81). This passage, the first to name the work Gus has been reading, implies that there is a greater affinity between the working-class Glaswegian student and the Afro-Caribbean modernist writer than between Gus and his own aggressive brother. Violent criminality is a more fundamental form of otherness than race or ethnicity. Once Gus has reluctantly offered the heavies information on Tony's possible whereabouts, he returns to Césaire:

> But it was strange how he felt on the opposite side of the book from that with which he had identified before Jim and his friend came in. He felt he was one of the people Aimé Césaire was talking about rather than to.
>     'In this disarming town, this strange crowd which does not gather, does not mingle: this crowd that can so easily disengage itself, make off, slip away...' [87].

Gus draws on Césaire's poem to interpret his own uneasy relation to his native land, and thus the episode offers corroboration of Alibhai-Brown's suggestion that the dislocating experiences of modernity are ones about which white Britons can learn from postcolonial thinkers.[23]

The book's next chapter takes up the implication that imported energies may be antidotes to local dysfunctions. Laidlaw visits one of Tony Veitch's professors, who speaks pompously but revealingly of the young man's potential: "'You get a lot of first-generation academics here.... Perhaps among them there's an Attila of the mind — if you'll excuse a racially mixed metaphor. Someone who will reanimate our rituals by attacking them. Tony had possibilities in that direction'" (90–91). Tony turns out to have been murdered, the collateral victim of gangster machinations, but at the end of the book Laidlaw and Gus go on a pub crawl together as "a belated wake" (252) for the dead man, and their fraternization serves to emphasize that Gus too is a potential "Attila of the mind." Thus, the book as a whole adumbrates the idea that some form of "racially mixed" future is desirable for Glasgow and for Scotland at large.

McIlvanney's work exemplifies the hybridization between "genre" and "serious" fiction that Brookmyre and Mina also accomplish in their own distinct ways. While they do not somehow create all-encompassing representations of cultural hybridization in contemporary Scotland, their books reflect several specific kinds of demographic and cultural mixing. Their black characters are both more prominent than Rankin's or McIlvanney's and more fully settled as Scottish. Racial and cultural otherness is both more evident in Brookmyre's and Mina's books, and less "other," less exotic or foreign. Both writers acknowledge the political concerns of their fiction, but they differ notably in their styles. Brookmyre relies most heavily on physical action, including liberal amounts of violence, and on satirical punchlines. Mina is just as witty and just as abrasive linguistically — both writers make copious yet often inventive use of profanity — but is more interested in psychological complexities.

## Christopher Brookmyre: Black Action Heroes and Beyond

Brookmyre's books offer intriguing plots, engaging third-person narrative voices, and sharp dialogue. They also rely on comparatively simplistic moral schemes: The protagonists are progressive, public-spirited, brave and witty; their antagonists are often neo–Thatcherite and always ruthlessly dishonest, hypocritical, and self-important. The protagonists are proudly though not chauvinistically Scottish; the antagonists are often contemptuous of Scottish aspirations. The underdog protagonists triumph; the overconfident antagonists are violently destroyed or spectacularly humiliated. These features are appealing to a reader who shares Brookmyre's sympathies, but what makes the books particularly interesting is their combination of what Brookmyre himself has described as "rant[ing]" with less direct and more allusively intriguing kinds of commentary on contemporary issues.

Brookmyre's third novel, *Not the End of the World* (1998), the only one not focused on Scotland, illustrates this combination well. Set in Los Angeles, it divides the protagonist function between a visiting Scottish photojournalist, Steff Kennedy, and LAPD Sergeant Larry Freeman, who team up to defeat a religious demagogue, Luther St. John, and his millennial conspiracy to engineer a tidal wave that will destroy the city. Freeman is African American, and on a superficial reading stereotypically so: The first passage that describes his appearance presents him as a "[g]iant bald black guy carrying a gun" and highlights his tactical use of his intimidating qualities.[24] Though the narrative often identifies him by his first name alone, his emblematic surname (which evokes his descent from once-enslaved Africans) keeps his race in view for the reader. In itself, as Reddy notes repeatedly, the creation of a powerful and sympathetic African American detective, or a black action hero, is no longer particularly remarkable; moreover, Brookmyre's use of Larry to voice commentary on American questions of race is not always particularly convincing. Early on, he is made to compare two notorious race-related events of the 1990s in Los Angeles, the trials of the police who beat Rodney King and the murder trial of O. J. Simpson, and to decide that the Simpson acquittal "had used race and prejudice to twist justice in a way that was even more ugly than in Simi Valley in '92" (45). This reads like an arbitrary piece of editorializing: The text does not offer a direct explanation for Larry's view, instead having him go on to think of both trials in relation to a "wave" of social tension or neurosis affecting the city. It suggests first that the "wave" is a real phenomenon, but implies almost immediately after that what Larry diagnoses as the widespread sense that "Things Are Getting Worse" is rooted in whites' nostalgia for an era in which they enjoyed unquestioned dominance (45–46). In other words, the book seems here to betray a short attention span for specific intersections between racial issues and other social and political matters.

Yet Brookmyre also uses Larry in less aggressive ways, giving him considerable space as a character in his own right. He is present in the text for almost ten pages before his race is mentioned, and his main concern is initially with regaining equilibrium, both on and off the job, after he and his wife, Sophie, have lost their only son to meningitis. Sophie has just become pregnant again, and the text explores everyday details of their relationship alongside the various other plotlines. Sophie's own race emerges even more gradually than does Larry's: Only in the eighth chapter, after she has been present in several lengthy passages, is there a clear indication that she is white. As she and Larry discuss Luther St. John and his hostility to miscegenation, she remarks, "'Well, I guess we're pretty much condemned'" (151). The non-specificity of the printed page allows Sophie to be established as an individual before she is identifiable by race; thus it serves to de-emphasize Larry's and Sophie's potential otherness as an interracial couple, and to reinforce their belief that fear of racial mixing is at best a contemptible superstition. It is perhaps unfortunate that Brookmyre's fondness for quick punchlines manifests itself in Larry's response to Sophie's remark: "'I sure hope so,' Larry replied softly, 'Because if heaven's full of those motherfuckers, I *want* my ticket to hell'" (151). Still, the depiction of Larry and Sophie's liberal form of family values serves to lend credibility to the book's attack on the religious right: Larry is treated not simply as an action hero, but as someone with a personal stake in the future that is to be preserved by the defeat of extremism. Furthermore, Brookmyre uses Larry and Sophie's interaction to debunk facile invocation of Yeats's "The Second Coming" as a universal prophecy. "Poem was written way back at the other end of this century, she told him, after our last collective bout of cataclysmic heeby-jeebies. This stuff, this end-of-the-world-as-we-know-it stuff, had all happened before" (49). Just before the final defeat of St. John's conspiracy, Larry offers a memorable, profanity-enhanced, diagnosis of the ethnocentrism that lies behind belief in the apocalyptic properties of the millennium: "It was just a date on a calendar. The *West*'s calendar. Islam wouldn't be getting around to the year 2000 for a few centuries yet. In Tibet they'd moved into the third millennium back in the fucking seventies" (477).

A *Big Boy Did It and Ran Away* and *The Sacred Art of Stealing* bring a similar mixture of modes and techniques to the depiction of a black Scottish detective protagonist, Strathclyde Police Detective Inspector Angelique de Xavia. Like Freeman, de Xavia is constructed both in cinematically vivid ways and in more literary and nuanced ones. Brookmyre uses her both as a distinctive kind of action hero and, particularly in the second of the two books, as a vehicle for meditations on the complexities of ethnicity and affiliation both within and beyond Scotland.

De Xavia first appears some forty pages into *A Big Boy Did It and Ran Away*, at a Special Branch briefing on the activities of the Black Spirit, a "contract terrorist" whose mercenary approach makes him especially daunting.[25] De Xavia knows that she stands out among her colleagues, but it is her sex and (small) stature that she sees as most likely to mark her as an outsider:

> 'What's she doing here? Positive discrimination, probably. Look at the size of her, too. Wouldn't want that backing you up in a ruck, would you? Must be a graduate fast-tracker. More qualifications than collars. All brains and no bottle.'
> Maybe that wasn't what they were thinking, but she'd certainly heard all of it in her time [41].

Her nickname, "Angel X," first used by a colleague soon after her arrival (42), can be read as a play on the name of Malcolm X and thus, retrospectively, as a marker of race, like Freeman's surname. However, as in *Not the End of the World*, Brookmyre uses the ambiguities of page and text constructively. De Xavia's racial heritage is, like Larry's, introduced gradually, and in the context of her professional activities:

> When she was nine, someone wrapped a dogturd in newspaper, placed it on her doorstep, set it alight, rang the doorbell then fucked off. Her father answered the door and immediately began stamping on the flaming parcel, covering his slippers in shit. That was roughly how audacious the Black Spirit's activities were. Neither perpetrator had the guts to look their victims in the eye [57].

Similar assaults on the homes of immigrants and visible minorities have been more than isolated occurrences in postcolonial Britain,[26] and since the text has not yet mentioned the color of de Xavia's skin, the passage is perhaps most immediately intelligible to readers already aware of the context of such attacks. The passage may be read not only as depicting the experience of one black character, but also as addressing the (possible) experience of a group of (possible) black readers. Such orientation toward a multiracial audience, according to Reddy, is comparatively rare in works by white writers "writing the other."[27]

As Brookmyre's narrative details de Xavia's background, it shows how her Belgian-Indian-Ugandan heritage and Scottish upbringing have familiarized her with more than one way of being "other." The book continues to emphasize the connections between her history and her choice of profession, in some ways more convincingly than in others. Here, for instance, is the passage in which she is first identified by skin color:

> Human experience taught that when people wanted to look tough, they picked on easy targets. A short-arsed megalomaniac picked Jews.... A bloated Ugandan dictator picked Asians. And endless halfwit nonentities in Leeside had picked the wee darkie lassie with the funny name.
>
> Consequently, she had serious anger-management issues around the whole bullying thing. And the whole racism thing, and the whole sexism thing, though they were really just parts of the same whole [58].

While the suggestion that de Xavia's encounters with racism have affected her views on issues other than racial ones is plausible, the text seems unhelpfully general here in labelling bullying, racism, and sexism as parts of the same "thing." When the passage turns to her parents' Ugandan experience of "having been expelled by Amin with a two-year-old son and a baby well on the way," the effect is somewhat like the editorializing one of Freeman's reflection on Los Angeles race relations: "[I]f some of the [Scottish] locals called them names or left turd-bombs on their doorstep, then it was still a lesser form of racial abuse than what they'd already survived" (58). This assertion is not necessarily wrong, but there is no real basis for the reader to judge it, because the account of what occurred in Uganda in 1972 is brief and relatively superficial. Alibhai-Brown, herself among the Ugandan Asians displaced by Amin's actions, notes that these were facilitated partly by the support granted the dictator by Britain and other Western powers which saw him as a bulwark against communism (75).

The terrorist plot against which de Xavia is mobilized also touches on postcolonial questions in ways which, taken alongside the references to Amin's Uganda, could appear to cast Africa as the heart of backwardness. The Black Spirit — a Scot called Simon Darcourt who has been driven to his vocation by a combination of egomania and rage at crimes committed against his own family — is the book's main villain. His ultimate employer is a terror-broker, an enigmatic middle-easterner known as Shaloub N'Gurath: "[t]he Bill Gates of international terrorism, [t]he anti–Kofi Annan" (107). His actual mission, however, is on behalf of an African dictator, General Aristide Mopoza, illegitimate military ruler of "the former British colony of Sonzola" (44). Mopoza resents British assistance to his democratic rivals, and has commissioned an attack on a British target. The Sonzolan situation bears a disquieting if inexact resemblance to the scenario of a neo-imperialist narrative such as the 1978 film *The Wild Geese*, in which British forces play a paternal, policing role on behalf of one group of Africans, dependently pro-western, against another one, brutally anti-western.[28] Tariq Modood has pointed out that one problem with the categorization of both Afro-Caribbean and South Asian Britons as "black" is that the two groups have sometimes been pitted against each other by cultural racism. Modood describes two contrasting patterns: In one, Afro-Caribbean blacks are seen as more readily assimilable into the British mainstream than South Asians, particularly Muslims; in the other, South Asians are seen as more disciplined than Afro-Caribbeans and thus as more desirable settlers.[29] The treatment of Africans in *A Big Boy Did It and Ran Away* could be seen as reinforcing, at least incidentally, the latter stereotype.

It is possible to suspect, thus, that de Xavia's background amounts to a convenient means of offsetting any impression of racism given in other parts of the book, or that the attention to her otherness within the police force amounts to a stratagem for giving her the maverick status that all good detective protagonists have. As she moves toward confrontation with the Black Spirit, de Xavia's personal history becomes just one of many threads. While her childhood confrontations with racism are shown to have affected her choice of career (59–61), her main interests as a police officer do not necessarily lie in the area of race relations, as she is obliged to explain to one of her superiors:

> He'd been told she spoke three other languages. What were they? Gujurati? [sic] Urdu? Hindi? That would be invaluable in working with 'her community'.

'What community?' she asked. 'Catholics?'...
'You're...? I mean...? I thought ... But ... You say you're a *Catholic*?'
'No. I was brought up one though. I went to a Catholic school. My mum's Belgian. They take it very seriously.'
'I'm sorry. I'd no idea."
She resisted the temptation to observe that, in the Glesca Polis, folk thinking that she was a Jungle Bunny rather than a Jungle Jim was probably the only reason she'd got this far [153].

While de Xavia is impatient with identity-labeling, this passage takes time to address its possible complications. The final short paragraph alludes idiomatically to the intersection in "Glesca" of two forms of otherness: "Jungle Jim" is rhyming slang for "Tim," which in turn stands—in the parlance of football fans, for example—for a Glasgow Catholic (the presumptive descendant of Irish immigrants, some of whom would have been christened Timothy). The suggestion is that de Xavia's visible racial heritage has been less of an obstacle to her than her religious heritage would have been, if made visible, in the Protestant-dominated police force. The second de Xavia book, *The Sacred Art of Stealing*, will take up the intersection of racism and sectarianism in an adventurous way. De Xavia's Glaswegian speech idiom, as illustrated here and throughout the book, is also noteworthy. Scottish poet and critic Robert Crawford points out that Scots, the everyday speech idiom of working-class and many middle-class Scottish people in urban areas, is a hybrid kind of English, "which frequently quotes, re-accents, and realigns elements of English vocabulary, mixing them in a rich impurity with alien elements (in the same way that some 'Black English' works)."[30] Both Brookmyre and Mina take Scots to a further level of hybridity—the same one illustrated in the quotations above from Aboulela and Qureshi—by presenting black characters who speak naturally in Scots.

The fact that de Xavia thinks and talks in Scots means that there is often little to mark her as a cultural other for the reader, especially when super-hero elements of her character are highlighted. Having worked out Darcourt's plan, which involves the demolition of a dam at Dubh Ardrain, a hydroelectric power-station, and the consequent drowning of thousands, de Xavia proceeds to defeat the terrorist almost single-handed: The final sixty-odd pages of the book see "Angel X" in full action mode. The de-emphasis on de Xavia's background seems double-edged in its significance: It may be read as reflecting the principle that ethnicity and heritage should not affect an individual's professional life, but the illegibility of her heritage during the action phases of the novel also offers readers the opportunity, if they want it, to discount the earlier material attacking racism.

However, de Xavia's return in *The Sacred Art of Stealing* (2002) revises the scope and emphasis of her character in ways that indicate that her ethnicity is not simply a device for Brookmyre. *Sacred Art*, though not sedate, is Brookmyre's most restrained book. Perhaps in deference to post–September 11 sensibilities, it relies far less on violence than do its forerunners, concentrating instead on refinements of characterization and satire. De Xavia in this version is less professionally single-minded, and, as the book opens, she is suffering from aftereffects of her exertions against Darcourt and of September 11 itself. She is uneasy at the violence she has had to employ, while her superiors are angry at the collateral damage to the power station. Moreover, she is unwilling to go public with her side of the story: "Having so long resisted senior officers' desires to sideline her into the window-dressing role of a visibly Asian and female figurehead, she was buggered if she was going to be Strathclyde Police's ethnic posterchild now."[31] At the same time, she knows that her visible otherness has already complicated her relations with white male colleagues: "The attainment of official 'all right' status in their estimation required that she 'didn't make a big deal' about her ethnicity. That this was precisely what they were doing was an irony they were tragically inequipped to grasp" (41). The renewed attention in *Sacred Art* to such aspects of de Xavia's experience reads as a tacit acknowledgement that *Big Boy* has been superficial in its characterizations.

De Xavia deals with the stresses of her life in ordinary ways: being an action hero, she exercises, and she also follows football (soccer). Her interest in football, like her action-heroism, but on a more prosaic and perhaps more convincing level, serves to challenge stereotypical British perceptions of South Asians as unathletic.[32] Moreover, Brookmyre uses her choice of team both to accentuate her individualism and to look at Scottish sectarianism from an unexpected angle: De Xavia is a keen supporter of Glasgow Rangers. This powerful club has long been associated with the Protestant elements that have traditionally enjoyed economic and social ascendancy in Scotland; it has also been linked with neo-imperialist bigotry, particularly in the eyes of the mainly Catholic supporters of its archrival, Glasgow Celtic. Brookmyre's books repeatedly mock the mindless zeal of certain fans of the "Old Firm," as the two big Glasgow clubs are known. While residual Scottish sectarianism may be an obvious satirical target, Brookmyre's treatment of it serves to acknowledge the diversities and contradictions within whiteness itself that both Alibhai-Brown and Reddy see as often-ignored by white writers.[33] More adventurous, however, is the way in which Brookmyre examines the constructive uses of football-fandom by having de Xavia embrace Rangers, which might be expected to repel her. Her adoption of the club dates back to her reaction against Celtic-supporting persecutors of her schooldays: "All she knew was that the people who hated her also hated Rangers, and they seemed to hate them for a lot of the same reasons. They were the others: different, alien, to be closed ranks against, to be defined as apart from, to be despised" (53). This passage serves pointedly to defamiliarize, and expose as outdated, the traditional sectarian opposition between Protestant and Catholic, establishment and underdog.

De Xavia's choice of team, like her choice of career, finds her appropriating and adapting colonial instruments to her own ends. In a small way, the choice — and her acceptance by mainstream Rangers fans — hybridizes Rangers, helping to shift the club away from its own stereotyped status as an emblem of intolerant Protestantism. But if de Xavia's support for Rangers presents cultural affiliation in Scotland as something increasingly elective, rather than given or dictated by ethnic heritage, it is not without its complications. She consciously avoids using her footballing sympathies as "a cheap route to acceptance and approval" from her police colleagues (50), so that her allegiance remains not fully integrated into her life. Football cannot solve all her problems, much as her presence in the police cannot overcome all of the force's blindspots as readily as she has overcome the Black Spirit in the more simplistic, action-based world of *Big Boy*.

On her thirtieth birthday, paged away from a Rangers match, de Xavia finds herself dealing with a bizarre bank robbery turned hostage-taking. She succeeds in getting into the bank by abseiling onto its roof, but herself falls hostage to the masked gang of robbers. The gang members, however, are oddly customer-friendly: They entertain their hostages with take-offs on modernist art and drama, whose creators' names— Chagall, Dali, Ionesco— they have adopted. The gang leader, Jarry, gets de Xavia's attention through his unconventional courtesy to his hostages, which the two of them discuss via allusions to *Waiting for Godot* (146). After the gang has cleverly escaped, she finds herself admiring their audacity and relishing the vexation of her self-inflated superiors (162). Her interest in Jarry is reciprocated: "He liked her accent, the sound of her voice" (172). They meet in a Glasgow bar, then travel clandestinely together to Paris. They each have professional motives— hers being to monitor the gang's activities, and his to utilize the police in his complicated scheme to gain revenge on an American gangster who has blackmailed him into crime and murdered his father. However, their developing personal relationship becomes just as important as the crime-based threads of the plot. Jarry is really an American called Zal Innez, and an artist by profession; he and de Xavia explore the Louvre. Their chemistry is enhanced by his own hybrid heritage: he is the child of a Mexican mother and a Scottish father who "went from Garnethill to Vegas" (306), but missed Glasgow and so "practically mythologised" it for his son (307). Innez's father even proves to have been an ardent yet non-bigoted Rangers supporter (302). This may be a conspicuous coincidence even by the standards of genre fiction, but it does allow the book to extend its distinctive take on racism, sectarianism and elective loyalties, as de Xavia explains to Innez the significance of Rangers to her own life:

> That philosophy I learnt at Ibrox [the Rangers stadium] still applies. I don't compromise in order to fit in, and I'm not giving in to any arsehole who wants to make me feel as if I don't belong wherever I put myself.'
> 'We're alike in a lot of ways,' Zal said. 'It's not that we don't belong, it's that we've learned we don't need to' [305].

As this passage emphasizes, vocation, not race or ethnicity, is the otherness that complicates their relationship. The passage also, though, sets up the end of the book, which will complicate easy ideas about self-definition.

The main crime plot resolves neatly: Innez and his colleagues defeat their gangster nemesis, in the process allowing de Xavia and her colleagues to arrest a leading Glasgow crime boss for drug-trafficking. However, the book's ending shifts back to complication and ambiguity. De Xavia and Innez are forced to part, though perhaps not permanently; meanwhile, the outcome of the crime plot has gained de Xavia a new level of acceptance within the police, but one she no longer wants: "After all those years of isolation and defiance, it was their efforts to make her feel she belonged that most confirmed she didn't" (404–05). The closing pages detail de Xavia's decision to leave Scotland to join an elite "pan–European counterterrorist operation" (324) based in Paris. The ending confirms the book's revision of *Big Boy* and implicitly acknowledges that no one narrative can be definitive in its account of the choices and complications of hybridity. It leaves the way open for a further de Xavia novel, but also leaves few clues as to the form it may take.

## Denise Mina: More Than "A Bit of the Other"

De Xavia certainly qualifies as a "post-colonial detective" according to the definition recently proposed by Ed Christian: "[T]hey are usually marginalized in some way, which affects their ability to work at their full potential; they are always central and sympathetic characters; and their creators' interest usually lies in an exploration of how these detectives' approaches to criminal investigation are influenced by their cultural attitudes."[34] Maureen O'Donnell, central character of Denise Mina's *Garnethill* trilogy, is not a police officer, but she too operates in ways that fit Christian's definition. Sexually abused as a child by her father, Maureen has also survived a breakdown brought on in her early twenties by the after effects of the abuse and by the inability of most of her lower-middle-class Catholic family to acknowledge what has happened to her. Like McIlvanney's Gus Hawkins, she uses intellectual interests to gain perspective on her home environment: She has a degree in art history, which she aspires to build upon, and she is a committed feminist. However, as the trilogy's first book, *Garnethill*, opens, she finds herself working at a dull job and involved in an unhealthy affair with a psychologist, Douglas Brady, whom she has met at Glasgow's Northern Psychiatric Hospital during her treatment for the breakdown. When Douglas is murdered in her flat — "at the top of Garnethill, the highest hill in Glasgow"[35] — she is a prime suspect. Like Brookmyre's de Xavia books, the trilogy depicts the police critically: Though not all bigoted or brutal, they are often self-interested or simply obtuse. Maureen must rely on her own mettle, and that of a few allies, in order to survive the complicated physical and psychological dangers that the initial crime unleashes on her.

Mina's characterizations are notable, especially next to some of Brookmyre's, for their complexity. The only member of Maureen's family who accepts her account of the abuse is her brother Liam, and he is also a drug dealer, though uneasy about this vocation. Maureen's other main ally, her best friend Leslie, is sympathetic but not always reliable. Douglas too is complex. His relationship with Maureen is predatory, since although he has not actually treated her, he knows her history and her fragility; he is also, as Maureen has just discovered at the time of his death, married. Yet he proves to have been killed because of his conscience-driven inquiries into a series of sexual crimes against patients at the "Northern," the psychiatic hospital. Their perpetrator and his killer, a fellow psychologist called Angus Farrell, has been one of Maureen's own doctors; in a further twist of irony, Farrell, a kind of Jekyll/Hyde figure, has been by far the most effective of those who have treated her. Maureen draws upon her memory of his professional help even as she struggles to uncover his personal crimes, to bring him to some form of justice, and — in the second and third books — to escape his counter-attacks.

The trilogy's black characters initially seem as incidental as Maureen's regular visits to the corner shop that one of them, Mr. Padda, runs. Over the 1350-page course of the three books, however, these characters are revealed as crucial presences both in Maureen's Glasgow and — in less straightforward and particularly interesting ways — in Mina's narrative.

During one of Maureen's early interrogations, DCI Joe McEwan, the ego-tistical detective leading the investigation of Douglas's murder, tries to provoke her by implying that feminism entails hostility to men. Her response is typically sharp: "'Yeah, feminists don't like men and Martin Luther King picked on white people. You don't know many feminists, do you, Joe?'" (178). Here Maureen aligns herself, as a feminist, with another principled form of "otherness." As a white person who embraces the mar-ginalized, she is a kind of mirror image of de Xavia, a black person who claims a place near the centre of power.

Black people provide Maureen with practical as well as rhetorical sup-port at key points throughout the trilogy. Pursuing her own reconstruc-tion of the night of Douglas's murder (which she is unable to remember, having been drunk), she asks Mr. Padda if he saw "anyone covered in blood walking down the road a week last Tuesday." His response both alludes wryly to the more barbaric rituals of Glasgow culture and hints at his and Maureen's mutual respect: "'No, dear,' he said, and smiled. 'Saturdays, yes, often, Tuesdays, no'" (285). Maureen's investigations pay off, allowing her to befriend one of the victims of Farrell's crimes. When the woman, Siob-hain McCloud, is questioned insensitively by the police and re-trauma-tized, it is her physician, Dr. Pastawali, "a tall Asian man in his fifties, with dark sad eyes" (307), who, although initially unwilling to be called out at night, succeeds in calming her. Like McIlvanney's nameless Indian doc-tor, but in more detail, Pastawali embodies a tribute to the contribution made to Britain by medical personnel from the former empire; his brief role also neatly emblematizes the trilogy's suggestion that multi-ethnicity offers potential therapy for some of Scotland's ills.

Like Brookmyre, Mina uses the indeterminacies of the page to avoid defining her major characters by race or ethnicity. The most important black character in *Garnethill* is a nurse, Shan Ryan, who has his own ideas about Douglas's death and is eventually persuaded, over the course of the book's longest and most crucial chapter (356–81), to share them with Mau-reen. Alongside its contribution to the novel's plot, the gradual and com-plicated way in which Maureen and Shan establish their alliance offers a microcosm of a process of bridging difference and overcoming mistrust. Shan appears on a list of former Northern staff that Maureen has obtained from a porter she knows from her time at the psychiatric hospital. Mau-reen initially reads Shan's name as "Sharon" (280). Once Shan's flatmate has explained the confusion, Maureen visits him at his workplace, even though he is a potential suspect now that she knows he is male. While his (Hindi) first name may have helped to obscure his identity for Maureen at first, it has also given her a clue to his heritage:

> She had guessed that he was half–Asian from his name and she was right. His skin was dark and he had shiny black hair but his almond eyes were khaki green.... . He stood noncommittally behind the honey-blonde nurse and looked at Maureen expectantly. His front teeth were large and straight and white, his broad lips seemed unusually red [360].

The details of Shan's appearance seem to cast him as exotic, and their effect is heightened by the juxtaposition of his colleague, a traditional figure of a nurse. Yet, Maureen's ability to predict his heritage from his name indicates that racial mixing is an established fact of Glasgow life: People such as Shan may be striking individually, but are not foreign collectively. The passage thus shows Shan as a kind of familiar "other."

Shan is wary of Maureen and insists that they go to Glasgow airport in order to discuss the case: "'Paki guy with green eyes talking to a white lassie? There aren't many places in Glasgow where that wouldn't be noticed'" (366). Airports, Shan implies, represent zones where cultural norms do not have their usual force. His application to himself of the derogatory epithet "Paki" suggests weary awareness of everyday racism in the city. Yet even as they hint at ways in which his routine experience is affected by perceptions of his otherness, Shan's words here, and throughout his and Maureen's talk, also voice his Scottishness. Moreover, Shan's reticence has as much to do with the case as with race: He suspects and fears Farrell, and with reason, since the psychotic psychologist has already murdered the helpful porter and is closing in on others who may be capable of exposing him.

Maureen is equally uneasy with Shan, but mainly because of his masculinity rather than his ethnicity, although his reassurances to her evoke his generalized awareness of his own otherness: "'I'm sorry if I gave you a fright. I forgot about what's happened to you. You don't even know who I am. I suppose I could be anyone to you'" (371). In a further gesture of trust-building, Shan then identifies Farrell to Maureen — though "in an undertone" that the reader cannot hear — as the Northern rapist. Shan and Maureen bond further when she offers him a drink: "'Auch,' he said, clearly gasping. 'Auch, aye, get us a whisky if they've got it'" (371). One ethnonational stereotype that the trilogy leaves unchallenged for most of its length is that which sees Scots as natural lovers of alcohol, though the indication that Shan too enjoys a drink is a canny repudiation of the idea that this fondness— and Scottishness more generally — is a genetic rather than a cultural phenomenon. Shan, who has worked with Douglas and been privy to some of his investigation of the rapes, reveals both the extent of the investigation and the depth of Douglas's guilt over his failure to stop Farrell (374–75). Shan and Maureen work out that Farrell (still unidentified to the reader) has killed Douglas to silence him and has manipulated the police into suspecting Maureen in order to divert their attention from Siobhain McCloud, who can link him to the earlier crimes. As the chapter ends, Maureen and Shan seal their alliance by agreeing to "go out and get pissed together one night" (381)—after Maureen has dealt with Farrell. Shan has both a structural and a moral role in the novel: While he takes no physical part in Maureen's detective-work, he gives her both crucial information and vital endorsement of her plan to go outside the law in her campaign for justice.

The resolution of the novel's main plotline is noticeably simpler than the interpersonal negotiations along the way. Maureen lures Farrell to a remote island holiday resort, Millport, where she gives him coffee spiked with bad LSD and leaves him, along with an untraceable note explaining what he has done, for the police. DCI McEwan suspects her involvement but can prove nothing. Before being overwhelmed by the effects of the drug, however, Farrell has taunted her about her father's abuse; meanwhile, Liam has warned Maureen that her father himself, who had fled Glasgow after abusing her, has returned to the city. *Exile*, the middle volume, sees Maureen struggling to deal with this knowledge. Farrell, incarcerated and recovering from his bad trip, is harassing Maureen with letters, and the police continue to question her about the events at Millport. Maureen is working ineffectively at the underfunded women's shelter that Leslie manages, and their friendship is fraying. When a client of the shelter, Ann Harris, disappears, Maureen devotes herself to detective work as a diversion from her own problems.

After an enigmatic opening section that proves to be linked to the disappearance, the book's first chapter finds Maureen waking beside a new boyfriend, who is at first simply a pronoun:

> She peeled their skins apart, trying hard not to wake him, but he felt her stir. He peered around at her through sleep-puffed eyes.
> "Kay?' he murmured.
> 'Yeah,' breathed Maureen.[36]

"He" is soon given a first name, Vik, but throughout the chapter he remains a sketchy presence, and one about which Maureen herself is ambivalent: "He was the only thing in her life that wasn't about the past but it was the wrong time for a fresh chapter and coy new discoveries" (12). Vik is in fact Shan Ryan's cousin, Vikram Patak. He takes on ethnicity even more gradually than has Shan; even his name is revealed incrementally. By itself, "Vik" could suggest Slavic heritage (Viktor), or simply be a variation on the standard "Vic." The full first name arrives in the book's fourth chapter, where Katia, an odiously pert co-worker of Maureen's who has also dated Vik, asks, "'And how's the lovely Vikram?'" (32). Vik(ram)'s name, like de Xavia's recollection of racist pranks against her family, hails readers who share, or are at least aware of, the character's background.

There is an important difference between the way in which Vik manifests in the book and the way in which he turns out to have arrived in Maureen's life: The book's narrative sophistication (its use, in theoretical terms, of the difference between story and plot) serves to develop his role and its significance gradually, even though his relationship with Maureen has — as we learn well into the book — begun abruptly and semi-accidentally:

> When Vik's cousin Shan had introduced them to each other in the Variety bar Maureen couldn't believe her luck. Vik was tall and slim, his hair as black as Guinness, his eyes deep brown and adoring. That first night they'd got drunk and giggly together and fell back up the hill to her flat at closing time [173].

Stuart Hall, in his 1992 essay "What Is This 'Black' in Black Popular Culture?," comments on the contemporary commodification of cultural heritage and cultural difference: "[T]here's nothing that global postmodernism loves better than a certain kind of difference: a touch of ethnicity, a taste of the exotic, as we say in England, 'a bit of the other' (which in the United Kingdom has a sexual as well as an ethnic connotation)."[37] Although the Guinness simile in the passage just quoted links him to Maureen's own Irish heritage, Vik *is* initially "a bit of the other" for Maureen, but he becomes considerably more than this for the trilogy: He is the major constructive presence in Maureen's life during the second and third books.

For Maureen, Vik's normality, not his blackness, is the most exotic thing about him, and also the most problematic for their relationship. She fears that his good nature is incompatible with her own "soiled and melancholy" condition (13); at one point she hides from him, unable to face his friendliness (104–105). Vik is not saintly and loses patience with Maureen's elusiveness; indeed, the description of their relationship quoted above comes midway through a chapter in which he confronts her about her reluctance to commit to him —"Is it because I'm black?" (172). They discuss matters while sharing a joint:

> 'Don't ye have some wisdom from the East to help me out?'
> 'Don't ask me, hen, I'm frae Wishaw' [178].

Vik's gentle rebuke to Maureen's half-joking Orientalism confirms his Scottishness; it also enables the text explicitly to disavow the idea that he represents wisdom, or anything beyond himself. "'I'm nice to you because I'm a nice guy and I like your bum,'" he adds (178). Yet the text soon hints at Vik's therapeutic qualities. At his prompting, Maureen tells him a little of her psychological history, and he responds with understanding and tact expressed physically: "[H]is fingertips hardly touched her skin as he soothed her" (179). But the next morning, after he startles her and she reacts violently, they quarrel and he departs in anger, though he leaves behind a lighter that will serve as a kind of proxy over much of the rest of the work. Maureen's inner struggle to create "a fresh chapter" with Vik runs concomitantly over the trilogy's final two thirds with her more material battles against Farrell and other antagonists.

Maureen spends much of the second half of *Exile* in London, where Ann Harris was last seen. As a Scot, Maureen herself becomes something of an other in London. Before she leaves, her brother Liam warns her about "pig ignorant" Londoners: "'[T]hey hate us, they hate the Scots'" (201). An ironic response from Leslie, however, suggests that Liam's words illustrate reciprocal Scottish prejudice: "'How dare they,' said Leslie, smiling at Maureen. 'Those racist pricks'" (201). The narrative goes on to suggest that racism is stronger in Scotland than in parts of Britain with larger black populations. Before catching a bus south, Maureen leaves Vik a message, and when he arrives to see her off just as the bus pulls out, a drunken fellow passenger misinterprets her attempts to communicate through the window: "'I know,' he said, smiling kindly, "I hate they Pakis too'" (231). This episode echoes when Maureen contacts Ann Harris's sister in London, and learns that the woman and her black English husband have felt unable even to visit Scotland because of racism (272).

While the narrative acknowledges that English anti–Scottishness is less virulent than other forms of prejudice, it also highlights Maureen's affinity with more visible others. The old classmate with whom she stays in London offers her pamphlets with "mesmerizingly bad drawings of Aryan Jesus telling some black people what to do" (287). Later, when Maureen's investigations have combined with her vulnerabilities to leave her endangered and bedraggled, she asks a passer-by for directions to a police station: "'Yes dear,' he said, 'down there, under the bridge, third on your right. Canterbury Crescent.' His accent was African and his yellow and brown eyes were sad and sorry for her" (387). The man embodies one particular form of cultural hybridity: He is at once a Londoner, a guide to the territory, *and* an African, and the text treats him as ordinary in both capacities.

London is depicted as a place where otherness, physical and cultural, is almost a norm. One of the most exotic people Maureen meets there is a woman who looks "like a tiny, very beautiful tropical frog." Yet the woman's voice reveals her as an expatriate Glaswegian, and their shared Scottishness draws them together:

> The woman smiled at her and leaned over, holding on to the bar. She held out her hand.
> 'Kilty Goldfarb,' she said.
> Tickled, Maureen barked a laugh. 'Fuck off,' she said. 'That's not your name.'
> Kilty laughed too, delighted at Maureen's reaction. 'It is,' she insisted. 'My family were Polish and my granny made up the name Kilty in honour of her new homeland' [254].

After Maureen has apologized and introduced herself, they share lunch at what Kilty refers to as "an exotic wee place," which proves to be a globally known one that serves "McFood" (256). Kilty becomes one of Maureen's staunchest supporters. Though her arrival is highly coincidental, it does allow the narrative to broaden and complicate its account of Scottishness still further. Kilty's name, like Shan's love of Scotch or de Xavia's love of Rangers, shows that Scottish identity is created or claimed, not necessarily given or inherited.

Maureen is also aided in London by another, less amusing, fellow Scot, Mark Doyle. He is the brother of Pauline Doyle, a friend from Maureen's time in hospital who has subsequently committed suicide. Awareness of Vik's continued interest has buoyed Maureen, but as *Exile* ends she is back in Glasgow and seemingly growing closer to Doyle on the strength of the traumas they have in common. Significantly, though, this development is conveyed through one of the text's rare excursions into Vik's point of view: Having seen Maureen with Doyle in a café near Garnethill (444–45), he repairs to the nearby Variety bar hoping she will stop in: "He sat on a bar stool, watching the door for four hours, pretending to chat to Shan about Gram Parsons and Motherwell's lineup ... but Maureen never came" (446). Vik here becomes the reader's proxy, trying anxiously to interpret Maureen's actions, but forced to wait for developments.

At the beginning of the trilogy's final volume, *Resolution*, with Farrell's trial upcoming and its outcome uncertain, Maureen appears worse off than ever. She finds herself contemplating drastic action to protect her sister Una's baby against her father, who has partially re-insinuated himself into the family, though alcoholism has left him enfeebled. Maureen's own drinking is out of control, as an episode in the corner shop indicates memorably. On this occasion, she is served by Mr. Padda Junior, the owner's teenage son, who combats his boredom by behaving "as if he was in a Bollywood musical": "'The usual?' he asked, pointing at her and pulling the trigger."[38] Having sold Maureen whisky, he remarks, "'You fairly knock it back, don't ye?'" (67). The passage is typical of the trilogy's tonal mixing: Padda Junior is amusingly annoying in his rudeness but absolutely and soberingly correct in his diagnosis, and Maureen's response—"She made a mental note to use another offy [off-license] in future" (67)—clearly arises from embarrassment rather than aversion to Indian films or their fans. A little paradoxically, Padda Junior's obnoxious behaviour helps to confirm Mina's respect for her Indo-Glaswegian characters: they are allowed to be individuals at the same time as they are shown as valuable parts of the city's evolving culture.

At home, Maureen uses Vik's lighter on a cigarette and finds herself remembering him as "the almost-boyfriend"—as, it emerges, she has been doing for several months. However, directly after a chapter which looks in on Farrell and his sinister plans for Maureen, Vik reappears. As they talk in bed, he again demonstrates tactful empathy; he also brings up Maureen's interest in art: "'My wee cousin takes me to exhibitions all the time and I kept expecting to see you there. She's training to be a curator. ... You should do that" (125). As Vik drives Maureen across the city the next morning, the text comments slyly on the way in which it has linked Vik to Maureen's hopes for an ordinary life: "She imagined being seen from the outside by some mystery viewer. She'd look happy, at peace, loved and cosseted, like a real person with a life and a future" (130). Maureen's obsession with her past, though, is powerful, and finally she decides she must kill her father. With Mark Doyle's help she embarks on a plan to do so, but at a crucial moment Doyle betrays the fact that he has been working for Farrell, and Maureen realizes that the psychologist has manipulated her into the attack in order to destroy her credibility (379–80). Maureen escapes the trap, but only barely. As the trial progresses, her allies rally around her and bond among themselves: Shan and Kilty begin dating (439), in a development that seems to draw on the neatness of traditional comedy (in which eligible and sympathetic characters are paired off) in order to evoke a hopeful hybrid future for Scotland.

Yet only in its final one-page chapter, after Farrell has been defeated, does the trilogy affirm Maureen's future. She sits contemplating a painting, in a way so detached as to suggest at first that she may be dreaming or delusional. Incrementally, the text fills in details: She is in the Winter Palace in St. Petersburg, and the reality of the situation is confirmed by the fact that she must "watch her time [because] [t]here was only one English-speaking AA meeting per week in St. Petersburg and it began in an hour" (461). And she is not alone:

> He sat down next to her on the bench and took her hand lightly in his.
> 'All right?' she whispered, still looking out of the window. 'Are ye having a good time?'
> 'Aye,' said Vik. 'Oh, aye' [461].

These, the final words of the trilogy, recapitulate Vik's contribution to the work as a whole: His presence is understated but vital. As in *Exile*, his perception closes the text; as in *Exile*, he takes on a structural importance beyond his immediate role in Maureen's life.

Vik, Shan, and the trilogy's more minor black characters are most important exactly because they are ordinary and largely peripheral to the world of violence, uncertainty, and betrayal in which Maureen is trapped. They are not action heroes (if any character is, it is Maureen); indeed they take virtually no part in the physical events involving Farrell, Doyle, or Maureen's father. They serve as a moral reference-point for the trilogy: a source of the stability that both the police and Maureen's own family fail to provide. Nicholas Christopher has observed that a classic noir narrative is typically devoid of "bystanders— innocent or even neutral,"[39] but in Mina's trilogy, such untainted characters— Vik above all, but also Shan and Kilty — show Maureen the way back from the noirish world. If Brookmyre's and Mina's use of black characters against "noir" might be seen as idealistic or schematic, such an impression is counteracted by these characters' integration into long narratives whose full complexity probably cannot be conveyed in an essay such as this one. Understatement is particularly difficult to analyze without distortion, but Mina's use of it allows her deftly to show, rather than ostentatiously to assert, the everyday value of people like Vik to contemporary Scotland.

## Conclusion

While both Brookmyre and Mina present black people as integral parts of Scottish society, they do so at a certain cost of de-emphasizing the other, non–Scottish heritages of their major black characters. Vik says little about his friends and relations other than Shan; there are brief references to his mother, but there are even fewer details of his family history than Brookmyre provides of de Xavia's.[40] However, any impression that Brookmyre and Mina ultimately champion what amounts to assimilationism, rather than genuine multiculturalism, is complicated by the fact that the endings of their narratives see their central characters either having left Scotland or planning to do so. Alibhai-Brown suggests that "[i]t might be useful ... to think European" for progressive Britons of all races or cultural backgrounds. "No single ethnic group in the European Union is big enough to be a majority," she notes, adding that "[t]here is something hugely reassuring" about this fact.[41] Brookmyre and Mina implictly endorse this suggestion that Europe itself is becoming a zone of cultural mixing and hybridization.

The attractiveness of cultural hybridity as a social ideal and a theoretical concept can lead to overestimation of the value of individual examples. Social anthropologist Pnina Werbner comments on what she calls "an unwarranted tendency to use ... artistic 'texts'—films, novels, poetry, popular music — as documentary springboards for global theorising about society and culture."[42] Brookmyre's and Mina's novels are only two localized examinations of hybridity. Stuart Hall remarks that popular culture "is *profoundly* mythic. It is a theatre of popular desires, a theatre of popular fantasies."[43] In these terms, Brookmyre and Mina might be best described as revising myths of noir, and of the detective genre more generally, in order to revise larger cultural myths of race and otherness.

## Notes

1. The tag "Tartan noir" is said to have been coined by James Ellroy: see Terrence Rafferty, "Tartan Noir," *Gentlemen's Quarterly* December 2002: 186. It is used also by British commentators, including crime writers themselves. It appears on the front cover of the British Abacus paperback edition of Christopher Brookmyre's second novel, *Country of the Blind* (1997), for example, where it is attributed to a newspaper review in *The Independent*. Profiling another leading writer associated with "Tartan Noir," Val McDermid, in February 2002 in the Glasgow *Sunday Herald,* Denise Mina comments on the evolution of British crime fiction:
Perceptions of crime fiction have fundamentally changed in the past twenty years, largely because of the work of writers like McDermid and [Ian] Rankin. The new wave of British writing came as a result of the influence of American urban noir.... British, and particularly Scottish, crime fiction has moved the genre into new disturbing areas.... McDermid says that straight literature "Became so self-reverential in the eighties and nineties that it all but disappeared up its own arse. The success of crime fiction shows that there is a place for narrative." Available at www.valmcdermid.com.
2. In a recent article, "Tough Guys with Long Legs: The Global Popularity of the Hard-Boiled Style" (*World Literature Today,* January–April 2004), American crime novelist and academic J. Madison Davis suggests that noir "retains its vitality around the world both because of its ability to carry serious social commentary and its malleability within its familiar form and style" (40). However, Davis seems to overlook the possibility that noirish sensibilities may be to some extent indigenous to cultures other than American ones.
3. According to 1991 Census figures, the non-white population of Scotland as a whole was only about 1.25 percent, but for Glasgow, Scotland's largest city, the figure was 3.25 percent. Just over 2 percent of the city's population identified as Pakistani, Indian, or Bangladeshi. This figure represents just under 15,000 people, more than half of whom were born either in Scotland or in England. The census also identified some

3000 Chinese and 1500 Afro-Caribbean Glaswegians. See Suzanne Audrey, *Multiculturalism in Practice: Irish, Jewish, Italian and Pakistani Migration to Scotland* (Aldershot: Ashgate, 2000), 68–69.

4. Yasmin Alibhai-Brown, *Imagining the New Britain* (London: Routledge, 2001), xii; see also Stuart Hall, "New Ethnicities," in David Morley and Kuan-Hsing Chen, eds., *Stuart Hall: Critical Dialogues in Cultural Studies* (London: Routledge, 1996), 441.

5. Alibhai-Brown, xii–xiii; see also Tariq Modood, "'Difference', Cultural Racism and Anti-Racism," in Pnina Werbner and Tariq Modood, eds., *Debating Cultural Hybridity: Multi-Cultural Identities and the Politics of Anti-Racism* (London: Zed Books, 1997), 169-70.

6. Maureen T. Reddy, *Traces, Codes, and Clues: Reading Race in Crime Fiction* (New Brunswick, NJ: Rutgers University Press, 2003), 154.

7. Alibhai-Brown, 4.

8. Julie Drew, "Cultural Composition: Stuart Hall on Ethnicity and the Discursive Turn." (Interview with Hall), in Gary A. Olson and Lynn Worsham, eds., *Race, Rhetoric, and the Postcolonial* (Albany: SUNY Press, 1999), 207.

9. Stuart Hall, "What Is This 'Black' in Black Popular Culture?" In David Morley and Kuan-Hsing Chen, eds., *Stuart Hall: Critical Dialogues in Cultural Studies* (London: Routledge, 1996), 471; see also Alibhai-Brown, 146.

10. Peter Stallybrass and Allon White, *The Politics and Poetics of Transgression* (Ithaca: Cornell University Press, 1986), 44; see also Hall, "'What Is This 'Black,'" 469.

11. Devine, Tom, and Paddy Logue, eds., *Being Scottish: Personal Reflections on Scottish Identity Today* (Edinburgh: Polygon, 2002), xii–xiii.

12. *Ibid.*, 2.

13. *Ibid.*, 138.

14. *Ibid.*, 217–19.

15. *Ibid.*, 282.

16. Ian Rankin, *Black & Blue* (London: Orion, 1997), 105–06.

17. Alibhai-Brown, 3.

18. Rankin, 115.

19. Alibhai-Brown, 109.

20. *Ibid.*, 109–10.

21. William McIlvanney, *The Papers of Tony Veitch* (New York: Pantheon, 1983), 23 Subsequent citations will appear parenthetically in the text.

22. Abiola Irele, Introduction to *Cahier d'un retour au pays natal*, by Aimé Césaire (Columbus: Ohio State University Press, 2000), lxxiii.

23. Alibhai-Brown, 4; see also Hall as quoted in Kuan-Hsing Chen, "The Formation of a Diasporic Intellectual: An Interview with Stuart Hall," in David Morley and Kuan-Hsing Chen, eds., *Stuart Hall: Critical Dialogues in Cultural Studies* (London: Routledge, 1996), 490.

24. Christopher Brookmyre, *Not the End of the World* [1998] (London: Warner Books, 2001), 17. Subsequent citations will appear parenthetically in the text.

25. Christopher Brookmyre, *A Big Boy Did It and Ran Away* (London: Abacus, 2001), 49. Subsequent citations will appear parenthetically in the text.

26. See e.g. Alibhai-Brown, 93–94.

27. See Reddy, 170–72, 186.

28. On *The Wild Geese*, see e.g. Ella Shohat and Robert Stam, *Unthinking Eurocentrism: Multiculturalism and the Media* (London: Routledge, 1994), 122–23.

29. Modood, 160–63.

30. Robert Crawford, *Identifying Poets* (Edinburgh: Edinburgh University Press, 1993), 7.

31. Christopher Brookmyre, *The Sacred Art of Stealing* (London: Abacus, 2002), 37. Subsequent citations will appear parenthetically in the text.

32. On this and associated beliefs, see e.g. Modood, 161.

33. See Alibhai-Brown, 113, and Reddy, 151–52.

34. Ed Christian, "Introducing the Post-Colonial Detective; Putting Marginality to Work," in Ed Christian, ed., *The Post-Colonial Detective* (Basingstoke: Palgrave, 2001), 2.

35. Denise Mina, *Garnethill* (London: Bantam, 1998), 9. Subsequent citations will appear parenthetically in the text.

36. Denise Mina, *Exile* (London: Bantam, 2000), 11. Subsequent citations will appear parenthetically in the text.

37. Hall, "What Is This 'Black,'" 467.

38. Denise Mina, *Resolution* (London: Bantam, 2001), 66. Subsequent citations will appear parenthetically in the text.

39. Nicholas Christopher, *Somewhere in the Night: Film Noir and the American City* (1997) (NY: Owl, 1998), 6.

40. Reddy discusses what she sees as the tendency of white detective writers to present black characters as comprehensible under white norms (161), but does not address the possibility that such presentation may change a reader's perception of the norms themselves (as fixed rather than evolving, for example).

41. Alibhai-Brown, 115.

42. Pnina Werbner, "Introduction: The Dialectics of Cultural Hybridity," in Pnina Werbner and Tariq Modood, eds, *Debating Cultural Hybridity: Multi-Cultural Identities and the Politics of Anti-Racism* (London: Zed Books, 1997), 7.

43. Hall, "What Is This 'Black,'" 474; original italics.

# About the Contributors

***Brad Buchanan*** is an assistant professor of English at the California State University, Sacramento. His scholarly and creative work has appeared in journals such as *Twentieth Century Literature, The Journal of Modern Literature,* and *Canadian Literature.* He is currently working on a book about the fiction of Hanif Kureishi, to be published by Palgrave Macmillan Press.

***Peter Clandfield*** is an assistant professor in the Department of English Studies at Nipissing University in North Bay, Ontario, Canada. He has also investigated questions of "murder and the other" in an essay on the television series *Homicide* (in *Closely Watched Brains,* 2001). His main research interests include contemporary Scottish literature, representations of urban and suburban redevelopment, and theories and practices of censorship.

***Brian Diemert*** is an associate professor of English at Brescia University College in London, Ontario. He is the author of *Graham Greene's Thrillers and the 1930's* (1996) and has published essays on twentieth-century British and American literature in such journals as *Genre, Texas Studies in Language and Literature, Twentieth Century Literature,* and *Style.* He is currently working on a book that explores the links between detective fiction and occultism.

***Julie H. Kim*** is an associate professor of English and women's studies at Northeastern Illinois University (Chicago). Her primary field of research is in sixteenth- and seventeenth-century British literature. She has published on Milton, early modern British studies, and film. She is currently working on essays on John Bunyan and on Milton and popular culture.

**Kate Koppelman** is currently an assistant professor of English at the University of Montevallo in Alabama. Her research interests include medieval studies, devotional literature, pedagogy, gender studies, and psychoanalytic theory. Her publications include articles in *Essays in Medieval Studies* and in *Teaching Literary Research Challenges in a Changing Environment*.

**Tim Libretti** is currently an associate professor of English and women's studies at Northeastern Illinois University. He has published articles and chapters in books and journals such as *Melus, Women's Studies Quarterly, Modern Fiction Studies, College English, Contemporary Justice Review, Radical Teacher, Amerasia Journal, Post Identity, Against the Current,* and *Nature, Society, and Thought*.

**Neil McCaw** is senior lecturer in English at University College of Winchester. His publications include *George Eliot and Victorian Historiography* (2000) and *Writing Irishness in Nineteenth-Century British Culture* (2004) in addition to other chapters and articles on philosophies of history, literary masculinity, and Englishness.

**Andrew Hock-soon Ng** teaches contemporary fiction, film studies and theories of authorship and writing at the School of Communications, Faculty of Arts, with Monash University, Malaysia. He is the author of *Dimensions of Monstrosity in Contemporary Narratives* (2004).

**Suzanne Penuel** is a doctoral student at the University of Texas and an instructor at the University of Mississippi. Her primary research interest is in early modern drama, and her previous published work includes an essay on the link between sixteenth-century religious conflict and father-child dynamics in *The Merchant of Venice*.

**John Scaggs** is a lecturer in modern fiction at Mary Immaculate College in Limerick, Ireland. He has published a book on crime fiction with Routledge, and has also published a number of articles on British and American crime fiction. The focus of his research is on contemporary fiction and narrative and critical theory.

**Marta Vizcaya Echano** has recently completed a doctoral thesis on U.S. Latina literature at the University of York, U.K. Together with formula fiction, her main research interests are ethnic American and postcolonial women's narratives, life-writing and literature for young adults. Her publication record includes pieces on Julia Alvarez, Esmeralda Santiago and Jessica Hagedorn.

# Index

241

Paul, Robert 6, 31, 38
Penuel, Suzanne 8, 51–70, 240
Pepper, Andrew 74
Phillips, Mike 213
Pilgrim, Anita Naoko 198, 199
Poe, Edgar Allan 4, 178
Poirot, Hercule 5, 192
Popular Culture 1, 4, 14, 73, 194, 196, 231, 236
Postcolonialism 3, 51, 52, 54, 55, 58, 59, 61, 62, 72, 217, 221, 222, 226
Postmodernism 10, 16, 32, 139, 140, 154, 155, 159, 231
Poststructuralist 52
Powell, Enoch 36, 72
Presbyterian 169, 173, 181
Protestantism 6, 11, 96, 98, 99, 107–109, 111–115, 165, 167, 168, 172, 173, 211, 223–225

Queerness 21
Qureshi, Robina 214, 223

Race Relations Act 3, 38, 124, 126
Rankin, Ian 10, 164–188, 211, 215, 216, 218
Reddy, Maureen 5, 67, 202, 212, 213, 221, 224
Reformation 96–98, 107–109, 112, 115, 167
Rendell, Ruth 3, 6, 8, 51–70
Richter, David 158
Roberts, Richard H. 159
Routley, Erik 31
Rowland, Susan 52, 53, 68

Sage, Victor 166, 167, 172, 177, 178
Said, Edward 25, 51, 52, 55, 61
Sambrook, James 140
Sayers, Dorothy 165, 168
Scaggs, John 3, 9, 10, 119–137, 240
Scarisbrick, J. J. 107, 108
Scottishness 10, 11, 39, 40, 164–188, 211–238
Sectarianism 33, 211, 223–226
Semite 123, 131, 135, 136

Separatism (Lesbian) 203, 204
Sexuality 2, 19, 21, 119, 189, 194, 200, 202, 203, 205–207
Sharpe, Jenny 62, 65
Simon, Ulrich 149
Sinclair, Iain 139
Solomos, John 127
Somalia 190, 200
Soyinka, Wole 42
Spark, Muriel 166, 178
Staincliffe, Cath 10, 189–210
Stallybrass, Peter 213
Stevenson, Robert Louis 164, 166, 170, 178, 179
Suleri, Sara 62
Supernatural 145, 155, 165, 166, 171
Sweeney, Susan Elizabeth 7, 138, 139, 192, 193
Swope, Richard 120

Tani, Stefano 167, 176
Tartan Noir 10, 173, 211–238
Taylor, Mark 122, 129, 131, 133
Templars 172, 180
Third World 62, 73, 75, 76, 82–84, 87, 88, 91, 92, 94
Thompson, Jon 3
Toland, John 141, 143
Tyndale, William 96, 109

Uganda 221, 222

Vizcaya Echano, Marta 10, 189–210, 240

Walton, Patricia 191, 192, 194, 206
Welsh, Irvine 214, 215
Werbner, Pnina 236
White, Allon 213
Wilson, Barbara 202
Wren, Christopher 141

X, Malcolm 220
Xenophobia 38

Yeats, William Butler 220
Yorkshire 97, 98, 100, 101, 108, 109